D1359806

ADVANCE PRAISE

"Bitcoin. Blockchain. Crypto. These days, you can't go a day without hearing about the blockchain revolution. While much has been written on the topic, little of it answers the underlying question: What is blockchain technology and why is everyone so excited about it? This book provides new perspectives for newcomers and industry veterans."

—Meltem Demirors, Chief Strategy Officer, CoinShares

"This book delivers a comprehensive profound treatment of the many ways blockchain is pushing us to fundamentally rethink the delivery of financial services."

—Dr. Peter Zemsky, Professor of Strategy and Dean of Innovation, INSEAD

"With its breadth of themes, this book provides a sweeping outlook for blockchain technology and the promise of its immense impact on the world of finance."

—Dr. Cathy Barrera, Founding Economist, Prysm Group

"Blockchain is poised to reshape financial services as we know it. This book arms its readers with the knowledge necessary to prepare for the coming transformation."

—Debbie Gamble, Chief Officer, Innovation Labs and New Ventures, Interac

FINANCIAL
SERVICES
REVOLUTION

ALSO BY ALEX TAPSCOTT

Blockchain Revolution: How the Technology Behind
Bitcoin and Other Cryptocurrencies Is Changing the World
(Penguin Portfolio, 2018) Co-author, Don Tapscott

Blockchain Revolution for the Enterprise
(INSEAD and Coursera, 2019) Co-instructor, Don Tapscott

Blockchain Revolution in Financial Services
(INSEAD and Coursera, 2020) Co-instructor, Don Tapscott

FINANCIAL SERVICES REVOLUTION

How **BLOCKCHAIN** Is Transforming
Money, Markets, and Banking

Edited with a preface by
ALEX TAPSCOTT
Co-Founder, Blockchain Research Institute

BARLOW BOOKS
fine books for enterprising authors

111 Peter Street, Suite 503, Toronto, ON M5V 2H1 Canada

Copyright © 2020 Blockchain Research Institute

The editor of this volume and its individual contributors have made every effort to provide information that was accurate and up to date at the time of writing. Neither the editor nor the contributors assume any responsibility for changes in data, names, titles, status, Internet addresses, or other details that occurred after manuscript completion.

This material is for educational purposes only; it is neither investment advice nor managerial consulting. Use of this material does not create or constitute any kind of business relationship with the Blockchain Research Institute or the Tapscott Group, and neither the Blockchain Research Institute nor the Tapscott Group is liable for the actions of persons or organizations relying on this material.

To refer to this material, we suggest the following citation:

> *Financial Services Revolution: How Blockchain Is Transforming Money, Markets, and Banking*, edited with a preface by Alex Tapscott (Toronto: Barlow Books, 2020).

To request permission for copying, distributing, remixing, transforming, building upon this material, or creating and distributing any derivative of it in print or other form for any purpose, please contact the Blockchain Research Institute, blockchain researchinstitute.org/contact-us, and put "Permission request" in the subject line. Thank you for your interest.

ISBN: 978-1-988025-49-0

Printed in the Canada

1 3 5 7 9 10 8 6 4 2

Publisher: Sarah Scott/Barlow Books
Book producer: Tracy Bordian/At Large Editorial Services
Book design (cover and interior) and layout: Ruth Dwight
For more information, visit **www.barlowbooks.com**

Barlow Book Publishing Inc.
96 Elm Avenue, Toronto, ON
Canada M4W 1P2

CONTENTS

LIST OF CONTRIBUTORS

Michael J. Casey (Chapter 2) is the chief content officer at *CoinDesk*, chairman and co-founder of Streambed Media, senior adviser at the MIT Media Lab's Digital Currency Initiative, and co-author (with Paul Vigna) of the bestselling book *The Age of Cryptocurrency: How Bitcoin and Digital Money Are Challenging the Global Economic Order.*

Alexis Collomb (Chapter 3) is head of the economics finance insurance and banking department at the Conservatoire National des Arts et Métiers and scientific co-director of the Blockchain Perspectives Joint Research Initiative within Paris-based ILB think tank. Alexis started his career in investment banking at Donaldson, Lufkin & Jenrette and later joined Citigroup.

Primavera De Filippi (Chapter 3) is a researcher at the National Center of Scientific Research, a faculty associate at the Berkman Klein Center for Internet and Society at Harvard University, a member of the Global Future Council on Blockchain Technologies at the World Economic Forum, and co-author (with Aaron Wright) of *Blockchain and the Law: The Rule of Code.*

Andreas Park (Chapter 6) is an associate professor of finance at the University of Toronto, appointed to the Rotman School of Management, the Institute for Management and Innovation, and the Department of Management at U of T Mississauga, and is the research director of Rotman's Financial Innovation Lab.

Klara Sok (Chapter 3) is a research fellow in social sciences at the Conservatoire National des Arts et Métiers in its Lirsa and the Dicen-IDF research centers, a founding member of the transdisciplinary Blockchain Perspectives Joint Research Initiative, and co-developer of OpenResearch, a blockchain-based open peer-review platform.

Alex Tapscott (Chapter 1) is a globally recognized speaker, investor, and adviser focused on the impact of emerging technologies. He is co-author (with Don Tapscott) of the critically acclaimed bestselling book *Blockchain Revolution: How the Technology Behind Bitcoin and Other Cryptocurrencies Is Changing the World.*

Bob Tapscott (Chapter 4) is a recognized IT strategist, author, consultant, and speaker, keynoting conferences on the topics of artificial intelligence, fintech, and blockchain. As a vice president or a CIO, Bob has led the Canadian technology efforts of Citibank, HSBC, and other Schedule II banks in Canada.

Fennie Wang (Chapter 3) is a lawyer turned entrepreneur in the blockchain space, leading strategy, legal, and partnerships at the ixo Network, UNICEF's first blockchain investment, and a US-qualified securities lawyer who practiced both securities defense and international capital markets with leading US law firms WilmerHale and Latham & Watkins.

Anthony D. Williams (Chapter 5) is co-founder and president of the DEEP Centre, an internationally recognized authority on the digital revolution, innovation, and creativity in business and society, and co-author (with Don Tapscott) of the bestselling book *Wikinomics: How Mass Collaboration Changes Everything.*

PREFACE

Alex Tapscott

As the Internet was the first digital medium for information, blockchain is the first native digital medium for value. Our research at the Blockchain Research Institute continues to look beyond the enterprise and the industry, to understand how blockchain will transform the economy and society at large. The financial services sector is a key lever in such transformation. Blockchain-based applications such as digital identities and smart wallets running in a trust-minimized manner on mobile devices will enable over a billion people to participate in the global economy.

This book looks at blockchain's impact on our notions of money, banking, and financial markets. In Chapter 1, we explore the nine major disruptions to our global financial system in the areas of identity verification and compliance with know-your-customer and anti-money laundering regulations; checking and value transfer services; savings and deposits; loans and credit accounts; trading and exchanges; venture capital and securities markets; insurance and risk management; financial analysis; and accounting and financial reporting. It's quite a list!

Facebook's new digital currency Libra is only the beginning. Even though seven of its original 28 backers have dropped out of the project—Mastercard, PayPal, and Visa among them—the project has the support of the Bank of England Governor, Mark Carney. He said that Britain must face up to the problems of its payments system. "In this day and age, those payments should be instantaneous, it should be the same as us exchanging a bank note online," he said. "It should be instantaneous, it should be virtually costless, and it should be 100 percent resilient."[1] We consider how the other FAANG companies—that is, Amazon.com, Apple, Netflix, and Google—might respond with their own digital tokens. The chapter provides direction for incumbents, innovators, and central bankers alike. Finally, we preview the world of financial services in the year 2030, so that readers get a clear sense of the unintended consequences of going it alone in financial services and the potential costs of doing nothing now.

In Chapter 2, Michael Casey lays out his vision for a token economy. A token such as bitcoin represents digital scarcity—finite, immutable, not copiable—in a global financial system where digital goods tend to be abundant, duplicative, and adaptable. What's more, tokens as programmable money could potentially automate internal governance over our common resources. As Michael writes, "It's money with a dynamic use"—not just a unit of exchange but also a direct means of achieving community objectives, a completely new approach to managing our increasingly digitized economy. With scarce digital tokens, communities with a common interest in value generation can embed their shared values into these tokens and use them as instruments of those values.

According to Michael, "The implications of imbuing digital money with policy and incentives" are far-reaching. A chasm has emerged between those who see a game-changing shift, not simply in fundraising activity or economic strategy but also in mitigating the tragedy of the commons, and those who warn of reckless *initial coin offering* (ICO) scams and an impending regulatory crackdown. Everyone should read Michael's lucid chapter and participate in the debate.

Speaking of ICO scams, the authors of Chapter 3 dig into the regulatory implications of blockchain-based systems, some of which qualify as ecosystems, such as Bitcoin and Ethereum, and some, as decentralized applications. While the ICO addresses the weaknesses of the initial public offering (IPO), it presents its own challenges, highlighted by some high-profile swindles that *WIRED* magazine called "straight-up trolling." Among them was Prodeum, which appeared on a Thursday, raised barely any money, and disappeared by the following Monday, along with its website, its press release, and its social media accounts.[2] Hacking is also a problem. The professional services firm Ernst & Young analyzed more than 300 ICOs and determined that roughly 10 percent ($400m) of the $3.7 billion raised had been siphoned off, with phishers nicking as much as $1.5 million a month.[3]

So ICOs represent a conundrum to securities law regulators. The US Securities and Exchange Commission (SEC) and its equivalents in other jurisdictions are gauging the level of regulatory oversight required to balance the viability of blockchain start-ups with the risk to investors, especially retail investors caught up in the hype. The chapter's all-star team of researchers—Fennie Wang, Primavera De Filippi, Alexis Collomb, and Klara Sok of Coalition of Automated Legal Applications (COALA)—deftly describes various legal solutions that could support ecosystems that are innovative and streamlined, yet fair for all stakeholders. It is among the most thoughtful and definitive studies to date.

In Chapter 4, Bob Tapscott explains how distributed ledgers will dramatically improve international clearance and settlement by replacing layers of complex systems for communicating with each other and adding fees and delays at each step of the payment process. With blockchain technology, proven mathematics instead of fallible or sometimes corrupt human beings will bolster users' trust in the system by providing a much-needed single version of the truth. In addition, dramatically reduced fees, micropayment capability, and mobile infrastructure will help a billion unbanked people to participate in the global economy. Bob details how our current payment system evolved, and what we can do to transform it for the digital economy. Blockchain start-ups are disrupting the banking industry's arcane procedures with distributed ledger technology. The incumbent powers may be slow to embrace blockchain; according to Bob, if they resist change, then they may find themselves without a role in the global economy. It's a powerful message.

Chapter 5 explores the possibility of blockchain transforming how we record, store, and manage information (not necessarily financial), with a deep dive into government use cases, though the same fundamental principles apply entirely to financial services. More than ever, engaged citizens expect to be heard and informed—indeed, to be active collaborators rather than passive recipients. They expect elected officials to spend tax funds wisely. Blockchain technology makes these goals easier to accomplish. In this chapter, Anthony Williams focuses on ways to simplify and improve government services through a single digital ledger for all government accounts. He assesses Canada's current general ledger system, compares it with best practices in places like Estonia and Sweden, and presents a possible blockchain-based solution. The analysis is not cheerleading; Anthony lays out the relevant challenges and implementation costs, including managing risk and connecting with existing policies and procedures.

The book's final chapter brings to mind the words of US Supreme Court Justice Louis D. Brandeis, "Sunlight is said to be the best of disinfectants." Transparency is critical to the robust functioning of markets, corporations, and governments. Consider the murkiness of Enron's balance sheet and the opacity of the US subprime mortgage market: the former contributed to the largest corporate failure ever at the time, the closure of a storied accounting firm with 85,000 jobs lost, and the convictions of several C-suite executives; and the latter factored into the 2008 market crash. Today trillions of dollars of underfunded derivatives—and some experts peg that amount much higher—threaten to trigger an economic crash that would make 2008 look like a tremor.

That's why transparency is one of the most important benefits of blockchain; it makes such obfuscation more difficult, if not impossible. For starters, two people cannot claim ownership of the same asset—the ledger will not allow it. That reminds me of the next part of Justice Brandeis' quote: "Electric light [is] the most efficient policeman."[4] The chapter's author Andreas Park is a finance professor at the Rotman School of Management. He studies equity markets and advises regulatory bodies on the economic impact of technology within the financial industries. In this final chapter, he demonstrates that transparency is a design choice and argues for public disclosure even on permissioned blockchains. His is a compelling argument, and one well worth considering for those weighing their public/private blockchain design options.

As you can see, this book is a preview of the fast approaching future of financial services, markets, and money. It is a global industry ripe for disruption, and blockchain start-ups around the world are targeting every aspect of it. Time has become the scarce commodity. Nobel laureate Robert Schiller observed, "Hesitation is often like procrastination. One may have vague doubts and feel a need to mull things over; meanwhile, other issues intrude on thought, and no decision is taken."[5] There are ideas and opportunities here for every forward-looking leader to act on now.

CHAPTER 1

THE COMING CATACLYSM

Blockchain and Financial Services

Alex Tapscott

 FINANCIAL SERVICES IN BRIEF

- In the first era of the Internet, software ate the world, transforming many industries in the process, from advertising and television to retail and education.[6] The second era of the Internet will make those changes look quaint, as blockchain disrupts finance, the foundation of all industries and human economic activity. It will rewire the deep structures of our economy.

- The stakes are high: the next era of money, commerce, and economic activity hangs in the balance. The dominant landlords of today's digital estate—Facebook, Google, and others—will no doubt use blockchain to control tomorrow's digital world. They will confront the keepers of the status quo: big banks with vast financial empires to protect and governments with systemic power and monetary policy to preserve.

- Banks and other financial intermediaries move money. The more they move, the more they store and the more they lend. Payment rails are the cardiovascular system of the industry's corpus, and money is the blood of global commerce. Without them, no other organ can function. Thus, the digitization of value is the first step to decoupling intermediaries from assets and migrating them to this native digital medium for value.

- We look at five disruptions to the industry: open finance and the digitization of financial assets; the "financialization" of everything; blockchains as trusted shared registers of truth; the strengths and limitations of *decentralized finance* (DeFi); and the role of self-sovereign identities.

- New decentralized models of finance and the emerging cryptoasset class will soon have incumbents—banks and digital conglomerates alike—scrambling to avoid obsolescence and irrelevance. Bitcoin and other cryptocurrencies will challenge the dogma of government-backed fiat currencies and, for the first time, billions of people will be able to connect to the global economy.

- We see both promise and peril in this new future. Authoritarian regimes that suppressed the first era of the Internet have already begun to capture this second-era technology for their own ends, a trend that will no doubt spread to societies that are more democratic in the absence of governance and public vigilance.

- With stewardship and responsible leadership, blockchain will usher in a new era of financial services that is more open, inclusive, efficient, secure, and free. If we get this right, new economic systems will emerge to generate greater prosperity for the many, rather than more wealth for the few.

INTRODUCTION

THE BLOCKCHAIN REVOLUTION IN FINANCIAL SERVICES

A week after I started my career in investment banking, Lehman Brothers went bankrupt, and the global economy went into a tailspin. At 22 years old, I had stumbled into a trial by fire. When the ashes settled from the financial inferno that ultimately engulfed many of the world's biggest banks, my firm was still standing, and I was (somehow) still employed. I was one of the lucky ones. For many of my generation, 2008 began a lost decade of structural unemployment, sluggish growth, political instability, and a corrosion of trust and confidence in many of our institutions. The financial crisis exposed the avarice, malfeasance, and plain incompetence that had driven the economy to the brink of collapse and had some asking, "How deep did the rot go?"

Amid this financial crisis, an anonymous person (or persons) named Satoshi Nakamoto invented the Bitcoin blockchain. Though he claimed at one point, "I'm better with code than words," Satoshi's brilliant and lucid white paper, "Bitcoin: A Peer-to-Peer Electronic Cash System," introduced a radical new concept: cash over the Internet—a way to move and store value without intermediaries like banks and governments.[7] What was remarkable about Bitcoin is that it worked, and it set off a spark that has caught on like wildfire and captured the imaginations of technologists, entrepreneurs, and business leaders. In January 2009, Satoshi said, "I would be surprised if, 10 years from now, we're not using electronic currency in some way. … If enough people think the same way, that becomes a self-fulfilling prophecy."[8] Today, bitcoin has a value of $200 billion, and the most powerful people in the world—from Donald Trump to Mark Carney (Bank of England), Steven Mnuchin (US Treasury), Jerome Powell (US Federal Reserve), and Christine Lagarde (International Monetary Fund)—are criticizing and praising it in equal measures.

Everyone seems to have a view, and these views seem to evolve rapidly.

Bitcoin also ushered in the Blockchain Revolution, referring to the underlying blockchain that makes fully digital assets like Bitcoin possible. Blockchains are permissionless distributed ledgers of transactions in a peer-to-peer (P2P) network where information (not necessarily financial) is recorded in a timely, secure, and tamper-resistant way. They exist and can be trusted because of mass collaboration, consensus, and code, not traditional intermediaries. They enable programmable scarce digital assets for virtually all forms of value. For the first time in human history, entities need not rely on banks and other third parties to move, store, coordinate, and manage value.

To be sure, Bitcoin remains the most important blockchain innovation to date, but innovators and entrepreneurs are using blockchain for much more. Blockchain is the first native digital medium for value in the same way that the Internet was the first digital medium for information. As such, we can use it for virtually any kind of asset, and it forces us to rethink the deep structure and workings of many industries, starting with finance.

FACEBOOK JOINS THE BLOCKCHAIN REVOLUTION— BUCKLE UP!

In June 2019, Facebook announced a plan to create money for the world to use. Libra is a bold new cryptocurrency project that could enable Facebook's 2.7 billion users to send money as easily as sending a message on WhatsApp.[9] The announcement rattled the doors of many powerful institutions, from banks and big tech to governments and money transfer services around the world.

Facebook has marketed Libra mainly as a way to bank the unbanked—a noble cause, to be sure. But it will attempt to deploy this coin across its platform, for use in all forms of commerce online and off, positioning Facebook as a powerful new player in the global financial system. It could change how, where, and with whom billions of people spend and save, borrow and loan, and otherwise finance and insure their lives and livelihoods. If Facebook succeeds—and that's a big *if*—then this shift will upend financial services, an exhilarating and worrying prospect. This is a watershed moment. Facebook is one of the largest landlords of our digital economy, and its actions are far-reaching.

First, Facebook is placing itself in the crosshairs of lawmakers and regulators as they wrestle for control over finance, money, and influence among citizen users. In the United States, lawmakers on both sides of the aisle criticized the plan and Congress demanded hearings. A few weeks later, President Trump tweeted, "Facebook Libra's 'virtual currency' will have little standing or dependability."[10] Jerome Powell, the chair of the Federal Reserve, added in testimony days later, "Libra raises serious concerns regarding privacy, money laundering, consumer protection, financial stability."[11]

Facebook faces the Sisyphean task of rebuilding the trust of users, governments, and other stakeholders. After Libra boss David Marcus testified before Congress, Jerry Brito of Coin Center told *The Wall Street Journal*, "Libra faces a huge challenge. ... It isn't a crypto issue, it's a Facebook issue."[12]

Second, by wading into the massive, complex world of financial services, Facebook is pitting itself against the big banks. Consider how Facebook, Amazon, Netflix, and Google have upended such industries as advertising, retail, and television. If I were a banker, I'd be quaking in my loafers. Finally, Libra, like Bitcoin, could forever alter the traditional role of fiat money in the global economy. Just as cellular technology allowed billions to leapfrog landlines, Libra's blockchain-based platform has the potential to obsolesce the Rube Goldbergian financial infrastructure in place today.

So far, Wall Street has been cautiously receptive. Major financial institutions such as Visa and Mastercard have nonbinding letters of intent to join Facebook in this venture, and they may have short-term opportunities for financial re-intermediation, as billions more begin to transact online. Facebook will need to play nice with banks, at least at first, by giving them a piece of the pie. However, in the long term, every aspect of the financial services industry will be up for grabs. Consider the unbanked: anyone living in Africa or South Asia is far more likely to have a Facebook account than a bank account. Consider the youth as well: tens of millions of young people have not yet opened a bank account and may never bother, but age 25 to 34 is the most common age demographic on Facebook.[13] Payment services could be just the first of Facebook's financial offerings.

Regulators and policymakers have been circumspect, with good reason. Facebook faces many implementation challenges to launching Libra and earning the trust of users and governments. It must make user privacy and security a priority. That said, Facebook has clearly thought about *governance*. Libra is governed by a not-for-profit Swiss foundation with potentially over 30 members. By putting up this big tent for other companies and organizations to participate in governance, Facebook is limiting its control over this platform. Still, this initial cabal is mostly large corporations driven by profit, not necessarily by bringing the unbanked online or lowering the cost of remittances to poor countries.

Even if Libra navigates the regulatory maze in the United States and Europe, Facebook faces another battle in the developing world. Libra will probably be a more reliable and useful store of value, medium of exchange, or unit of account than many of the world's smaller and more marginalized currencies. If a country decides to devalue its currency to make exports more competitive or investment more attractive, individuals will be able to opt out to a "hard dollar" digital alternative. Those living in Venezuela may not fully trust Facebook, but they'll probably trust it more than the tin-pot dictator devaluing their currency. To a lesser extent, this alternative store of value could pose problems for the world's wealthy countries as well as for those who value their monetary sovereignty.

Policymakers in North America and elsewhere should keep an open mind. If they ban Libra, then a Chinese Internet giant like

Baidu or Alibaba could launch its own coin, with the backing of the authoritarian regime interested in tracking and profiling users. In the days before Bitcoin, Tencent launched a project called QQ Coin, which users could purchase for one yuan on a nonrefundable basis. QQ Coins soon became commonplace for online payments before the Chinese government cracked down on them.[14] More than 10 years on, we can imagine private sector actors launching something hand in glove with totalitarian governments. That should concern democratic leaders and cause legislators to regulate rather than prohibit. We will explore this issue and other far-reaching implications in this research.

What does Libra mean for bitcoin and other cryptocurrencies? Because it will be a *stablecoin*—meaning that its value will be pegged to a basket of traditional currencies—its price will not be as volatile as bitcoin. Libra could be a more effective medium of exchange for payments where counterparties expect some predictability. But, it is not a threat to bitcoin itself. The Bitcoin blockchain remains the most consequential computer science invention in a generation. It laid the rails for a new Internet of value that could do for assets what the Internet did for information industries like the news media. The unstoppable force of blockchain is on a collision course with the heretofore immovable object of global finance. Buckle up.

Bitcoin is "digital gold," a phrase popularized by *New York Times* writer Nathaniel Popper.[15] It is a decentralized currency not controlled by governments or corporations, with a fixed supply curve, and with very strong security—all qualities that, by design, Libra never will have. If anything, Libra could prove to be the widest and fastest avenue, or on-ramp, to bring billions into a digital financial industry.

Finally, Facebook will face competition from its biggest rivals. In the coming months and years, many big technology companies will likely launch their own cryptocurrencies. In an interview, Cameron and Tyler Winklevoss, co-founders of Gemini, said, "We expect within 24 months that all the FAANGs will have their own crypto-currency."[16] They added that other companies, like Starbucks, with their own digital rewards program would be obvious candidates to follow suit. The banks, ever more conservative, will follow suit.

Amazon is the juggernaut in e-commerce in North America and elsewhere. Does anyone expect Jeff Bezos to allow Libra on Amazon, without launching an alternative? Unless you want the payment rail for your business running on some other company's infrastructure, with that company capturing most of the upside, then you'd better get your act together and design a coin.

LIBRA: THE LATEST INNOVATION

Facebook's foray into cryptocurrencies should surprise no student of technology. After all, the digital revolution has transformed nearly every aspect of our lives, except banking. Financial intermediaries depend more or less on pre-Internet technologies. Libra is simply the latest innovation to punch holes in the old model, establishing the battle lines for the future of our digital economy.

The stakes are high: the next era of commerce, economic activity, and money is uncertain. Computer scientists are rewiring the economic power grid, and software engineers are recoding the order of human affairs, exposing our lack of understanding of fundamental concepts like privacy, free speech, and the role of large corporations in our lives. As the digital landlords of this new economy—Facebook, Google, and others—challenge the supremacy of big banks, decentralized cryptocurrencies like bitcoin force us to confront our understanding of money, value, and the fortress of regulations erected around these concepts, originally to protect those who used the system, and now to preserve the status quo. This is ultimately a struggle for control, as many parties—totalitarian governments in China and elsewhere, legacy financial institutions, big social media companies and other digital conglomerates, technology upstarts, and other stakeholders— vie for even greater influence.

Human beings have become increasingly comfortable with software and technology replacing human actors in many industries and many facets of daily life. Finance is the largest, most consequential, and thus far most immovable industry of them all. The legacy banking system, digital conglomerates like Facebook, free and open cryptocurrency platforms such as Bitcoin, and, of course, governments are heading inexorably for a collision of historic proportions. The crash will be cataclysmic. Prepare for impact.

BLOCKCHAIN TRANSFORMATION FOR FINANCIAL SERVICES

CRYPTOASSETS AND OPEN FINANCE

"They say that software is eating the world. Soon, tokens will be eating the world," said Tyler Winklevoss. He's right. Blockchain is the first native digital for value: we can use it to program virtually every asset under the sun. In the latest edition of *Blockchain Revolution*, we provided a taxonomy of these assets to help the reader understand their many differences. They were cryptocurrencies (bitcoin, Zcash, litecoin), platform tokens (ether, ATOMs, EOS), utility tokens (Augur's REP), securities tokens (theDAO, Munchee's MUN, Vocean's crypto bond), natural asset tokens (carbon, water, air), crypto collectibles, stablecoins, and crypto fiat currencies (Venezuela's petro, China's forthcoming crypto yuan).[17]

In this section, we are going to focus on digitation of existing financial assets in the form of securities tokens and fiat-backed stablecoins. This is the world of *open finance*, which differs from *decentralized finance*, which we discuss later. Open finance refers to the opening up of traditionally closed, analog, and proprietary systems to blockchain and digital assets. Open finance will prove to be an opportunity and challenge for incumbents, regulators, and market actors everywhere.

Consider equities. The global "stock market" is really a loosely knitted patchwork of local and regional exchanges, banks, broker dealers, custodians, clearinghouses, regulators, asset managers, fund administrators and other market participants and intermediaries.

Though order books and market making are largely digitized, the underlying function of how these different parties actually clear, settle, custody, and register ownership of assets is antiquated.

Blythe Masters, former managing director of investment bank J.P.Morgan and former CEO of Digital Asset Holdings, told us,

> Bear in mind that financial infrastructures have not evolved in decades. The front end has evolved but not the back end. It's been an arms race in technology investment oriented toward speeding up transaction execution so that, nowadays, competitive advantages are measured in nanoseconds.[18]

She was referring to high frequency trading: "The irony is that post-trade infrastructure hasn't really evolved at all." Blockchain holds the potential to reduce radically the cost, complexity, and friction in markets by allowing market participants to connect, clear, and settle peer to peer instantaneously.

0x, an open protocol that enables P2P exchange of assets on the Ethereum blockchain, is a pioneer in this regard. Though not all the assets traded on this exchange are financial, some are. So far, 0x has conducted over 713,000 transactions worth $750 million.[19] As underlying platforms like Ethereum, Cosmos, Polkadot, EOS, and others scale, so too will the capacity of the applications and financial business use cases that employ them. tZERO, a subsidiary of publicly traded Overstock, has made great strides in this area as well. In the summer of 2019, Overstock announced that shareholders of the publicly traded company would receive dividends as a digital token listed on tZERO. Patrick Byrne, former CEO of Overstock, said of the move, "Five years ago, we set out to create a parallel universe: a legal, blockchain-based capital market. We've succeeded."[20] Byrne has reasons to be optimistic that this parallel universe of digital assets will create challenges and opportunities for new entrants and incumbents alike.

Securities tokens not only reduce friction, cost, and complexity.

They also enable broader participation in capital markets because they lower barriers and allow us to imagine building liquid marketplaces for a wide variety of assets, from real estate to private equity and venture capital (VC). Greater transparency, market depth, and liquidity should improve price, access, and the overall healthy functioning of markets.

Not all assets will work as tokens. But we see tokenization working when several conditions are satisfied:

1. Is there an established or untapped demand for an asset?

2. Do people or institutions want to buy the asset but can't currently?

3. Are there high barriers to transferability or liquidity in an asset?

4. Are transaction costs high, spread too wide, or are other barriers so prohibitive that market participants choose to avoid the asset class altogether?

5. Is blockchain required to digitize the asset—that is, the asset simply isn't workable in a traditional system?

6. Is the industry highly consolidated or highly fragmented?

If the answer is yes to a majority of these questions, then the asset is a likely candidate for securities tokens, and a highly fragmented market should make experimentation or innovation easier. Tokenized equity, debt, and real estate already exist. We may eventually see tokenized sports teams, music catalogs, wine portfolios, fine art, and event tickets, to name a few. Securities tokens may help improve access to wealth creation for average people by lowering barriers to entry and expanding investment options.

This opportunity is not without challenges: it lacks technology, business, market, and regulatory infrastructure. Anthony Pompliano, co-founder and partner at Morgan Creek Digital, believes that securities regulators "took the idea of the rich get richer and … wrote it into law. They took the best performing assets with the best returns and put them behind a firewall."[21] He was referring to the Securities and Exchange Act of 1933, which limited many investment opportunities to high-net-worth individuals. He called it a "violation of the American dream."[22] If these kinds of investment opportunities remain limited to the richest of the rich, then we haven't really democratized the benefits of blockchain-based financial innovation.

Consider Props. Props is a native digital token created by the popular video application YouNow, though it can work inside any application. YouNow was granted special authorization by the SEC to do a Regulation A offering of its token, approved in July 2019, and already launched. Think of Props as stock options for the gig economy, for people like Uber drivers, homeowners who let their houses on Airbnb, or content creators. On YouNow, these people can earn money by sharing something on the platform. Otherwise, they can't participate directly in the value creation from the growth of currently popular platforms such as Uber or Airbnb. Similarly, Uber drivers may get paid for completing a ride, but they don't get a piece of the $75 billion that Uber is worth. The so-called "sharing economy" is really an "aggregation economy," where powerful platforms capture most of the value, and contributors get the crumbs.

With Props, contributors to platforms like YouNow, and soon perhaps Uber, Airbnb, and others, can get paid for their contributions *and* earn Props tokens. The supply of Props is finite and grows at a predictable rate, and so the more apps using the native token, and the more people earning and holding them, the higher the value of Props. Any application can plug into the Props *application programming interface* (API) and allow contributors to start earning real value in Props. Founders and investors will no longer be the sole beneficiaries of platform growth. In the context of financial services, we can view Props both as a new payment rail for organizing contributors in a network and as an incentive mechanism, like equity, for staying on the platform and adding value to it. Already, 200,000 people are using Props on YouNow with 100,000 Props transactions per day. The plan is to add more apps as time goes on. As Props becomes ubiquitous, other applications may be compelled to offer it to contributors—and, *voilà*, a new digital economy is born.

This new cornucopia of digital tokens will need common standards, with groups like the Enterprise Ethereum Alliance (EEA) helping to lead the charge. Marley Gray of Microsoft, who is a key contributor to the EEA's Token Alliance, told us that common standards "remove the obstacles for defining assets. Blockchain should be just like using the payments network today. People should just use it."[23] He added, "You don't need to understand the blockchain to use tokens. Let's get to the point where we are actually driving business value. Let's abstract this, make it common. Commoditizing tokens so any industry or company can create them."[24]

If different assets exist inside of silos that don't speak to one another, then tokenization will have limited impact. Only through common standards and interoperability can tokenization reach its full potential. Fiat-backed stablecoins, such as Tether, USD Coin, and Libra are other examples of open finance. Not all stablecoins are backed dollar for dollar by reserves; and some, such as DAI created by MakerDAO, exist entirely in the cryptoasset world.

Already, stablecoins have exploded in value, and for good reason. They offer an easy way to move value peer to peer instantaneously at a fraction of the cost of traditional payment systems like Venmo. "[T]he aggregate total on-chain transfer volume across the largest stablecoins has now surpassed Venmo's total payment volume," according to TradeBlock, a provider of digital currency trading tools for institutional investors. TradeBlock found that fees—those of merchants and related Venmo services—dwarfed the fees involved in transmitting stablecoins over the Ethereum blockchain: "Across the five largest ERC-20 tokens, customers spent just $827,000 in Ethereum network fees to transfer more than $37 billion. Over this same period, fees and fees on associated services paid to Venmo are expected to reach $150 million."[25]

Given this explosive growth, Facebook, Walmart, and J.P.Morgan—and perhaps Google and Amazon—are including stablecoins in their growth plans.[26]

Cameron Winklevoss said, "We are going to see many companies issuing coins," adding that, "a company like Facebook with its size and stature is very encouraging in validating the general idea of better and new payment rails powered by crypto. Whether it's Libra or not [that succeeds], time will tell." Consider Amazon: "You can pretty much get a package anywhere in the world. What you can't do is get paid for that product. Amazon Coin could create the ability to extend the payment system to the edges of the earth."[27] No doubt, Libra is but the opening volley in this new competition among the world's tech behemoths.

Pompliano believes Libra is a positive development but that it is also good for bitcoin and other cryptocurrencies. He said, "It's the token density theory—if you set up a restaurant across the street from another restaurant, traffic at both restaurants typically goes up. Everyone's foot traffic increases as you add density. So with each legitimate crypto that gets created and gets added it increases the overall value proposition of Bitcoin."[28] Ryan Selkis, founder of Messari, summed it up simply by saying Libra will act as a "lead blocker" for other cryptoassets.[29]

Not everyone is so optimistic about corporate coins. "I'm not afraid of nuclear meltdowns or terrorist attacks. The only thing I'm afraid of is Facebook's cryptocurrency," said Ethan Buchman, co-creator of Cosmos. "Facebook perfected digital colonialism. While the early colonialist companies enslaved bodies, Facebook enslaves minds. This will be [its] historical legacy."[30] With Facebook settling with the US Federal Trade Commission for $5 billion and with the SEC for $100 million, while getting grilled by lawmakers, its road to launch Libra will be a hard one, and Facebook's leaders will need to earn back the trust of those they let down. That's a daunting challenge.

Still, the technology has its own momentum, which makes

it unlikely at this point to be derailed. Financial markets—from stocks to bonds and everything in between—will be unrecognizable. Incumbents that bet big on blockchain will survive this coming revolution.

FINANCIALIZATION AND DIGITIZATION OF EVERYTHING

If land was the most important asset of the agrarian age, and oil was the most important asset of the industrial age, then data is the most important asset of the digital age. Information is the foundation of our digital economy and the lifeblood of some of the world's largest and most profitable companies, such as Facebook and Google. Consider the reordering of the world's most valuable companies over the last 20 years (Table 1-1).[31] In this period, data has replaced oil as the main driver of business value in the world, and information behemoths have displaced the industrial giants.

TABLE 1-1

THE WORLD'S MOST VALUABLE COMPANIES OVER TIME

LARGEST BY MARKET CAP, OCTOBER 1997	LARGEST BY MARKET CAP, APRIL 2019
General Electric (USA)	Microsoft (USA)
Roya Dutch Shell (Netherlands)	Apple (USA)
Microsoft (USA)	Amazon (USA)
ExxonMobil (USA)	Alphabet (USA)
Coca-Cola (USA)	Berkshire Hathaway (USA)
Intel (USA)	Facebook (USA)
NTT (Japan)	Alibaba (China)
Merck (USA)	Tencent (China)
Toyota (Japan)	Johnson & Johnson (USA)
Novartis (Switzerland)	ExxonMobil (USA)

Source of data: RankingTheWorld, "Top 10 Most Valuable Companies in the World (1997–2019)," Video, YouTube.com, YouTube LLC, 28 April 2019.

We create all these data, yet we don't own them—the digital landlords do. This is problematic because it means we can't use that data to better organize our lives, we can't monetize it, and it can fall into the wrong hands.

Information is one example of an asset that has had no open, transparent marketplace where stakeholders can discover price or exchange its value. This is part of a much broader problem that the digital age has exacerbated. Many assets have been outside market forces and susceptible to overuse or capture by large intermediaries. Like water, air, or the oceans, powerful companies exploit the data and, in turn, the people who created it.

In a major research report for the Blockchain Research Institute, technology theorist Michael Casey suggested that tokenization and digital scarcity brought about by cryptoassets represents a solution:

Blockchain technology, and the cryptocurrencies, tokens, and other digital assets that it has engendered, may be moving us toward a model of programmable money that incorporates an automated internal governance of common resources and encourages collaboration among communities. Digital scarcity, when applied to these tokens treats our increasingly digitized world differently from the pre-digital one. It raises the possibility that our money may itself become the tool for achieving common outcomes.

Developers of new decentralized applications are tokenizing all manner of resources—electricity and bandwidth, for example, but also human qualities such as audience attention for online content or fact checkers' honesty. ... Once a community associates scarce tokens with rights to these resources, it can develop controls over token usage that help manage public goods. It's dynamic money whose role extends beyond that of a unit of exchange, money that's a direct tool for achieving community objectives.[32]

In his report, Casey lays out a new taxonomy for these tokens and suggests at least five different types: media, identity, honesty, decentralized computing, and the environment.

The potential is very significant for these tokens to enable new economies around assets that were either previously in the commons (such as the environment) or captured asymmetrically (such as our identities) by a few large technology intermediaries. Moreover, we can tokenize everything of value to ensure creators receive fair compensation. Now, individuals can capture the value from the data they produce in their online selves, choosing to keep it private or provide informed consent for its use, making money in the process. Individual artists can receive fair payment for the music they create as their songs roam the Internet collecting royalties. People can enter agreements enforced by smart contracts and verified by oracles in prediction markets. These capabilities will no doubt spread from the trivial (sports betting) to more meaningful markets like derivatives markets.

The lines defining "financial services" will begin to blur as everything becomes an asset and everyone becomes a market participant.

BLOCKCHAINS AS STATE MACHINES

Blockchains are timely, accurate, shared trusted snapshots of the state of affairs of a network or other entity, from corporate accounts to a global supply chain or voting registry. They are a new form of record keeping. Let's call it *triple-entry accounting*. Double-entry bookkeeping is often credited as being foundational to capitalism and our modern way of life, allowing vast amounts of financial information to be organized and understood. Blockchains will do likewise.

Blockchain Research Institute author Anthony Williams wrote, "As transactions recorded onto the ledger would be instantly searchable and publishable, the blockchain-based ledger could also boost ... transparency, fulfill and expedite ... auditing requirements, and improve the integrity of accounts."[33] In other words, it would be a shared version of the truth.

In finance, this shared ledger would enable market participants to see more clearly what Ethan Buchman called "the plaintext corporation—a representation of a corporate state that is easily human and machine readable."[34] Having reliable and timely insights into the state of these networks helps to detect concentrations of risk or funding shortfalls. Williams outlines four advantages to this capability in his report, "Consolidating Multiple Ledgers with Blockchain":

1. Automation of reconciliation and reporting: instantly verifiable transactions would eliminate the need for time-intensive off-line or batch reconciliation processes between different systems.

2. Transparency and granularity: stakeholders gain near real-time visibility into individual transactions conducted across a network or entity like a corporation.

3. Reduced fraud: a blockchain solution would ensure that financial records are tamper-proof and would reduce the scope for entering fraudulent transactions or falsifying information. The use of cryptographically linked blocks would ensure that no one could alter or delete records without detection.

4. Value-added auditing: a blockchain ledger would allow auditors (and other stakeholders) to verify a large portion of the most important data behind the financial accounts of companies, governments, and other parties.[35]

Consider the myriad ways a blockchain-based ledger could radically simplify the inner workings of the financial services industry:

The distributed ledger cannot be edited, even by an individual who holds all of the access keys. The stockholder record can be appended, but retroactive adjustments to the record cannot be made. This process generates a highly dependable audit trail that clearly—and indisputably—indicates how each stockholder acquired stock and from whom. That trail would be essential in a court of law, should a plaintiff dispute who the stockholders were at a given moment.

Eliminating paper records is a significant win, but there are potentially even greater efficiencies to be gained by speeding up incorporations, mergers, acquisitions, IPOs, and other sophisticated commercial transactions. Blockchain-based smart contracts, for example, will make it possible to update, delete, and act automatically upon records when specific conditions are met, like option expirations. Other possibilities include automatic updates to reflect name and address changes and amendments to collateral descriptions and secured parties.[36]

The upside to this is that the cost and time necessary to conduct a financial audit would decline considerably. Auditors could deploy more automation, analytics, and machine-learning capabilities such as automatically alerting relevant parties about unusual transactions on a near real-time basis. Supporting documentation—contracts, purchase orders, and invoices—could be encrypted and securely stored or linked to a blockchain. These improvements would free auditors to spend time where they could add more value, such as analyzing complex dealings, recommending improvements in public spending process, and ensuring adequate internal controls and processes to measure and report on their performance.

A NEW MODEL FOR IDENTITY

We might think of the Internet economy as "digital feudalism," in which digital elite own vast amounts of the virtual landscape. We serfs work this land, searching, learning, publishing, collaborating, and conducting business. But the digital landlords are capturing the real value—the data we throw off as we go about our lives—and monetizing it themselves. "Imagine if General Motors did not pay for its steel, rubber, or glass—its inputs," said Robert J. Shapiro, an economist. "That's what it's like for the big Internet companies. It's a sweet deal."[37]

Privacy is the foundation of freedom, yet these digital landlords are irrevocably violating our privacy and other human rights. Look at China's blockchain-based social credit scoring system for evidence of that. Blockchain and cryptocurrencies could have either a positive or a negative effect. Blockchain could enable greater privacy and autonomy over our personal information or could exacerbate an already bad situation. To wit, Libra and similar initiatives by big banks and other incumbents might consolidate even more valuable data—about people's economic lives—into the hands of a few all-powerful intermediaries and use blockchain-based platforms as tools for greater surveillance. China for one sees value in the trackability of cryptocurrencies over paper yuan.[38]

When considering privacy and identity in the context of Facebook's ambitious new Libra project, Meltem Demirors, chief strategy officer of CoinShares, said:

> The question is not about whether Facebook has the right to do it [launch Libra]. There [must] be two things: consent—consent to the rules of the system. You need choice to exit a system with all of your data intact. These are complex problems. One of the issues with the blockchain industry is [that] we are trying to create simple solutions to complex problems.[39]

This speaks to a much broader issue identified in a Blockchain Research Report by Greg McMullen, Primavera De Filippi, and Constance Choi of COALA. In their report, "Blockchain Identity Services," the authors argued that we increasingly rely on "governments or corporations, which manage unique identifiers and centralized private data repositories relating to specific certificates or attributes. These centralized authorities, often representing single points of failure, are often associated with problems of data privacy violations, data abuse, and leaks."[40] This is problematic for a number of reasons:

The blurring of boundaries between private data markets and markets for identity management services has intensified the situation. On one hand, services marketed as identity management by providers such as Facebook or LinkedIn are collecting enormous troves of personal information and developing highly profitable business models of private data brokerage. On the other hand, data brokers such as Experian, which have built lucrative and opaque business models on the nonconsensual profiling of individuals, are now marketing their services to the very individuals being profiled.

These systems operate with little to no transparency about the kind of information collected, how it is used, and who it is shared with or sold to. Data subjects have no visibility into the security, accuracy, or usage of the information held by these platforms. The original gatekeeping function of identity verification has evolved into a complex and opaque process of data collecting, profiling, and selling for purposes well beyond identification. As these platforms became essential parts of our daily lives, they gained the power to dictate the terms of data collection and use, often to the detriment of us as subjects. The development of national identity management systems such as Aadhaar in India and the social citizen score in China leads to identification creep and the surveillance state.[41]

The COALA team argued, "With blockchain technology, individuals have the potential to reclaim sovereignty over their identities and personal data from centralized entities, such as corporations and digital platforms, and to benefit from the value of their own data."[42] In other words, individuals can have self-sovereign identities that they own and control themselves.

So, the solution is not to ask governments to protect privacy through laws like the EU General Data Protection Regulation. New approaches to privacy and ID management give citizens ownership of their identities, the facts of their existence, and the data they create as they live their lives. Through self-sovereign identity technologies, we could record and store immutable facts and other personal data in a virtual black box and manage access to these data through smart contracts. The self-sovereign identity is one the pillars of the Blockchain Research Institute's "Declaration of Interdependence: Toward a New Social Contract for the Digital Economy" and will be critical to the transformation to a more open, inclusive, and private financial system.[43]

DECENTRALIZED FINANCE: THE GOLDEN NINE

"Decentralization of finance is really the democratization of finance. It's about eradicating barriers," said Ethan Buchman, co-founder of the Cosmos Network.[44] In *Blockchain Revolution*, we broke down the financial industry into seven components: moving value, storing value, lending value, exchanging value, funding and investing, accounting, and risk management and insurance. We're adding this ninth category, "analyzing value," to reflect the growing importance of data and information in the global economy and the proliferation of ventures offering services in this area. Today there are literally dozens of projects and companies launched or launching to disrupt these pillars of our financial reality (Table 1-2).

Ethereum has emerged as the leading platform by far for decentralized finance applications, with many projects coming from ConsenSys. The breadth of projects is impressive. James Beck of ConsenSys said, "From stablecoins, decentralized exchanges and wallets to payments networks, lending and insurance platforms, key infrastructural development, marketplaces, and investment engines— the decentralized finance ecosystem is flourishing."[45] Joseph Lubin, co-founder of Ethereum and CEO of ConsenSys, added,

What's now emerging is a vast spectrum of decentralized finance: On one hand, open finance platforms that empower individuals around the world to engage with new and remodeled financial systems. On the other hand, decentralized finance solutions are changing the approach of established institutions by bringing decentralized solutions into play.[46]

TABLE 1-2
THE GOLDEN NINE

FUNCTION	BLOCKCHAIN IMPACT	BLOCKCHAIN	PROJECT NAME
1. Authenticating identity and value	Verifiable, robust, and cryptographically secured identities will ensure know-your-customer/ anti-money laundering compliance.	Corda	BlockOne IQ
			DreamzChain KYC
			Whistle Blower
		Ethereum	3Box
			Bloom
			SelfKey
		Hyperledger	Blinking
			BlockR (REALTOR® Association Blockchain)
			HealthVerity
2. Storing value	Payment mechanism combined with a reliable store of value will obsolesce typical financial services.	Bitcoin	Blockstream Green
		Corda	21st Century Banking
			Piston Vault
			PropineCustody
		Ethereum	Argent
			MyEtherWallet
			Trustology
3. Moving value	Transfer of value in very large and very small increments without intermediary will dramatically reduce cost and speed of payments.	Bitcoin	Lightning Peach
		Corda	B2P for Procure-to-Pay
			Wildfire
		Cosmos	e-Money
		Ethereum	DAI
			TrueUSD
		Hyperledger	Aabo
			LedgerKitchen
			TEKO LLC
		Ripple	RippleNet

FUNCTION	BLOCKCHAIN IMPACT	BLOCKCHAIN	PROJECT NAME
4. Lending value	Parties can issue, trade, and settle debt peer to peer, relying on blockchain-based reputation scores; more accessible to the unbanked and the entrepreneurial.	Corda	BSOS AR Financing
			Invoice Discounting Platform
			Letter of Credit
			Loan-Finance Application
			Promissory Note Loan Platform
		Ethereum	Compound Finance
			Cred
			Lendoit
			MakerDAO Collateralized Debt Position
5. Funding and investing	New models for peer-to-peer financing, recording of corporate actions such as dividends paid automatically through smart contracts. Titles registry to automate claims to rental income and other forms of yield.	Corda	Automated Issuances
			TINA
			Unlisted Share Trading
		Ethereum	ConsenSys Digital Securities
			Mattereum
			Melonport
		Hyperledger	D3Ledger
			OmegaX
			Peloton Blockchain
6. Exchanging value	Blockchain takes settlement times on all transactions from days and weeks to minutes and seconds. This speed and efficiency also creates opportunities for unbanked and underbanked to participate in wealth creation.	Corda	Digital RFQ
			Shipping Trade Finance Platform
			Three parties DvP Atomic TX
		Cosmos	Binance Chain
			Kira Interchain Exchange
		Ethereum	Augur
			Bounties Network
			DutchX
			Ethlance
		Hyperledger	Aid tech
			Altoros
			healthDigit
			Smart Block Laboratory

FUNCTION	BLOCKCHAIN IMPACT	BLOCKCHAIN	PROJECT NAME
7. Insuring value and managing risk	Using reputational systems, insurers will better estimate actuarial risk, creating decentralized markets for insurance. More transparent derivatives.	Corda	Adappt
			B3i Reinsurance
			Interest Rate Swap
			Personal Auto Claims Management
			Workers Comp Claims Process
		Ethereum	Etherisc
			VouchForMe
		Hyperledger	Energy Savings Insurance (ESI)
			openIDL (open Insurance Data Link)
8. Analyzing financial data	Cutting-edge information is as critical as ever. Public blockchain-based data flows are readily auditable and may serve as oracles in smart contracts.	Bitcoin	Block Explorer
			Cryptocurrency Data Feed
		Corda	Property Listing
			Topaz
		Ethereum	Augur Leaderboard
			Prediction Global
			Stablecoin Index
		Hyperledger	Ocyan
9. Accounting for value	Distributed ledger will make audit and financial reporting real time, responsive, and transparent; will dramatically improve capacity of regulators to scrutinize financial actions within a corporation.	Bitcoin	Crystal Blockchain
			Verady
		Corda	BlockProvenance
			Cheque Verifier
		Cosmos	BigchainDB
		Ethereum	Sweetbridge Accounting Protocol
			XribaBooks
		Hyperledger	Avanza Innovations

Replacing old infrastructure with the new is daunting and raises many questions: What problems are we trying to solve? Are we subbing out big companies for small unproven ventures? Will these ventures help with inclusion? Will the transformation truly democratize finance or simply consolidate wealth in the hands of a new set of large stakeholders in powerful blockchain networks like Ethereum and Bitcoin?

How does decentralized finance differ from open finance? Collin Myers of ConsenSys put it on a scale of 0 to 10, where 0 is creative destruction and 10 is incremental change: "Open finance is a 9 to 10 innovation—an improvement on what we have today. Decentralized finance is a 0 to 1 innovation—creating a parallel financial system that will allow humans to send value and organize in ways we have never experienced before."[47] To Myers, Libra is not an example of decentralized finance, but it could help pave the way: "Libra is a Trojan horse to get people comfortable with transacting and utilizing digital currencies. Ten years from now, we will look back on Libra as an intermediary step enabling the core blockchain community to get where we want to be, which is a truly permissionless and open source financial system."[48]

In the meantime, why is everyone so excited about decentralized finance? Rune Christensen, founder of MakerDAO, said, "The main advantage and characteristic of DeFi is very similar to open source software in that it's really about unlocking network effects and the value of people being able to work together seamlessly and in a permissionless manner without intermediaries." According to Christensen, for something to be considered a DeFi *decentralized application* (Dapp), it must satisfy the following three requirements: it is difficult to shut down, it runs on a blockchain, and it is trustless.[49] From Christensen's perspective, the benefits are fivefold: lower costs, efficient accounting, total transparency, low switching costs, and broader access.

Decentralized finance has replaced ICOs as the dominant use case for the Ethereum network. A nascent marketplace of dozens of Dapps running on Ethereum represent, in aggregate, a very meaningful chunk of Ethereum's native token, ether. According to the website defipulse.com, around $400 to $700 million of ether is locked in these DeFi applications at any given time (Table 1-3).[50]

TABLE 1-3

VALUE LOCKED IN THE TOP 10 DECENTRALIZED FINANCE APPLICATIONS

NAME	BLOCKCHAIN	CATEGORY	LOCKED ° (IN $ MILLIONS)
Maker	Ethereum	Lending	$255.7
Compound	Ethereum	Lending	$93.0
InstaDApp	Ethereum	Lending	$23.8
Synthetix	Ethereum	Derivatives	$20.4
Uniswap	Ethereum	DEXes	$15.9
Nuo Network	Ethereum	Lending	$14.1
dYdX	Ethereum	Lending	$10.3
Dharma	Ethereum	Lending	$10.1
Lightning Network	Bitcoin	Payments	$8.5
WBTC	Ethereum	Assets	$5.8

Source of data: defipulse.com, as of 14 Aug. 2019.

Part of the benefit of DeFi applications is anonymity or pseudo-anonymity. Traditional financial intermediaries require you to provide proof of who you are (authenticating value), but many people don't have an identity to provide or are unwilling to reveal it. Demirors sees this as a key attribute of DeFi:

> If you abstract out the need for an identity and centralized intermediary, we suddenly create an open world marketplace that is defined by a completely new set of criteria, where everything that is programmable and tradable can be traded 24/7. The realm of possibilities of what you can now do—markets, assets, structure—start to change.[51]

Consider MakerDAO, the largest and most successful DeFi Dapp. The associated stablecoin DAI: MakerDAO is "digital financial infrastructure that aims to create unbiased currency and unbiased access to credit for everyone," according to its founder

Rune Christensen. More simply, MakerDAO views its mission as a logical step from Bitcoin. "Bitcoin was supposed to be better peer-to-peer-cash. Bitcoin doesn't make good cash. It's an excellent store of value and a check on central banks but it is not good cash," said Greg Di Prisco of MakerDAO. How does Maker solve these perceived shortcomings? "Maker is a decentralized central bank. Everyone has the ability to generate money against their own assets. Traditionally, you need a commercial bank to act as intermediary," but now anyone who owns ether can do so instead.[52]

Individuals can create the stablecoin DAI by collateralizing it with ether. Crucially, the smart contract is set up so that each DAI must be over-collateralized. So, for example, if you pledged $150 equivalent of ether to the MakerDAO smart contract you could conceivably create $100 of DAI, but no more. The goal is to ensure that DAI doesn't "break the buck," that is, maintain its peg to the USD. The decision to choose the USD was more practical than philosophical. Right now the USD is the global reserve currency and the most widely recognized medium of exchange so it was logical to start with that reference point.

Considering how volatile ether is—in the past three years, it has skyrocketed from $20 to over $1,400 before crashing below $100 and now sits at $200—we might wonder how something collateralized in such a volatile asset could possibly maintain its peg to a comparatively steady one. With DAI, if the value of ether drops below a preset threshold, the smart contract will liquidate the ether locked within it to ensure that the contract is always properly collateralized and the price maintained. An added buffer is a stability fee individuals pay into the system when they create a DAI.

If this all sounds a bit far-fetched, consider that DAI has gone through a trial by fire. Launched in 2018, it has withstood the collapse in the price of ether while maintaining its peg. The smart contract manages all of the mechanics of this process autonomously. Right now, the value of DAI sits at around $90 million (and the total value locked in Maker is $300 million) but MakerDAO plans to grow aggressively by opening up collateral to any kind of asset, most likely in 2019.

The upside is that anybody can generate new money without an intermediary. You become your own bank. Today DAI is used by a small but growing group of technologists and hobbyists but Rune Christensen has bigger goals: "The way DAI scales in the long run is not so much about the existing crypto world. It's about tokenizing other assets—[that is,] claims on property, stocks, or bonds."[53]

Core to DAI's road map is understanding that, while DAI is built on Ethereum, there will not be one blockchain to rule them all. There will be different trade-offs for different kinds of use cases and the industry will need to build bridges. Christensen wants MakerDAO to be a "blockchain transcendent distributed application."

As he put it: "By creating beachheads where you get some level adoption you open up the industry to a world of possibilities."[54] Today, bankers might be understandably relaxed about the potential threat of these nascent and small-scale projects. DAI is a rounding error in the grand scheme of things. But big things start small: once innovations have been proven to work, it's hard to go back. As Demirors said about DeFi, "It's early stage, but these are important experiments to prove out a set of ideas. Now that the world has been exposed to these ideas, they can't be put in the box."[55]

Still, DeFi is not a stand-alone category within financial services. Bill Barhydt, CEO of Abra, said that decentralized finance is a spectrum:

If you're operating purely within the Bitcoin realm and you're not touching the banking system, and individuals are holding their own keys, it is a purely decentralized application. You are interoperating with all the Bitcoin nodes out there. But, if you're using Abra to buy synthetic hybrid Apple shares, Abra is your counterparty, so it is quasi-decentralized. ... Anything that integrates into the physical world introduces trust.[56]

With that integration, it creates opportunities and challenges for the world's leading financial incumbents, which we discuss next.

CHALLENGES AND IMPLICATIONS

How many incumbents realize that their money-making platforms are burning, their tools for managing the economy are weakening, their approaches to tracking criminals are grossly infringing upon the privacy rights of law-abiding citizens, and their efforts at economic development and financial inclusion depend too much on redistributing wealth—and that the risk of doing nothing is greater than the risk of taking a leap into the great unknown? As Eric Shinseki, retired US Army general, said, "If you dislike change, you're going to dislike irrelevance even more."[57]

THREAT AND OPPORTUNITY FOR INCUMBENTS

With paradigm shifts, leaders of the old are often last to embrace the new, if they survive to embrace it at all. So why did Blockbuster not create Netflix, and why did Sears not create Amazon? One reason is the innovator's dilemma, where disruptors of old paradigms have trouble disrupting themselves, largely because of good management. Harvard Business School professor Clay Christensen explained:

> The very decision-making and resource allocation processes that are key to the success of established companies are the very processes that reject disruptive technologies: listening to customers; tracking competitors' actions carefully; and investing resources to design and build higher-performance, higher-quality products that will yield greater profit.[58]

That's not to say that incumbents sit idly while start-ups sprout up around them. Quite the opposite. Don Sull, former professor of strategy and entrepreneurship at both Harvard and London business schools, found that leaders of successful companies double down on what made them successful, investing more in outdated technology, rather than directing funds to innovation. Sull called this phenomenon *active inertia*: "When the world changes, organizations trapped in active inertia do more of the same."[59] "Organizations trapped in active inertia resemble a car with its back wheels stuck in a rut," Sull wrote. "Managers step on the gas. Rather than escape the rut, they only dig themselves in deeper."[60]

Many so-called digital transformation projects often fall into the camp of doing more of the same but with a digital gloss. Often, those initiatives are unsuccessful and wasteful. To wit, according to Steve Zobell of *Forbes*, 70 percent of all digital transformation initiatives do not reach their goals.[61] Despite spending $1.3 trillion on digital transformations, approximately $900 billion went to waste.[62]

However, sometimes leaders of old do embrace the new. IBM has so far navigated multiple shifts—from punch cards to mainframes, PCs, and the Internet. FedEx has been an innovator in supply chains and shipping for 40 years; it now has a big vision for how FedEx will become a financial services company with open standards built on blockchain.[63] Facebook perhaps sees itself doing the same with the launch of Libra. What each of these examples has in common is a focus on the problems that customers are trying to solve.

In financial services, blockchain is often touted as a magic cost-saving elixir, poised to cut fat, waste, and complexity from existing markets. This may very well be true, but it is far from the whole picture. Stating blockchain can cut X cost from a market segment assumes that the market segment itself will continue to exist. History tells us that technology not only disrupts industries but also can eliminate them altogether.

Incumbents are not sitting on the sidelines. The strategies of J.P.Morgan and Fidelity reflect the differing approaches that incumbents are taking. J.P.Morgan is representative of what some of the leading financial institutions are doing in this space. The bank launched Quorum, a permissioned implementation of the Ethereum network. The bank touted Quorum as a variant of public blockchain technology with strong permissions and privacy. This focus on privacy is understandable, since many financial transactions are sensitive and require anonymity. To wit, J.P.Morgan integrated Zcash's zero-knowledge proofs into Quorum as early as 2017. Also in 2017, the bank launched its own Interbank Information Network, which the bank touted as the industry's first scalable, P2P network powered by blockchain.[64]

The bank remains active in the space. In 2018, it showcased Dromaius, a prototype for blockchain transactions. At the time, Christine Moy, head of J.P.Morgan's Blockchain Center of Excellence, said the project could "streamline operations, help with cost savings, and overall make the experience of transacting or issuing a financial instrument like this more seamless and simplified."[65] In February 2019, the bank announced that it was the first major US bank to "successfully test a digital coin representing a fiat currency." In a press release, it said, "The JPM Coin is based on blockchain-based technology enabling the instantaneous transfer of payments between institutional clients."[66]

While J.P.Morgan's efforts in this space are laudable, they are still largely focused on reducing cost, complexity, and friction within existing financial markets. They have not embraced cryptoassets and the senior leadership remains skeptical of bitcoin and others.[67]

Compare J.P.Morgan's approach to Fidelity's. One of the most storied financial institutions in the United States, Fidelity has long advocated the benefits of cryptocurrencies and the underlying blockchain technology. As early as 2014, CEO Abigail Johnson was touting the benefits of bitcoin, and Fidelity has mined bitcoin for some years.

Perhaps because Fidelity is a privately held company, it can focus on long-term disruption over short-term profits.

We weren't surprised when, in 2018, the asset management giant launched Fidelity Digital Assets, a separately managed subsidiary. Helmed by Wall Street veteran Tom Jessop, Fidelity Digital Asset is creating a suite of products and services to make it easier to buy, sell, and store digital assets. Initially, it is focusing on bitcoin and other well-established cryptocurrencies. Fidelity, however, also either manages or administers nearly $6 trillion of customer assets, and we can reasonably speculate that Fidelity Digital Asset's initial foray into cryptoassets is cultivating the knowledge and talent needed to migrate existing securities and financial products onto the blockchain. Either way, by embracing the native cryptoasset industry, Fidelity is positioning itself to build new businesses, which will likely attract many new and younger customers.

Increasingly, financial firms fall into one of these two categories: focusing on costs or focusing on revenues. We believe that, by focusing on the latter, financial incumbents will not only survive but also thrive in this new era of digital disruption.

RETHINKING CENTRAL BANKING

Central banks themselves are coming to terms with the threats and opportunities of blockchain technologies, from cryptocurrencies to distributed ledgers. On one hand, cryptocurrencies—whether bitcoin, Libra, or something else—require central banks to confront the possible end to government monopolies on money. But blockchain is also a powerful tool that governments will likely exploit for their own ends, and that could be a good thing too. The rise of blockchain technology has renewed "[d]ebates over the wisdom of these policies [and] led to a revival of interest in classical monetary economics," according to New York University professors David Yermack and Max Raskin.[68]

Christine Lagarde, nominated for the presidency of the European Central Bank (ECB), captured the threat and opportunity of blockchain and cryptocurrencies in an interview with CNBC: "I think the role of the disruptors and anything that is using distributed ledger technology, whether you call it crypto, assets, currencies, or whatever. ... [T]hat is clearly shaking the system." She added, "We don't want to shake the system so much that we would lose the stability that is needed."[69]

Let's start with the potential existential impact of blockchain. Monetary policy is a key lever that governments can pull to influence the economy and exert sovereignty over people. For most of bitcoin's 10-year existence, the notion that it could actually threaten or replace fiat currencies was more of a thought experiment than a real risk.

Yet, within the decade, that discussion has spread from Internet forums and mailing lists to the US Congress, the International Monetary Fund, the US Treasury Department, and the White House. Throughout July 2019, a number of high-ranking US government officials opined on bitcoin and the risk (or lack thereof) to the US dollar's reserve status. President Trump said in a tweet,

I am not a fan of Bitcoin and other Cryptocurrencies, which are not money, and whose value is highly volatile and based on thin air. Unregulated cryptoassets can facilitate unlawful behavior, including drug trade and other illegal activity. ... We have only one real currency in the USA, and it is stronger than ever, both dependable and reliable. It is by far the most dominant currency anywhere in the World, and it will always stay that way. It is called the United States Dollar![70]

That some blockchain-enabled currency could displace the US dollar or at the very least disrupt conventional fiat currencies is no longer a far-fetched idea and may even be likely. Governments have not always been good stewards of fiat currencies and monetary policy, and the lack of strong stewardship has created an opening for bitcoin or alternatives.[71] Adam Hayes of the University of Wisconsin suggested that we are "moving away from today's human-fallible central bankers and toward a technocratic, rules-based algorithmic approach."[72] He blamed modern central banks that "have failed to stem macroeconomic crises, and may have, in fact, exacerbated negative outcomes by incentivizing excessive risk-taking and moral hazard via unconventional monetary tools such as quantitative easing and negative interest rates."[73]

Central bankers must also contend with the reality of corporate and other private sector digital currencies such as Facebook's Libra. The Libra blockchain could grow very quickly, making it one of the largest central banks in the world, accountable to shareholders but not necessarily to citizens. It could become too big to fail, making the bailout of AIG (American International Group) look like chump change.[74] This systemic risk, combined with the real risk that individuals opt out of local payment infrastructure and money in favor of global corporate coins, should raise concerns for central bankers. In an op-ed for *The New York Times*, Matt Stoller, a fellow at the Open Markets Institute, wrote about the threat that such a private currency scheme could present: "What happens if all users want to sell their Libra currency at once, causing the Libra Reserve to hold a fire sale of assets? If the Libra system becomes intertwined in our global economy in the way Facebook hopes, we would need to consider a public bailout of a privately managed system. Sorry, but no thanks."[75]

Stoller doesn't think that government should allow the launch of any private global payments system that taxpayers would have to bail out because it had become too big too fail. During the Congressional hearings on Libra, House Financial Services Committee Rep. Gregory Meeks (D-NY) suggested that a successful Libra "would absolutely make [Libra] a systemically risky financial institution, and we would expect [the Financial Services Oversight Council] to designate [Libra] as such."[76]

Stoller also raised a concern regarding national sovereignty. To his mind, a public currency scheme dependent on the consensus of a large number of private nodes wasn't a democracy, no matter how decentralized the network or open the protocols: "Today, American bank regulators and central bankers are hired and fired by publicly elected leaders. Libra payments regulators would be hired and fired by a self-selected council of corporations. There are ways to characterize such a system, but democratic is not one of them." [77]

Another concern is what Libra might do to many economies in the developing world, where more people have a Facebook account than a bank account. They may choose to transact and store value in Libra rather than the local currency. India has been openly hostile to Bitcoin, shutting down exchanges and considering jail time for users and Bitcoin entrepreneurs.[78] They may not be able to bully Facebook and other big tech companies so easily, but they could target merchants and users of Libra, if they saw Libra as a threat.

If Libra is successful, it may cause people to rethink fractional reserve banking. Today, commercial banks typically lend up to 10 times as much money as they hold on deposit. This expansion of money in the form of new credit can help fuel economic growth but raises systemic risks when depositors get jittery and demand their money back. The bank in turn calls its loans leading to a credit crunch and economic crisis. As Bill Barhydt of Abra said, "If Libra has 100 percent reserves, they are killing the fractional reserve system."[79] Perhaps people would prefer having money "on deposit" with a bank that does not create so much new money.

Finally, many central bankers are contemplating what a digital fiat currency could do, and many projects have already been launched. In 10 more years, we expect the landscape of global currencies to look very different from how it does today, with those governments who embrace this technology faring better than those who do not. "The blockchain technology behind digital currencies has the potential to improve central banks' payment and clearing operations, and possibly to serve as a platform from which central banks might launch their own digital currencies," wrote professors Yermack and Raskin back in 2016. "A sovereign digital currency could have profound implications for the banking system, narrowing the relationship between citizens and central banks and removing the need for the public to keep deposits in fractional reserve commercial banks."[80]

Governor Mark Carney of the Bank of England is perhaps the most sophisticated proponent of a new financial order and has spoken openly and often about digital currencies. For example, as his tenure as governor comes to an end, Carney dropped a bombshell on the old-world financial order. After six years of combining financial innovation with a calm stewardship of the UK economy in a time of great turmoil, he proposed the biggest change in the global financial system, perhaps since the 1944 Bretton Woods agreement.

On 23 August 2019, central bankers from around the world assembled for their annual Jackson Hole Symposium. Trump's reactionary tweets may have dominated the 24-hour news cycle, but Carney's speech was one for the ages.[81] Those assembled will remember his words for years to come. Calling the mainstream view of international policy cooperation anachronistic and out of touch with our changing world, Carney argued for replacing the US dollar as the global reserve currency with a synthetic global currency backed by a basket of digital government-issued digital currencies. "Such a platform would be based on the virtual rather than the physical," he said.

Carney suggested that this international stablecoin could resemble Facebook's Libra. More likely, it would mix the attributes of fiat currencies, cryptocurrencies like bitcoin and its underlying blockchain technology, and possibly private sector initiatives like Libra.

In the storied halls of high finance, challenging established dogma is hazardous, potentially career-ending—the US dollar has been the reserve currency for 75 years. Where iconoclasts like Jeff Bezos, Richard Branson, Elon Musk, and Mark Zuckerberg were largely outsiders to the citadels of publishing, retail, transportation, and media, Carney is an insider with the power to effect change. With an insider's knowledge of how our global systems work and a disruptor's view of the future, this is a potent and rare mix of leadership attributes.

The speech surprised some, but Carney had long foreseen how digital technology would change our institutions and our money. In 2016, he said, "Fintech may deliver a more inclusive financial system, domestically and globally; with people better connected, more informed, and increasingly empowered."[82] In the same speech, he announced the Bank of England would begin a pilot for a digital fiat currency.

The global world order is changing as digital technology disrupts industries, strains our institutions, and forces us to rethink basic social constructs like money. Many countries should read Carney's words and deeds carefully because they could benefit from this kind of leadership in three ways.

First, many countries should create their own digital fiat currencies. The Bank of England found that replacing a portion of payments with a digital currency could boost global domestic product by three percent, lower barriers to financial inclusion, and empower consumers.[83] It went so far as to develop three models for central bank digital currencies, with design principles and balance sheet implications.[84] Private industry grows and innovates through experimentation and risk-taking. Government, in albeit a more measured and cautious manner, can do likewise.

Second, political leaders should work with industry to address the regulatory challenges of the emerging fintech and blockchain industries. Carney is acutely aware of these challenges. In his August 2019 speech, he said,

The Bank of England and other regulators have been clear that, unlike in social media, for which standards and regulations are only now being developed after the technologies have been adopted by billions of users, the terms of engagement for any new systemic private payments system must be in force well in advance of any launch.[85]

In other words, money is regulated, governed, and managed differently from information. The new Internet of value will require leadership exquisitely attuned to these challenges and prepared to chart a new course.

Finally, by becoming a model user of technology, by streamlining laws and regulations, and by funding education and training initiatives, a national government could set off a Cambrian explosion of new business development and lay the foundation for a global innovation economy centered within its borders.

So far, many of the actual government cryptocurrencies have been proposed or poorly implemented by authoritarian regimes such as Venezuela, Iran, and Turkey. The People's Bank of China has taken a few bold steps. Leaders in the Federal Reserve, ECB, and others stall at their peril.

ONBOARDING THE UNBANKED

Blockchain has been touted as a solution to banking the unbanked. Indeed, there are promising though limited signs of it in places like Venezuela, where those who have access to computers, electricity, and the Internet (a clear minority in a struggling country) can opt out of the inflationary death spiral of the local currency and store and move value digitally.

Still, the promise of solving the financial inclusion crisis remains largely unfulfilled. Perhaps, as Demirors told us in an interview, financial inclusion is not always a technology problem. "It's an education, policy, monetary, hardware, social problem. It is very naive to say complex problems have simple solutions."[86] There is no doubt much truth to this. However, we view these problems not as reasons blockchain will fail to onboard the world's unbanked, but as implementation challenges to be overcome.

World Economic Forum founder and executive director Klaus Schwab said, "Our collective inability to secure inclusive growth and preserve our scarce resources puts multiple global systems at risk simultaneously." He added, "Our first response must be to develop new models for cooperation that are not based on narrow interests but on the destiny of humanity as a whole."[87] Financial inclusion is foundational to building this more inclusive model for global growth. Without access to financial services, billions are unable to participate fully in the global economy.

Blockchain Research Institute author Rachel Robinson summed up the status quo as a "network of heavily regulated intermediaries [facilitating] transactions between parties by reconciling transaction data and assuming some of the inherent risk to make the current financial system possible."[88] She noted:

> This network was developed piecemeal, in response to different needs at different times and using different technologies. Within this network, financial institutions maintain proprietary ledgers of transactions with minimal transparency into each version. Therefore, these institutions, and all market participants must invest in costly software to reconcile transaction data, which remains vulnerable to error and fraud. They must also submit to periodic audits to ensure their proprietary ledgers have been recorded accurately.[89]

The upshot is that many financial intermediaries are unwilling or unable to bank billions of people because the cost of doing so is prohibitive or those individuals lack an acceptable identity, which banks need for complying with *know-your-customer* (KYC) or *anti-money laundering* (AML) regulations.

Blockchain applications are making access to financial services a reality. We need more work in this area. Barhydt's Abra is one of the most successful cryptocurrency applications. Outside the United States, Abra's fast-growing markets include Canada, the Philippines,

Singapore, Hong Kong, Turkey, Mexico, Russia, Southeast Asia, and the United Kingdom.

Ultimately, this is a complex problem with no easy solution. Among other things, we need to accelerate the adoption of new forms of identity. If individuals can bootstrap a persistent digital ID, they will be able to access banking and credit more easily.

PREVENTING CRIME WHILE PRESERVING RIGHTS

Since bitcoin's early days, naysayers have condemned the cryptocurrency as a tool for laundering money or buying illicit goods. Critics argued that, because the technology was decentralized, lightning quick, and peer to peer, criminals would exploit it. To be sure, criminals are always one step ahead of the law in harnessing the latest technology. Marc Goodman, author of *Future Crimes*, wrote, "Exponential times lead to exponential crimes."[90] So this criticism of bitcoin falls under the category of human beings wanting to harm other human beings. Criminals will use the latest technology to do it.

But there is nothing unique to bitcoin or blockchain technology that makes it more effective for criminals than other technologies or other media of value such as paper bills. In fact, as the industry has matured, many authorities now believe that digital currencies could help law enforcement by providing a record of suspicious activities, maybe even solving a multitude of cybercrimes, from financial services to the Internet of Things.

Bitcoin and blockchain technology could potentially discourage criminal use. First, even criminals must publish all their bitcoin transactions in the blockchain like everybody else. The old Watergate adage, "Follow the money" to the crook, is actually more doable on the blockchain than through other payment methods. Bitcoin's pseudonymous nature has regulators dubbing bitcoins "prosecution futures" because they can be tracked and reconciled more easily than cash, still the dominant payment medium for criminals.

Second, while blockchains ensure a degree of anonymity, they also provide a degree of openness. If past behavior is any indication of future intent, then we should expect corporations known for spying and countries known for waging cyberwarfare to redouble their efforts because value is involved—money, patents, access to mineral rights, the titles to land and national treasures. It's as if we've placed a big bull's-eye on top of the Internet. The good news is that everyone will be able to see the shenanigans.

CONCLUSION: PROMISE AND PERIL

THE WORLD IN 2030

The year is 2030. The crypto space race among global superpowers has been underway for a decade. The US dollar is now one of two major digital fiat reserve currencies. China was first to launch a fully digitized renminbi, creating a parallel currency regime in 2022. The US Federal Reserve migrated the dollar to a blockchain in 2025.

For most democracies in the world, the US dollar had been, by necessity and by choice, the settlement currency for global business for nearly a century. But China's crypto yuan has become an instrument of state-sponsored mercantilism and surveillance capitalism around the world. Each of the now-180 countries participating in the new Silk Road has agreed to adopt China's currency standard in exchange for generous Chinese loans and access to China's ever-expanding middle class of consumers. Crypto yuan is also the currency of choice (sometimes, by coercion) among African businesses with ties to the Chinese state and state-owned companies. The Communist Party of China has exclusive visibility into all the transactions on its proprietary and permissioned platform. The United States and China are waging an economic war for influence in the world with their two competing visions for the future.

Inside China, the government has outlawed print cash; all individuals must use crypto yuan. All transactions contribute to their social credit scores, which determine whether they get to spend or save money, invest in property, pay for basic utilities, earn an education, or get a job, with everything denominated in the new state-backed crypto yuan. There is no forgiving or forgetting missed payments, defaults on loans, or unfortunate purchases. There is no escaping the errors of youth or the sins of parents.

The euro still exists but, with the Union teetering and many members participating in the Silk Road initiative, the ECB has been unable to adopt a new technology standard, and the currency has fallen further from use. The pound is digitized, too, but with yet another BREXIT delay and the country's election of its sixth prime minister since the UK referendum, no one is paying much attention.

Corporate currencies are now a reality of life for billions. Facebook was the first to announce its plans but failed to launch Libra after a bruising fight in Washington, DC. Only after the Chinese Internet giants began aggressively exporting the crypto yuan did the US government decide to allow its corporate champions to do likewise with their own version of the US dollar. Amazon, Google, and Facebook are now effectively shadow central banks with trillions of dollars in reserves, banking billions of people, some of them within alternative economies along the Silk Road.

In many emerging markets, the rise to prominence of these corporate currencies has destabilized governments that have lost sovereignty over their own currencies. India has banned not just Bitcoin, but Facebook, Amazon, and others. The United States responded by imposing sanctions on India. For individuals, the upside has been financial inclusion without state surveillance. Now everyone with a smartphone can move, store, and manage value. The flipside is indentureship to corporate oligopolies.

Is this scenario unrealistic? Perhaps. It is certainly speculative. But consider how much the world has changed in the first 10 years of the Bitcoin blockchain. We are on the second half of the chessboard. The better question is, is this future desirable? Do we want the corporate landlords of today's digital economy dominating the next era? Do we want governments to wage their own battles in the technology arena with the human rights of billions of bystanders at stake?

WHAT CAN WE DO?

In July 2019, the US Congress held hearings on Libra. By extension, bitcoin and all blockchain uses are also on trial. It makes for great political theater but is also revealing the nuance and depth of knowledge within government. In one particularly gripping sequence, North Carolina Rep. Patrick McHenry said, "The world that Satoshi Nakamoto, author of the Bitcoin white paper, envisioned is an unstoppable force. We should not attempt to deter this innovation. ... And those that have tried have already failed."[91]

Rep. McHenry is right. To those who have been in this industry since the early days, this is a remarkable admission and demonstrates how fast things have evolved. We welcome the position that this innovation is worth fostering. We also expect government to be far more involved in the evolution of this industry than in the Internet, because the Internet dealt with information and media, whereas blockchain deals with money and assets, areas where government has historically played and should continue to play a more active role.

There is a lack of clarity today over how to categorize crypto-assets from a regulatory perspective—as securities, commodities, currencies, or something else altogether? The SEC initially took the approach that almost all token sales were securities (except bitcoin and perhaps ether), at least until proven otherwise. However, on 10 and 11 July 2019, the SEC did grant two different projects, Blockstack and YouNow, coverage under the new Regulation A categorization.

The law firm of Cooley LLP pointed out that the announcement came "nearly two years after the DAO report and a year and half after Chair Jay Clayton stated that he had yet to see an ICO that did not have a sufficient number of hallmarks of a security."[92] Cooley summarized the grants:

> The [Blockstack and YouNow] offerings were qualified under Tier 2 of Regulation A and cover: (1) for Blockstack the offer and sale of stack tokens to current holders of nonbinding vouchers, to qualified purchasers and the distribution of the stack tokens for noncash consideration pursuant to the issuer's bounty program; and (2) YouNow to distribute up to $50 million prop tokens as in-app rewards.[93]

These grants were positive steps, marking an alternate path forward. However, whether other token offerings can qualify at minimal cost and regulatory burden remains to be seen. In the meantime, several high-profile cryptocurrency and blockchain companies have voiced concern and frustration over the ongoing lack of clarity from regulators. For example, Goldman Sachs–backed Circle moved much of its operations offshore; its CEO Jeremy Allaire said, "The lack of regulatory frameworks significantly limits what can be offered to individuals and businesses in the [United States]."[94]

So far, the response in government broadly to the rise of blockchain technology has been fragmented, piecemeal, and lacking a broad and clear message from government. Perhaps what we need is a new "Telecommunications Act" for the blockchain economy. The US Telecommunications Act of 1996 was a significant overhaul of broadcasting and media regulations that for the first time included consideration of the Internet. Section 230 of the Act stated, "No provider or user of an interactive computer service shall be treated as the publisher or speaker of any information provided by another information content provider."[95] This opened up the floodgates for the Internet revolution to occur free of concern over being caught in the snag of retrograde regulations.

We could draw a similar analogy to companies like Circle. If "blockchain service providers" were not held directly liable for the misbehavior and misuse of users, then there would be a lot less certainty and investment. This is a delicate and complex question. On one hand, we want blockchain innovation to flourish; on the other, we should not falsely equate the issues of the Internet of information—violations of privacy, publicity, moral, Fifth Amendment, and intellectual property (IP) rights—with the potential issues of the Internet of value, such as terrorism financing and money laundering. Both activities are certainly possible by "users" of "blockchain platforms," especially when these "users" could be decentralized autonomous organizations set in motion by hostile regimes. In a research report for the Blockchain Research Institute, Joel Telpner wrote:

> When regulators face an industry in a state of rapid evolution or revolution, that is, high uncertainty, regulators have three possible responses. They can make new laws through rulemaking and potentially through enforcement actions. They can refrain from taking any action and simply observe, study, and learn. Or they can watch developments and periodically issue reports, guidance, or threats. They may end up requiring some combination of the above. But determining which approach is optimal, we believe, must start with a process of informed questioning.[96]

We agree. Regulators must take a light-touch approach, recognizing that technology innovation renders them unable to absorb all information and take appropriate action. Additionally, the very nature of certain blockchain innovations, such as Bitcoin, makes regulating a difficult challenge. Bitcoin should be lightly regulated, but large corporations that seek to transform financial markets ought to be subject to scrutiny. Indeed, their centralized nature makes it far easier to do so. As Ryan Selkis, founder of Messari, told us, "Congress wanted a throat to step on. Facebook makes a good throat to step on. There is no entity to bring before Congress for decentralized cryptocurrencies like bitcoin."[97] A collaborative approach with industry and a broad-based, simple, and clear set of policies will work best.

Beyond regulation, governments must also be model users of blockchain, which will in turn help to usher in a better, more efficient, and more inclusive financial marketplace. As we advocate in this report, governments should use blockchain for their own fiat currencies, to reduce complexity and cost, and improve access to financial services. A truly native digital fiat currency could turbocharge the economy, improve monetary policy, and help reach those who are unbanked or underbanked.

Incumbents must see blockchain not only as a way to reduce complexity and save costs but also as a new platform for creating and moving value. Focus on future revenue opportunities and not merely on cost cutting, and you'll be better positioned. The rise of Facebook and the launch of Libra should serve as a wake-up call: finance is the foundation of all sectors and virtually all human economic activity and production. The transformation has already begun. Embrace blockchain or perish.

CHAPTER 2

THE TOKEN ECONOMY

When Money Becomes Programmable

Michael J. Casey

 ## TOKEN ECONOMY IN BRIEF

- Blockchain technology, and the cryptocurrencies, tokens, and other digital assets it has engendered, may be moving us toward a model of programmable money that incorporates an automated internal governance of common resources and encourages collaboration among communities. Digital scarcity, when applied to these tokens, treats our increasingly digitized economy differently from the pre-digital one. It raises the possibility that our money itself becomes the tool for achieving common outcomes.

- Developers of new decentralized applications are tokenizing all manner of resources—electricity and bandwidth, for example, but also human qualities such as audience attention for online content or fact-checkers' honesty. Whereas media coverage has focused on the billions of dollars these token issuers have raised, it's the radical new economic design that promises a lasting impact on society. Once a community associates scarce tokens with rights to these resources, it can develop controls over token usage that help manage public goods. It's dynamic money whose role extends beyond that of a unit of exchange, money that's a direct tool for achieving community objectives.

- This chapter explores the far-reaching implications of imbuing digital money with policy and incentives. We can envisage a future of digital barter in which different assets are traded directly and people no longer need to store a common currency like the dollar or even bitcoin. The token economy might even free people from the economic distortions and periodic crises that centralized monetary systems have experienced through the centuries.

- As regulators start cracking down on ICOs, development may stall, and that looming threat stands as a call for stricter governance measures to protect investors and users. But the token phenomenon has piqued the collective imagination of hundreds of thousands of hyper-intelligent people now pouring new ideas into the space. This chapter does not predict where this orderless process of iterative innovation will take us; instead, it explores early signs of important, highly disruptive change.

A PREFACE TO THIS CHAPTER

In the immediate months after the report on which this chapter is based went to print, the already booming market for ERC-20 tokens went into overdrive, experiencing one of those late-stage exponential rallies that never ends well.

Predictably, after that spectacular boom had taken the crypto-currency market capitalization to a staggering $830 billion in early January 2018, history's lessons were confirmed as the market did a brutal one-eighty. The price of everything collapsed as the once virtuous circle of self-reinforcing demand for ether and tokens turned into its converse, and a vicious cycle of loss-covering sales pushed prices to the floor.

In public discourse, the "to the moon" bulls who'd flaunted their crypto wealth with very public displays of decadence were displaced by the "told you so" bears: lawyers who'd warned that, within the flood of ICOs, most were more than likely illegal; developers who'd dug into the projects and discovered many built on plagiarized white papers or, at best, flimsy forked code; and seasoned investors who'd predicted that those taking the "greater fool" approach to investing would face their day of reckoning.

The whole affair significantly set back the standing of cryptoeconomics in the public eye. With mainstream press focused singularly on roller-coaster price activity of cryptoassets, the powerful idea that tokens could fuel decentralized platforms and run protocols that incentivized individual behavior toward common objectives hardly got coverage. Instead, the talk was of Tulip Mania, of fortunes lost, of lessons learned the hard way.

Meanwhile, the SEC, in a series of guidance statements followed by numerous cases against ICO issuers, clarified that most, if not all, the token offerings that had come to market in the 2016–2018 wave, were securities offerings. Since the vast majority had not been registered as such and were sold to the public without the appropriate protections and warnings, founders remained vulnerable to legal action unless they'd taken stringent measures to keep their tokens out of the hands of American investors.

But the core idea that tokens promise new efficiencies—that they could overcome the frictions, trust barriers, and rent-seeking that inhibit the centralized global economy—was far from dead. There was a shift to security tokens, established either as digital claims on real-world assets such as real estate or bonds, or offered to the public in *security token offerings* (STOs) in venture fundraising, all on the understanding that they would be fully compliant with securities regulations.

The concept took on with financial institutions. Banks such as Société Générale and Santander sold blockchain-based bonds, as did the World Bank. Also adopting it were start-ups such as Blockstack, which raised $23 million in a first-of-its-kind, SEC-approved public

STO of its "stacks" tokens, the proceeds of which were to be used to build out the architecture of its decentralized Internet software.

Still, the real promise lay in the far more radical idea of a utility token, the concept that ignited the ICO boom—the notion of a digital unit that takes it value not from some defined asset such as a building or a claim on future earnings such as bond or a stock but from its purpose within the blockchain network itself. Utility tokens hold the real promise of decentralization because they regulate the behavior of all participants in the system, through incentives and costs rather than through a centralized entity.

The ICO boom and bust, however, revealed a chicken-and-egg problem: it was almost impossible to identify a utility value in tokens that were sold on the open market before their network was built. By default, that meant regulators would view those initial offerings as speculative investment contracts and, by extension, as sales of unregistered securities. There was a timing issue. How does a token become a utility token? How does it lose its security status?

Influential legal minds, including some from the regulatory sector, have been tackling those questions. Securities regulators in several countries (e.g., Singapore and Switzerland) issued guidelines to define explicitly which types of tokens would constitute securities and which ones were utility tokens, though they did not always use the latter phrase.

In an important speech, Director of the SEC's Division of Corporation Finance William Hinman laid out a case for how a token that was native to a blockchain could evolve over time from being a security at its outset to losing that status as its underlying network and functionality grew. His remarks were interpreted as a sign that the SEC viewed Ethereum's initial offering of ether tokens as an unregistered security token but that ether could not be traded freely on exchanges without requiring such compliance.[98]

Similar thinking about a token's evolutionary capacity was behind the *simple agreement for future token* (SAFT) vehicle designed by

Cooley LLP to help start-ups raise funding with accredited investors, using instruments that would later be convertible into tokens once the network was sufficiently functional and decentralized. It's still unclear where the SEC stands on the SAFT.

This back-and-forth between regulators and the market is inherently unpredictable and meandering. But with each new case and each issuer's new effort to devise a structure that stays compliant but fulfills its decentralized objectives, clarity will slowly emerge. In other words, the dream of the token economy remains well and truly alive.

INTRODUCTION TO THE TOKEN ECONOMY

Throughout 2016 and the first eight months of 2017, developers of decentralized software applications raised more than $1.6 billion via a new tool dubbed the ICO that was first launched in early 2014.[99] By late July 2017, secondary-market trading in the tokens they'd issued had given the pool of cryptocurrencies, cryptocommodities, and cryptotokens to which they belonged a combined value of $95.6 billion, up from $7 billion at the start of 2016.

The phenomenon has made many developers and cryptocurrency enthusiasts very rich and revealed a new crowdfunding model that some see as a threat to Silicon Valley's venture capitalists. Skeptics, on the other hand, make comparisons to the South Sea Bubble, in which shares in an 18th-century British trading company rose rapidly on hype and speculation, only to collapse when the returns didn't live up to the hype. A chasm has emerged between those who see a game-changing shift, not only in fundraising activity but also in economic strategy, and those who warn of reckless ICO scams and of an impending regulatory crackdown. Both deserve to be considered.

If token fans are right, something quite profound is at stake: a new economic system that challenges the basic tenets of 20th-century capitalism. These negotiable tokens blur the lines between "product," "currency," and "equity." In theory, their in-built software can regulate how users behave with each other—so that computer owners can trade excess storage across a decentralized network, for example, or social media users can earn income for their content and attention. They combine self-interest and market pricing signals with a governance system that protects a common good.

For tokens to be viable, however, we need a major overhaul of our auditing processes and commercial regulations to keep issuers honest. If those goals can be met, this emerging token economy offers society an entirely new paradigm of money and value exchange.

A SOLUTION TO THE TRAGEDY OF THE COMMONS?

In his influential essay, "Tragedy of the Commons," about 19th-century farmers grazing their cows on common land, the ecologist Garrett Hardin posited that communities that depend on a shared, unregulated resource will ultimately deplete it as individuals are incentivized to pursue self-interest to the detriment of the common good.[100] Hardin recognized a coordination problem caused by a lack of trust, where well-meaning actors can't avoid overusing a common resource due to their concern that others might "free-ride" on their goodwill.

Ever since that 1968 essay, the word *commons* has come to refer not just to natural resources such as land, water, and food supplies but also to human-created resources such as public infrastructure, and even intangible concepts such as free speech. It is now used frequently in the context of designing policies to ensure free, public access to those resources.

Over the years, Hardin's thesis has been used to justify the role of *external governance*—that is, the state—in regulating and protecting scarce resources that constitute a *public good*. Yet, more recently, some economists have demonstrated that his rather cynical view of human nature doesn't always hold true. In particular, the late Elinor Ostrom, who won a Nobel Prize in 2009 for her work studying how fishermen in Maine self-organized to develop ingrained norms of behavior that helped protect the region's lobster fishery, argued that various communities have proven capable of coming up with effective *internal governance* to manage resources. However, while there are many instances of such common-interest practices around the world, their success relies more on art than science. Internal governance is often contingent on common cultural practices and close personal ties within a community.

Developing a universal model for internal governance has been challenging, especially within the many microeconomic settings in which it is difficult to identify and practically regulate misuse of the common resource. Now, with the advent of blockchain technology and the cryptocurrencies, cryptotokens, and other digital assets that it has engendered, we may be moving toward a model of programmable money that can deliver a more automated system of internal governance over common resources.

Once a community incorporates programmable software into its shared medium of exchange, it can embed usage rules straight into the monetary unit itself. We can use it for some transactions but not for others, and we can program its value to rise in concert with proof of an improvement in the state of the public resource. Tokens thus offer a way to codify into money itself a function that executes the community's expectations regarding people's distinct *rights* to common property and the associated obligations that come with those.

According to Ostrom and Schlager's taxonomy, these may include distinct rights of *access, withdrawal, management, exclusion,* and *alienation*.[101] If we can capture these quasi-legal notions in a token, it becomes a meta-asset, a thing of value that is simultaneously a governance vehicle. It's money with a dynamic use that extends beyond its role as a stable and exchangeable unit of value, to a direct means of achieving community objectives. The great promise of the token economy is that it might solve the Tragedy of the Commons.

INITIAL COIN OFFERINGS: A NEW BREED OF META-ASSET

This promise of profound economic disruption, along with a special breed of speculative mania, is driving explosive investment in these meta-assets. Between 2016 and mid-2017, developers of new decentralized software applications sold $1.6 billion worth of these tokens in ICO events. In the secondary market, this new class of crypto-assets has soared in value, with the collective market capitalization surging from $7 billion at the end of 2015 to a peak of $148 billion in mid-2017, according to *CoinMarketCap.com*.[102] This phenomenon has also seen bitcoin's dominance of the wider market of cryptocurrencies wane somewhat.

Bitcoin's proportional value of all tokens tracked by *CoinMarketCap.com* dropped from 87 percent of the total market capitalization as of the end of 2016 to 46 percent in late August 2017. This river of money into the new tokens has fueled a surge of creative activity, inspiring ideas and fueling an ever-widening ecosystem of open-source development that generates its own feedback loops of exponential innovation. In a mark of how extensive this has become, the range of industries to which new token-based solutions are now being pitched looks as broad as the makeup of the global economy itself. It includes social media, shipping logistics, energy, health, academic research, and insurance, to name just a few.

A new cryptoasset class had been born, one that Goldman Sachs told clients in August 2017 is "getting harder for institutional investors to ignore."[103] By then, many seasoned investors were also concluding that this new asset class was in the midst of a spectacular bubble and overdue for a major sell-off. In one noteworthy ICO, a project called Gnosis—which intends to let people trade tokens in a market based on the success (or otherwise) of any prediction—raised $12.5 million in a 12-minute sale of just five percent of the total tokens outstanding.

With the founders still holding the other 95 percent, that left the platform's total valuation at a whopping $300 million.[104] Then, within a month, its price nearly quadrupled to over $1 billion, earning what Silicon Valley would call "unicorn" status—all for a project that ostensibly has no users and no clear path to market. In pretty much all ICOs, the ideas on offer are far from fully tested, and many have little more than a white paper behind them. FOMO—"fear of missing out"—may be driving this euphoria as much any consideration of value propositions.

The concerns now are that an overabundance of incoming money is distorting incentives for the suddenly rich developers who've established these concepts and, perhaps worse, that many have done insufficient legal due diligence to protect themselves from securities law. Either way, a shakeout of some sort seems inevitable. If that forces a more mature development of this market, with appropriate regulations, best practices, and institutions to monitor and hold the industry to account, then such a correction would be positive.

But it would be a pity if the losses set back the more promising aspects of this new approach to value generation, exchange, and resource management. The intent of this chapter is to draw out that grand potential while suggesting ways to bring more order and security to this nascent investment market.

THE ADVENT OF DIGITAL SCARCITY

Both the enthusiasm for meta-asset investing and their potential to tackle the Tragedy of the Commons can be traced to bitcoin, the very first cryptotoken. Not only did this invention turn the imagination of thousands of developers toward designing applications for a decentralized, disintermediated economic future, it also established a precedent for the software-driven internal governance of a scarce public resource. In coming up with the blockchain, a distributed public ledger that a community of currency users could share as their record of the truth, Bitcoin's pseudonymous founder, Satoshi Nakamoto, created a public good, a commons in need of protection.

Its integrity had to be assured despite the possibility that individual validators of that ledger, known as *bitcoin miners*, might be incentivized to act maliciously and enter false data that would allow them to "double-spend" their bitcoin balances—in other words, to engage in digital counterfeiting. There was no centralized authority to keep all the actors honest, no external governance, which had been the failure point for all prior attempts to create a decentralized currency with no centralized authority in charge. Without such an authority, a permissionless ledger that did not require identification of the user was always vulnerable to these abuses. Like the cattle herders on the commons, individual actors could not trust other people to act honestly.

Satoshi Nakamoto beat this limitation. By embedding a unique set of software-driven rules into the Bitcoin protocol, he incentivized the otherwise unidentified participants in the network to maintain the ledger's integrity for the good of the whole while simultaneously seeking profits out of self-interest. The key was a special *proof-of-work* (PoW) algorithm that compelled miners to perform an electricity-burning computation task before they could earn the right to receive bitcoin rewards. That "skin in the game" made it prohibitively expensive to take over the network and doctor the results. It incentivized them to come to a consensus on a truthful ledger with all the other miners. It was a unique marriage of self and common interest. With it, Nakamoto achieved something remarkable: he solved the Tragedy of the Commons.

In addition to its PoW consensus system, which compels even unidentifiable rogue players to act honestly, there's another powerful idea behind Bitcoin that has helped frame new ideas around how cryptotokens can help communities manage common resources: that of "digital assets." Because PoW assures the integrity of the (uppercase *B*) Bitcoin ledger and protects against double-spending of (lowercase *b*) bitcoin currency, each unit of that currency can be treated as a unique item. For the first time, we have a form of digital value that cannot be replicated—unlike a Word document, an MP3 song, a video, or any other software vehicle for transmitting value that pre-existed Bitcoin. In one fell swoop, Nakamoto created the concept of *digital scarcity* and brought digital assets into existence.

Digital scarcity, when applied to a token such as bitcoin or some other digitally tokenized medium of exchange, allows a new approach to managing our increasingly digitized economy and its microeconomies within. With scarce digital tokens, communities with a common interest in value generation can embed their shared values into the software's governance and use these meta-assets as instruments of those values. Once they associate scarce tokens with rights to scarce resources, they can develop controls over token usage that help manage that public good.

Here's one hypothetical example: A local government that wants to reduce pollution, traffic congestion, and the town's carbon footprint might reward households that invest in local solar generation with negotiable digital tokens that grant access to electric mass-transit vehicles but not to toll roads or parking lots. The tokens would be negotiable, with their value tied to measures of the town's carbon footprint, creating an incentive for residents to use them.

It's an example of a direct, token-led strategy for promoting conservation of the natural environment. It's also potentially a way for economists to put a price on externalities such as pollution. But the concept extends far beyond managing resources in the natural environment. With tokens that mediate the exchange of spare computer storage across a decentralized network, we could share use of otherwise wasted disk space on people's hard drives. Or with "reputation tokens" that reward adjudicators for making provably honest judgments about prediction market outcomes, we could promote and protect the public good of "honest judgments."

TOKENS AS POWERFUL INCENTIVES

The implications of imbuing digital money with policy and incentives are far-reaching. The concept aligns with the goals of a *circular economy*, where all participants in a supply chain have incentives to minimize waste and constantly recycle parts and materials. Designers of new social media platforms could encourage pro-social behavior and accurate information by requiring skin-in-the-game tokens that put a computing tax on bots and other automating tools of fake news.

We could tokenize everything from electricity to bandwidth. All of that would potentially bring new market efficiencies down to micro-transaction levels, enabling an Internet of Things economy to silently, automatically manage our economic activities with far more precision and less waste than was ever conceivable in the world of nonprogrammable, analog money.

For this world to emerge, however, many token users need to believe in them and, by extension, to use them. At this stage, even transactions in bitcoin, the biggest and most established cryptotoken, represent a tiny proportion of global commerce. What's more, this requirement for legitimacy faces potential conflicts with the investment part of token craze. There's a real risk that easy money flowing into this sector is incentivizing founders of these ventures to focus not on the integration of the tokens into their platform but on amassing a store of outside reference currency, such as bitcoins or dollars, earned from preselling tokens. This hoarding trend could stall progress toward the technology's greater purpose.

If all that tokens become is a crowdfunding tool to bypass SEC regulations in pursuit of nonaccredited investors, then their disruptive impact will be limited. If the vast majority of investors are simply participating in a speculative bubble with no interest in the utility value of the tokens themselves, then a retrenchment is likely—both in the tokens market and in the pace of innovation around it—especially once the SEC starts filing selective lawsuits.

The risk of such a crackdown is serious, partly because the taxonomy within which regulatory thinking resides allows no flexibility. Using pre-cryptocurrency terminology, regulators looking at fundraising exercises will decide whether the asset being sold was either a "currency," a "commodity," a "security," or a presold right to the future delivery of a product. In US markets, to avoid falling foul of the *"Howey* test" with which courts have defined the concept of a security, lawyers have advised token issuers to describe their ICOs as examples of the latter: as the sale of something that holds utility, a tool that can be *used* to do something beyond storing and transferring monetary value.[105] (Many also include a disclaimer telling US investors they cannot participate in the sale—though many Americans appear to be ignoring those pleas.)

To be sure, it's this utility value that makes tokens interesting. But a fair analysis of their function must recognize that almost all of them share some of the qualities of currencies, commodities, and securities. Ideally, cryptotokens would be best viewed as an amalgam of all these categories or as something that transcends them. As Benjamin Roberts, CEO and co-founder of Citizen Hex, an Ethereum liquidity company, said, "[A] token is not just value. And it's not just data. It's both together in a wrapper, a format or abstraction that you can put around something. This is a new thing—sending value and information bundled together."[106]

BALANCING INNOVATION AND REGULATION

The either/or classification of existing financial regulations makes no room for this expansive interpretation and so raises the risk of a draconian response by an SEC bestowed with wide, discretionary powers. If it tries to ram these square pegs into the round holes of a pre-digital world's financial system, it could send a harmful message about this sector's prospects and drive innovation offshore.

On 25 July 2017, the SEC offered a hint of its thinking. It advised that it had reviewed the tokens issued by the now-defunct cryptoinvestment fund the DAO and decided that they amounted to unregistered securities.[107] The SEC chose to take no action against the founders, but it used the statement to warn that other tokens might well fall into the same category. At the same time, the SEC seemed to keep the door open to excluding other tokens from such conclusions and emphasized that it wanted to encourage innovation in capital-raising, suggesting it was willing to engage with the token industry on defining these rules going forward. The Chinese government took even more draconian action in early September. It explicitly banned the use of ICOs to raise money.[108]

Securities laws around the world hold fundraisers to strict disclosure requirements, mostly because societies feel a need to guard unsophisticated investors from unscrupulous pitchmen. The challenge, then, is to find strategies that maintain sufficient protection without stymieing a nascent technology. In this case, the industry needs an appropriately flexible mix of new standards, self-regulatory bodies, and best-practice models for the emerging token market so that it fosters widespread trust. An equivalent buildup of more sophisticated investment vehicles dedicated to buying and holding meta-assets, as well as specialized token analysts, a system of ratings, independent journalists, and institutions such as self-regulatory bodies, would help it earn legitimacy and stability.

Any new laws should be sufficiently permissive to encourage the kind of risk-taking that characterizes the investor profile for this sector. They include many who are fed up with earning puny returns on regulated investment options and want a share of the action that well-funded venture capitalists experience, thanks to their privileged status as professional investors. (It should be noted, however, that venture capitalists, hedge funds, and other accredited professionals are among the biggest participants in ICOs.)

"VCs see this as a real potential threat. You can see it in their body language," said Cornell cryptographer and cryptocurrency expert Emin Gün Sirer, an adviser to various token-issuing start-ups. He explained:

> [Retail token investors] realized that VCs get far more in these new business models and [those same small investors] are eager to take on similar risks. They might find sometimes they really regret the decisions they've made, but this community also seems quite independent and at home with the consequences of its actions. You don't see people organizing against "so and so" and saying "let's create a regulatory push." That's very exciting on its own.[109]

Democratizing the investor pool is a way of simultaneously democratizing opportunities for small business entrepreneurs. It opens up new avenues for developers to fund their ventures. These new funding tools have the potential to bootstrap a global ecosystem of organizations and freelance developers creating Dapps. The VC funding model demands returns on equity, which prioritizes monopoly capitalism and centralization; it bets on the very same intermediating entities that blockchain technology intends to disrupt. Now investors can steer money to those working on decentralizing solutions, a group that is, in effect, building public goods.

The token funding model is a way to pay for an open infrastructure of protocols and governance systems that facilitate peer-to-peer exchange and new decentralized economies within everything from voting to energy systems. Some engineers are getting very rich on this process, which may itself pose a risk of re-centralization. But gains are arguably more widely shared in this new, decentralized form of platform economics. It seems significantly more distributed than the economy of smartphone app development, for example, where "free app" models enhance the phone but not the app developers' income.

Vitally, in transferring value to open-source developers, tokens could ensure that, for the first time, a core component of the new Internet architecture is monetized for profit and is more rapidly built out. In the words of 21.co CEO Balaji Srinivasan, tokens can be thought of as "paid API keys," in that developers of Dapps need to buy and deploy them to work on a decentralized protocol that other developers have built.[110] The funds injected by these Dapp developers help pay for the protocol developers' work in building the open platforms. That creates a very different model from that of the pre-Bitcoin Internet.

A GOLDEN AGE OF PROTOCOLS?

Previously, the development of the important base-layer open protocols that underpin the Internet's open network infrastructure was a not-for-profit undertaking. Network software such as the *transmission control* and *Internet protocols* (TCP/IP), which manage the Internet's core packet-switching function, or the *hypertext transfer protocol* (HTTP) for websites and the *simple mail transfer protocol* (SMTP) for e-mail, were developed by universities and nonprofit bodies. Commercial, for-profit private entities weren't directly incentivized to work on these protocols. Where they did partner with nonprofit labs, it was largely motivated by the development advantages of having access to the underlying technology and the engineering talent working on it.

For the most part, however, for-profit companies steered their resources toward the commercialized proprietary applications that ran *on top of* the open protocols. The problem for the nonprofit entities was that those commercial players had deeper pockets, which made it hard for the former to compete for talent. In the end, the biggest companies got to shape, indirectly, the development of open protocols since it was their donations that kept the universities moving ahead.

As Albert Wenger and Fred Wilson from Union Square Ventures argue, we may be entering the "golden age of open protocols" in which value is captured by those who develop the most used open platforms.[111] A case in point: the soaring value of the Ethereum protocol's native token, ether, due to the popularity of the Ethereum-based ERC-20 token standard for ICOs.

These permissionless open protocols, upon which anyone with a token can start developing any idea, are another form of a public good, a commons. That's what TCP and IP have been, and their maintenance has required stewardship by a range of international bodies acting in the public interest. By steering funds directly to the developers of these protocols, the token economy could now more directly incentivize the build-out of this vital architecture. In other words, tokens address the Tragedy of the Commons for both those using Dapps to change economic outcomes and those developing the infrastructure on which those Dapps run.

Yet here, too, there is a need for caution. The biggest risk according to Lucian Tarnowski, CEO of BraveNew, an online community-building platform, is that developers become too powerful, leaving the communities that depend on their software as "slaves to the algorithm." He worries about engineers' inclination to build monolithic, math-based blockchain protocols that cannot accommodate the great many ways real human beings lead their lives. "Rigidity is really dangerous as it creates this master-slave dependency," Tarnowski said.[112]

One group of token developers is focused on this problem. The Economic Space Agency (ECSA), which is supported by an array of technologists, economists, anthropologists, and other social theorists, is building systems that would be secure from fraud without depending on validation by an overarching global blockchain such as Bitcoin or Ethereum—instead applying a narrow, peer-to-peer form of computer security that's based on the least-authority principles of *object capabilities*.[113]

In theory, that should allow groups of people, however small, to jointly issue their own unique tokens based on localized smart contracts that captured their community's interests and weren't beholden to the developer-established rules of the global protocol. ECSA founder and CEO Akseli Virtanen wants the system to be so simple that it promotes the "ritual of the ICO," in which people and entities are constantly making newly tokenized offerings of their services to others.[114]

Whether they lie in ECSA's complicated object-capabilities technology or within the cross-ledger interoperability of Ripple Labs' Interledger project, Cosmos' "Internet of Blockchains," or Polkadot's "Parachain," solutions are emerging that drive the process away from the "maximalist" notion that all economic activity must gravitate to a dominant blockchain. If so, then we're moving to a multi-token world where not only is the Dapp behind each token unique but also the distributed trust governance system is greatly varied and a matter of user choice.

Putting a reliable market value on all these tokens may still require a centralized reference currency but, depending on how efficiently they can be traded, their prices might one day simply refer to each other. It's possible, in other words, to envisage a future of digital barter in which different assets are traded directly and people no longer need to store a common currency like the dollar or bitcoin. It might even free people from the economic distortions and periodic crises that centralized monetary systems have experienced through the centuries.

Of course, the fiat currency-dominated world monetary system is a very long way from such a decentralized structure. Nonetheless, the rapid change of this current period suggests that we may be entering one of those 200-year turning points when humanity's system of money goes through radical change. The ever-growing pool of interested investors, developers, and potential users in these tokens and meta-assets is only accelerating the innovative drive behind them. There may well be a setback if and when regulators start collectively cracking down. But the token phenomenon has piqued the collective imagination of hundreds of thousands of intelligent people who are now pouring new ideas into the space. We cannot predict where this orderless process of iterative innovation will take us, but we would be unwise to assume that a significant, highly disruptive change is not looming.

THE BAT: A NEW PARADIGM FOR ONLINE ADVERTISING?

On 31 May 2017 at 2:34 pm GMT, the start-up Brave Software Inc. opened a public crowdsale of its *basic access tokens* (BATs). Twenty-four seconds later, the entire offering pool of one billion tokens was sold out. Brave had raised $35 million in a whirlwind ICO that left many hopeful investors bitter about being left out. Over the summer, as ICO mania took over and billions of dollars flooded into this new blockchain-based investment class, others would raise as much as six times Brave's haul to successively establish new records for the biggest crowdfunding exercises in history.

But it was the speed of the Brave sale that was striking. While it raised concerns about heavyweight investors muscling less nimble players out of the pool and limiting the breadth of the tokens' distribution, the intense demand also reflected the buzz attached to Brave's unique value proposition: that it could fix the Internet's dysfunctional advertising model. BATs are an integral component of Brave's attempt to improve the measurement, pricing, and alignment of demand and supply.

By inserting a token into a tripartite market of users, publishers, and advertisers, the Brave team believes it can bring more order, transparency, and pricing precision to it. It's a real test case for how a programmable token could incentivize participants from different, opposing sectors within a market to come together and improve that market's efficiency.

It's a nut worth trying to crack—again. In contrast to the Internet's early promise of bringing precision, analytics, and direct-to-customer marketing to advertising, representatives of all three stakeholder groups generally agree that the online ad industry is seriously broken. For users, the scourge of banner ads and unsolicited promotional videos is not only deteriorating the website experience but also costing them bandwidth. (By one estimate, $23 a month of people's mobile phone bill pays for ads they don't want.[115])

For advertisers, bots that generate fake traffic data have inflated rates for unworthy websites, resulting in an estimated $6.5 billion in losses for the industry in 2017, according to the Association of National Advertisers.[116] Meanwhile, plunging CPMs (the standard costs-per-thousand measure of impressions by which ad charge-out rates are set) are hurting mainstream publishers as their sites compete with the relentlessly expanding supply of alternative online content from blogs and social media.

Perhaps inevitably, consumers are turning to ad-blocking software, with some 86.6 million mobile and desktop devices using these services as of early 2017, a trend that will leave labor-intensive newsrooms starved for the funds needed to produce quality journalism. [117] The result: an ever-deteriorating quality of information, and a distorted set of incentives that makes it profitable for "fake news" providers to capture markets and earn ad dollars.

In economic terms, this breakdown constitutes a failure to establish an acceptable price for the principle scarce resource around which all advertising markets revolve: *user attention*. At its core, this business entails publishers capturing their readers' and viewers' limited amount of attention and then delivering it to advertisers. It's a market that's open to distortion because users aren't paid directly for providing this resource; instead, publishers share it with advertisers under an unspoken quid pro quo in which the users receive, in return, sought-after news, information, and entertainment.

In the online experience, however, poor or fake page-view metrics and an ever-growing supply of available content have distorted the market further. Meanwhile, the real cost to users is arguably much higher, since they are also handing over massive amounts of valuable personal data—part of a new asset that *The Economist* described as a 21st-century resource on par with what oil was in the previous century.[118]

Users are giving up something of great value and getting a deteriorating experience in return, while publishers and advertisers—unable to accurately measure user attention, let alone capture it—are playing with phantom numbers to devise pricing schemes.

Brave applies a two-pronged strategy to this problem, combining a powerful, specially tailored, self-branded browser with the BAT. The Brave browser has two core functionalities that differentiate it from more widely used competitors such as Chrome and Internet Explorer: it blocks ads by default and, with sophisticated analytics, it collates and anonymizes data from users that indicates how much time they spend looking at certain content. Users can receive BATs for selectively turning off the blocker to view certain ads and can use those tokens to reward publishers of content that they appreciate.

Currently, this functions as a donation option only, not as a form of payment or subscription. But in permitting per-article micropayments that were impossible with traditional payment systems, it creates a revenue model that may enable media companies to free themselves from a dependence on ads. Meanwhile, to place ads with publishers of content on the system, advertisers must first acquire BATs and then pay those tokens to publishers, on terms defined by the attention metrics generated by the latter's content.

Together, these features are intended to create an ecosystem in which attention is more directly and precisely valued. Compared to the existing model, this idea seems intrinsically fairer: for providing attention, users earn tokens that capture progressively more value as more advertisers enter the market for BATs and drive up their price. Users can then choose either to cash out those tokens into traditional currency or to transfer small amounts to publishers to reward and encourage the content they appreciate.

It also suggests that publishers will have stronger incentives to legitimately earn readers' and viewers' attention. Without a subscription component for news, this model doesn't necessarily reward quality journalism or disincentivize "click-bait" approaches to capturing user attention. But a fairer deal for all should indirectly foster a healthier ecosystem of news and information.

As with the many other tokens developed in this new age of cryptocurrency, BATs differ from traditional money in an important way: they are programmable. Whereas any two consenting parties can exchange a mainstream currency such as the dollar anywhere, and for any transaction, a cryptotoken contains software logic that limits and proscribes what it's used for. Money, under this construct, is no longer a neutral intermediating element of the transaction; it can capture the common values and interests of all parties who've agreed to use it.

This new form of money contains within its logic the chosen governance of the community. In the case of BATs, this governance emerges from its software's interaction with the browser, at which point it determines who can earn or receive it and the terms and conditions attached to those rights—all occurring within the context of the transaction itself. This is why the BAT is vital to Brave's model: it provides a hitherto unavailable market mechanism for the community to arrive at a trustworthy price for attention, a resource that traditional money was unable to isolate and recognize. In this sense, Brave, as with other cryptotoken issuers, is in the business of improving resource management.

The BAT is one of a number of early attempts by software developers to deploy programmable money to reshape economic outcomes. For now, it's too early to tell whether it will work. Much like the platform models behind Amazon, Alibaba, Uber, and other digital behemoths, success depends on generating network effects—on how widely an idea is adopted and reinforced in a positive feedback loop. For Brave, that will hinge on the future liquidity of the market for BATs. If the tokens are simply hoarded by investors and don't enter into widespread circulation, their value won't accurately represent the market for user attention within Brave browser content and the system will fail to offer an alternative to the existing one. Brave needs critical mass.

On that basis, critics questioned the narrow investor base that engaged in Brave's 24-second initial token offering. Only 130 buyers could get into the deal, and the top 20 of them controlled more than two-thirds of the total issuance.[119] It's unclear how many of those participants were part of presale arrangements with committed investors.

Many wondered how such a small pool could generate a network effect. Secondary-market sales helped expand the pool somewhat—with the BATs ownership base growing to more than 7,000 holders in the six weeks after the ICO. That left the top five investors with just 30 percent of the ICO tokens, a wider distribution than most of the ICOs of the same period.[120] Still, even though broad-based buzz has been fostered among the broader cryptoasset investment public, there's no way to know yet whether this level of distribution is wide enough to promote sufficient token liquidity for a functioning microeconomy.

Brave has another answer to the risk of concentrated ownership. In addition to the extra 200 million tokens it set aside to compensate both in-house and external developers of its open-source software, it established a 300 million–strong "user growth pool" to attract new users. Brave will distribute these in return for unique downloads of its browser and for other forms of user participation in the network. It sees the token as a tool to bootstrap adoption, to foster network effects.

"Early on we saw this as something that would allow us to stake users with initial grants," said Brave CEO Brendan Eich. The strategy was shaped by Eich's decades in Silicon Valley, where the veteran engineer created the ubiquitous Web programming language JavaScript in the 1990s and went on to co-found browser developer Mozilla. Over time, he realized that venture capitalists were reluctant to fund the marketing and handout cost of acquiring users and that tapping new equity or debt to do so diluted the ownership stakes of the founders and early investors. "But with a token, it can be disbursed to users without credit consequences," he adds, arguing that by contrast to a dollar worth of equity or debt, "the BAT is a social credit currency; it doesn't have this inflationary property."[121]

Still, there are concerns about Brave's "flash" ICO, primarily that it was undemocratic. Vitalik Buterin, founder of Ethereum, on whose blockchain the BATs' so-called ERC-20 tokens are issued, pointed out that one BATs bidder had paid an exorbitant $2,220 fee to get a transaction pushed to the front of the queue and argued that the problem lay with capped fundraising goals.[122] Separately, there were questions about whether Brave, in eschewing the nine-figure intakes of other token issuers, had raised enough money for its development needs.

One month after its offering, after posting a host of new engineering jobs intended to double the size of its team, Eich complained to *CoinDesk* that he was having a hard time hiring Ethereum talent, a direct result of the competition for developers that the ICO frenzy has unleashed. Yet others have lauded Brave, in restricting the number of tokens sold, for not putting the management's interests over those of its investors and its users. These people argued that giant, uncapped ICOs, such as Ethereum competitor Tezos' record-breaking $232 million raised over 12 days in July 2017, end up diluting small holders and create a moral hazard, as founders no longer have an incentive to deliver on their promises.[123]

The most important test of these differing token sale strategies will be whether they aid or hinder the token's evolution into what it is supposed to be: not a financing vehicle, but a utility token that engages the functionality of the platform to which it belongs. ICO issuers must prove that their tokens aren't just speculative instruments, they are also "products," as software with a utility function. The question has intrigued lawyers and regulators, who are addressing whether these new, ambiguous methods of value exchange can be distinguished from securities and, if so, whether they should be exempt from the rather onerous laws and restrictions that apply to the latter.

How things pan out will likely determine whether investors and users lose or make money, and what their legal response might be. This response will likely shape the regulatory standard-setting, and institution-building for this nascent industry and asset class. There's a lot resting on whether the tokens actually do what their issuers say they will do.

The early experimenters in this new trial-and-error approach to fundraising and decentralized network development are guinea pigs. So, too, are the hordes of investors pouring money into these offerings, often without appearing to have done much due diligence. Brave's and every other token-based project have inevitably had their flaws, but those mistakes are part of the learning process and inform the improvement of future offerings.

Notwithstanding the dangers of get-rich-quick mania, small investors have a rationale for scrambling to buy into opportunities like Brave's rapid-fire $35 million deal: they sense a unique opportunity to get in on the ground floor of a transformational phenomenon. Token technology has the hallmarks of a once-in-a-century economic paradigm shift. That's too tempting an idea to forego.

THE TOKEN LANDSCAPE: CRYPTOCURRENCIES, CRYPTOCOMMODITIES, AND CRYPTOTOKENS

One of the striking aspects of the rapidly expanding universe of block-chain-backed tokens and meta-assets is their sheer variety. Every week,

TABLE 2-1

CRYPTOASSETS IN THE TOKEN LANDSCAPE

CATEGORY	EXAMPLES
Cryptocurrencies	Bitcoin, Litecoin, Zcash, Monero
Cryptocommodities	Ethereum, Tezos, EOS
Cryptotokens	AdChain, Augur, BAT, Civic, Climate Coin, Exergy Token, Filecoin, Gnosis, Maidsafe, Ocean Coin, Po.et, Sia, Storj, Userfeeds.io

new white papers address novel use cases. It's not only in the different Dapps but also in the function of the tokens within the emerging digital economy. Using distinctions drawn by cryptoasset analysts Chris Burniske and Jack Tatar, we'll address a sampling here under three categories: cryptocurrencies, cryptocommodities, and cryptotokens (Table 2-1).[124]

These classifications aren't entirely precise. For instance, we can use Ethereum's ether token as economy-wide payment vehicle (cryptocurrency) and as an access token that's a required input for the development of Ethereum-based applications (cryptocommodity). Still, distinctions are possible and we make them, based on the core conceptualization of each token. We label ether a cryptocommodity.

Within each category are multiple alternative coins or "altcoins"—yet another interchangeable word for non-bitcoin cryptocurrencies and tokens—with competing value propositions, business models, and underlying protocol designs. Collectively, they represent different visions, both competing and complementary, of how the digital economy will evolve. Each appeals to an identifiable community with specific interests and values.

In offering new governance models, these altcoins sometimes try to overcome flaws of the dominant cryptocurrencies and blockchains—such as the energy-intensity and capital intensiveness of Bitcoin's mining industry or the security vulnerabilities in Ethereum's code.

But in all cases, the open-source development model means the ongoing process of copying, altering, experimenting, and iterating creates a reinforcing feedback loop across all software models. While each cryptoasset example below offers a distinct choice of decentralized commerce model for the various constituents it seeks to attract, none is static by any means. All exist within a dynamic, changing, and unpredictable ecosystem where permissionless, open innovation will shape the evolving infrastructure of a future decentralized, token-based economy.

Note: This survey excludes a discussion of so-called permissioned blockchains, though much corporate research and development is going into this technology, mostly because it typically does not involve the issuance of native tokens of floating value.

CRYPTOCURRENCIES

Cryptocurrencies are tokens whose primary role is to facilitate payments or act as a store of universal value. Each cryptocurrency competes not only with the others but also with government-issued fiat currencies and traditional stores of value such as gold. Cryptocurrencies are agnostic about how they are used. Importantly, while acting as media of exchange between users, they are often deeply integrated into the underlying blockchain's governance system—generally as rewards to incentivize miners or transaction validators to maintain the integrity of the ledger.

Bitcoin: The grandfather of cryptoassets

Bitcoin's pros and cons provide critical reference points for framing the features of all other token offerings.

Unique protocol features of Bitcoin

The defining feature of Bitcoin (BTC) is its PoW consensus algorithm, which compels miners to conduct an otherwise pointless computation task—some describe it as an intensive mathematical puzzle—in parallel to validating transactions and updating the blockchain ledger. Only by incurring the resource costs of that "hashing" exercise can they earn the right to compete for bitcoin rewards and to contribute to the consensus that validates each new block of transactions in Bitcoin's perpetually updating ledger.

Miners' investment in this effort, both in electricity and equipment costs, represents their skin in the game to force their honesty. They can boost their chances of winning bitcoin rewards by adding more computing power, but the PoW algorithm attaches real costs to that and exponentially increases them as competition in the network intensifies. This formulation wards off a particular miner's accumulating more than 50 percent of the Bitcoin network's overall hashing power, a threshold that defines consensus in the network. It's not impossible for a miner to break the consensus and doctor transactions; but, based on the market dynamics and signaling effects from launching such an attack, it is extremely, prohibitively expensive.

Eight and half years and 120 million transactions into its life, this system has continued to hold up. The Bitcoin ledger has never been seriously compromised. No one—not a hacker, not a bank, not a government—has been able to take it over and alter, or censor, transactions.

The quality of proven censorship resistance turns out to be quite valuable for a payments and asset recording system. It's a welcome alternative where national currencies such as Venezuela's bolivar are being debased and where capital controls and centralized, gatekeeping banks lock billions out of the financial system and add cost to everyone else's financial dealings.

These qualities underpin the investment appeal of bitcoin, which as of late summer 2017 had risen a stunning 4.6 million percent since the founding of the first major bitcoin exchange in July 2010. (Burniske and Tatar say bitcoin's return makes it "the most exciting alternative investment of the 21st century.")[125] The gain reflects the accumulative popular recognition that this apparently unbreakable system of value exchange constitutes a public good, a unique new, digital system of value management that, like gold, defies control by any centralized party, be it a government, a bank, or any other institution. Notably, these increases in the value of the Bitcoin ecosystem only add to its security because it greatly increases the cost of a "51 percent attack."

Rising values also mean that the developers who look after Bitcoin's code are incentivized to protect it. MIT Media Lab Director Joichi Ito describes bitcoin's market capitalization, which stood at $48 billion in late July 2017, as a "bounty" that encourages coders to come up with battle-tested security structures before making any changes. "This high valuation causes a great deal of caution and testing before anything is deployed on its network, but we can be quite sure that many, many people have been thinking about how they can break the system and have so far failed," Ito said.[126]

In the context of an evolutionary, open-source system that, by design, is open to attack, this combination of value, proven strength, and rising awareness is, for the time being, creating a powerful, positive feedback loop. More security adds to bitcoin's appeal, which boosts the system valuation, making it more expensive to attack and increasing the caution of its engineer stewards, which only makes it more secure. And so on.

Yet, Bitcoin is flawed in ways that constrain its ability to scale to a level that would make it a major part of the global financial system. (As of this writing, Bitcoin could process seven transactions a second compared to Visa's network capacity of more than 24,000.) These limitations have led to numerous altcoin "forks" of the original Bitcoin idea, each with tweaks and upgrades to resolve some of these challenges. But how long can Bitcoin sustain its first-mover advantage and the network effects that come with that, when money is now flowing into alternative cryptoassets that have a superior design? How nimbly can developers make changes to Bitcoin's protocol to allow it to compete with these alternatives?

Three fundamental challenges are worth considering. Each has created opportunities for the alternative cryptotokens that we'll explore below.

First, Bitcoin's PoW mining algorithm encourages an arms race of ever more powerful, industrialized computing farms, which deploy specialized machines based on *application-specific integrated circuits* (ASICs), to do nothing more than the hashing work. Miners must now deploy these expensive, high-powered computing arrays to compete successfully for bitcoin rewards, and that creates a barrier to entry for smaller, less wealthy participants. The ASIC buildup has led, if not to the emergence of entities that can control more than 51 percent of the network, then to a kind of non-colluding oligopoly of heavily capitalized competing miners.

Inevitably, these big players wield significant clout over the governance of the network, leading to what some see as a de facto centralization, in direct contradiction of the decentralizing mission of this technology. Since this arms race involves deploying ever more electricity to run the network, Bitcoin's expansion presents a serious environmental threat. At the time of writing, Bitcoin's network consumed an estimated 14.5-terawatt hours of power a year, more than the entire nation of Slovenia.[127]

Second, Bitcoin's open-source community has no clear democratic mechanism for smoothly resolving disputes over contentious changes in the source code, which pits different vested interests against each other. The three main interest groups are:

1. Miners, who ultimately decide what does and doesn't go into each block of transactions and are paid in fees and fresh bitcoin issuances

2. Venture-backed businesses, which run exchanges and digital wallets and facilitate the users' transactions that generate those fees

3. Developers, who are the engineers tasked with contributing updates to the code.

No group is monolithic in its views—there are clear differences of opinion among miners and across different developers, for example—but profit motives are skewing the positions of each side. The more value at stake in the network, the more intransigent their positions, the more irreconcilable their differences. This deep community dysfunction plays out in bitter arguments on Twitter and Reddit and encourages dangerous games of chicken, with each side threatening to adopt measures that could split bitcoin into two different, incompatible currencies.

We saw this dysfunction during the Bitcoin "civil war" over competing proposals to increase the blockchain's capacity. That long-running argument boiled down to a binary choice. One option, supported by one powerful block of miners, would raise the capacity of each 10-minute block beyond the current 1MB worth of data— some wanted 2MB, others 8MB, still others no limit at all.

The other side, promoted by a group of core developers, would maintain the existing 1MB limit and instead insert a protocol change known as Segregated Witness, or SegWit, that compressed data to increase the amount that could fit within the 1MB limit and would help to activate a protocol known as the Lightning Network that could be built on top of Bitcoin. That was contentious for miners, in part because Lightning's system of provable "off-chain" payment channels enables users to increase transaction throughput and avoid paying miners' fees for on-chain transactions.

To resolve an apparent standoff, take-it-or-leave-it code adjustments were proposed as "hard fork" changes that would force people's hands because the choice would invalidate certain types of transactions. Eventually SegWit was implemented under a compromise agreement by which miners promised to adopt the coding change in July followed by an increase to 2MB in November. But this wasn't enough for some in the "big block" crowd, who suspected there would be no follow-through on the second phase. So they forked the Bitcoin code on 1 August 2017, offering a new "Bitcoin Cash" protocol that allows for 8MB blocks. This split Bitcoin into two incompatible coins.

Far from the existential threat it was once thought to be, however, the split prompted a surge in the price of the original 1MB Bitcoin, which got as high as $5,000 in late August, more than double its level from a month earlier. This reaction, it seemed, reflected both the market's appreciation for the SegWit innovation and the fact that this option attracted the most talented and passionate developers to it.

Bitcoin Cash briefly breached $800, but was clearly assigned much lower value by the market, a reminder that developer talent is a key factor in the logic of investment decisions. Still, the split is not easily explained to outsiders and confuses the Bitcoin "brand." The discord has no doubt left many mainstream consumers and enterprises unnerved by the unpredictability and legal uncertainty of Bitcoin's unruly system of governance.

Third, Bitcoin is a poor protector of user privacy. Often erroneously described as an "anonymous" currency that criminals use to hide their transactions, the public ledger keeps track of all transactions; even though user names are hidden behind pseudonymous alphanumeric addresses, its permanently assigned addresses are easily tracked. With network analysis, we can now follow users' transactions relatively easily. This concerns not only libertarians who care about freedom of commerce but also companies for whom a public transaction record would undermine their competitive advantage.

Just as important, the very idea of traced coins goes against the expectation that money be fungible, that the value of each equivalent unit of a currency is the same regardless of its history. Traceability of bitcoin transactions undermines that principle. Consider the high premium that bidders paid when the FBI sold bitcoins it had seized from Silk Road drug marketplace owner Ross Ulbricht. They viewed these particular coins as "whitewashed" by the US government's brief ownership, making them devoid of seizure risks, which other bitcoins could not guarantee. That differentiation is counterproductive to the functioning of money.

Financial governance of Bitcoin

Unlike most other cryptoasset projects, where the founding developers are known individuals, the identity of the person or persons who created Bitcoin remains a mystery. That changes the debate about how incoming funds are used, since it obviates the need for founders to self-impose constraints on their use to foster trust among token-holders. (Satoshi Nakamoto appears not to have touched some one million bitcoins he mined early in the cryptocurrency's life—perhaps because that would identify him and subject him to demands from both within and outside the Bitcoin community.)

The neutralization of the founder question doesn't remove politics from questions of fund allocation within the Bitcoin ecosystem. The main non-founder entities that currently earn revenue from Bitcoin's expansion and usage still face pressure from users, especially now that Bitcoin is reaching capacity limits and after the protocol halved miners' bitcoin reward payouts in mid-2016, making transaction fees a more important source of income for them. (Bitcoin rewards are halved every 210,000 blocks—more or less every four years, based on an average block time of 10 minutes—as part of a schedule designed to limit the total future issuance to 21 million bitcoins by the year 2140.)

In this environment, the clearest moneyed, for-profit interests in the financial governance of Bitcoin are defined by two groups: miners, who are rewarded with fees and freshly issued bitcoins for their role in providing the system's vital security infrastructure; and venture-capital-backed entrepreneurs, whose businesses pay many of the fees that go to miners to support that. The questions these groups often clash over are: How should the cost of building, sustaining, protecting, and developing Bitcoin's ecosystem be apportioned? What is the right approach in the long-term interests of the wider community of users? That was the essence of the 1MB versus 2MB block-size debate.

Related complicating questions are: How to reward the people who, in this open-source environment, are developing the source code of the core protocol even though they get no direct income or monetized gain from that work? How to align interests, since the absence of an ICO, pre-mine, or in-protocol mechanism for funding coding work leaves developers dependent on private companies for their livelihood?

In Bitcoin's early years, the not-for-profit institution Bitcoin Foundation, funded by donations from Bitcoin-related start-ups, paid for the salary of the then-lead developer Gavin Andresen. Then MIT Digital Currency Initiative took in funding to support developers, under the same principle of avoiding conflicts of interest. MIT DCI now pays for two core Bitcoin developers to continue their work.

But many others working on the core code need to put food on the table. So, at various times, wallet providers, exchanges, and payment processors have employed Bitcoin developers. In recent years, developers employed by the privately funded company Blockstream have done a significant amount of the work. Those salary providers might well be mostly motivated by a desire to develop the "commons" of Bitcoin's core code for the good of all, but their business interests won't align with everyone in the Bitcoin community. That naturally makes outsiders wary of their motives.

The governance question for cryptocurrencies such as bitcoin is not how should founders most responsibly manage the early influx of proceeds from a one-off ICO (as with altcoins), but how should new funds generated within the ecosystem be distributed? What's emerged from Bitcoin's successes and failures is the need for transparency and awareness around the interests of developers, miners, and businesses differently impacted by competing proposals for protocol changes.

The goal is to find the best mix of policies that serves the community's shared long-term interests in security, ease of use, and value creation. Bitcoin's challenge is how to get a deeply divided community to reach compromises in the most effective, costless manner. Investors and users of its technology will need to weigh whether it has the capacity to do so.

Litecoin: Silver to bitcoin's gold

Litecoin (LTC), created in October 2011 by developer Charlie Lee, was one of the first altcoin copies of Bitcoin, with a few important changes that sought to make the coin more universally accessible. For many years Litecoin's token was the second most valuable cryptoasset after bitcoin and is often described as the "silver to bitcoin's gold." While it has fallen behind Ethereum's ether and Ripple's XRP, litecoin remains an important benchmark for altcoins and a closely watched experiment.

Unique protocol features of Litecoin

The key distinguishing feature of Litecoin's protocol is its use of the Scrypt (pronounced "ess crypt") mining algorithm, which requires more amounts of high-speed RAM than does Bitcoin's algorithm; computers cannot easily exploit the massive raw hashing speed of the parallel processing functions that ASIC machines' specialized chips permit. In theory, that should mitigate the trend toward concentrated mining power because smaller players using cheaper, RAM-dependent *graphics processing units* (GPUs), can still compete. The design has not been entirely "ASIC-resistant," as ASIC rigs for mining litecoins are now available. But Scrypt's "memory hard problem" has nonetheless curtailed the trend toward a Bitcoin-like industrialized arms race in mining.

Another distinction is that Litecoin's PoW algorithm is designed so that miners will on average resolve their computing challenge and finalize a block of transactions every 2.5 minutes, whereas Bitcoin blocks take 10 minutes. Users wait a shorter time for the confirmation of transactions. It also accelerates the issuance of tokens; but, since

Lee wanted a money supply schedule similar to Bitcoin's, he adjusted the monetary policy so that the total future issuance would run to 84 million coins, as opposed to Bitcoin's 21 million, and set the halving of the litecoin payout reward to every 840,000 blocks. In effect, we can make fairly accurate price comparisons between litecoin and bitcoin by multiplying litecoin's price by four or by comparing total market capitalization. As of late July 2017, Litecoin had a market capitalization of $2.3 billion, according to *CoinMarketCap.com*—a valuation one-twentieth that of Bitcoin.

Financial governance of Litecoin

Although Charlie Lee is easily identified, he has generally avoided conflict with users and investors who might otherwise worry about a founder's motives, partly because there was no "pre-mine" of coins or any presale of tokens to the public to fund operations. Lee and other early users just began mining litecoins on Litecoin's own terms, competing with each other for rewards. As early adopters, they have no doubt profited well as litecoin's value has risen, but many view those as fairly won profits. Because of that, and as with Bitcoin, the community isn't wondering what founders or developers are doing with their earnings.

As for the distribution of costs and rewards within the Litecoin ecosystem, we could argue that Scrypt's constraints on ASIC mining have created a more equitable spread of wealth, which may have mitigated the political tensions that arose in Bitcoin once concentrated miners accumulated high-stakes interest in a particular protocol rule set. That was evident in the relative lack of discord between miners and developers over Litecoin's move to adopt SegWit, which soon paved the way for Lightning Network integration. Litecoin miners seemed to recognize that a SegWit-led scaling improvement would drive up the cryptocurrency's price, which would more than offset the lost fees over which Bitcoin miners fretted. Sure enough, after it implemented SegWit following a daylong negotiation, its price soared from $3.77 per litecoin on 1 March 2017 to $44.32 in late July that year.

Was Litecoin's relative success in implementing a protocol change been because, paradoxically, it has been less successful than Bitcoin? With less monetary value tied up in litecoins, the ecosystem's competing interests have smaller fortunes at stake, which lets users place more speculative bets on change. There are nowhere near as many people using litecoin for transactions, which means fewer wallet providers and other service providers with interests in how it develops. Network effects generate value for all stakeholders in cryptoassets, but their relative absence can also help to resolve sticky problems around governance and the distribution of funds. Everyone can treat Litecoin as a useful "living lab" in which to test ideas before applying them to the bigger networks of larger cryptoassets.

The reason behind Litecoin's smooth adoption of SegWit may also be a function of Charlie Lee's influence. As Litecoin's de facto leader, he came out in strong support of the change. Importantly, Lee himself is not remunerated by direct distributions from the Litecoin ecosystem; for most of its existence, he has worked for cryptocurrency wallet and exchange provider Coinbase, which, although not a neutral party, had far bigger business interests in bitcoin and ether than in litecoin.

Like all founders of successful open-source projects, Lee has been aided by an army of volunteer coders who seek not immediate financial gain but projects that interest them or benefit their own pet projects. (On that score, Litecoin's embrace of SegWit appears to have enhanced its "cool factor," as the protocol attracted a surge of developer engagement after the move.) With the launch of the not-for-profit Litecoin Foundation in March 2017 to steer donations toward funding continued developer contributions, Litecoin now has a vehicle for paying for its protocol's upkeep, with Lee himself leaving Coinbase to run the foundation full-time with a $1 salary.

No doubt Lee is well sustained by the store of litecoins and bitcoins he has accumulated over the years, but he also wants to see his brainchild succeed. How would Litecoin fare without him? We don't know. That's a reminder that the personalities, principles, and circumstances of the people who launch cryptoassets are a relevant consideration for investors in those tokens—even as these strive to function as leaderless, decentralized systems in which no CEO or other form of authority can exercise centralized command.

Zcash and Monero: Pro-privacy

The development of sophisticated big-data-driven network analysis services such as Elliptic and Chainalysis to better track and identify individual users of bitcoin prompted a backlash among developers who felt that a better, more private cryptocurrency was needed. For people like influential cryptographer Zooko Wilcox-O'Hearn, who sees privacy as "a human right, a necessary condition for the exercise of free choice, of morality, of political participation and of intimacy—of everything that is most important as humans," this privacy limitation was a call to action.[128]

Adding more privacy into a cryptocurrency was easier said than done, however, because the miners would have to ascertain the legitimacy of transactions and of the state of the ledger without checking the transaction history of the account in question. Yet Wilcox and others knew that certain tricks of cryptography would allow computers to confirm that a change in the state of a ledger has legitimately occurred without knowing its underlying components. In other words, they could prove that funds weren't being double-spent without knowing addresses involved in the transaction. So, these developers got to work on the problem, the outcome of which were new, pro-privacy cryptocurrencies, the most important of which are Monero (XMR) and Zcash (ZEC).

Unique protocol features of Zcash and Monero

In the case of Monero, the privacy solution is something called *ring signatures*, where any member of a group of signers controlling authorizing keys could digitally sign transactions. No outsider could determine which member of the key-holding group owned the particular account or address from which a cryptocurrency transfer occurred. For Wilcox, the creator of Zcash, the solution lay in something called a *zero-knowledge Succinct Non-Interactive ARgument of Knowledge*, or zk-SNARK.

Zero-knowledge cryptography is a powerful means by which a third party can prove that someone else's claim is true without knowing all the details behind it. Thus zk-SNARKs gave rise to Zcash, where miners on the network can verify that transactions are legitimate even though the details behind them are so heavily encrypted as to obscure the accounts from and to which they are going. Importantly, Zcash also provides some opt-out tools for users so that, were a third party such as a bank or regulator require access to information, they could selectively divulge data without breaking the chain of privacy beyond that.

In creating new currencies, the developers of both Monero and Zcash took the opportunity to tackle not only Bitcoin's privacy problem but also other issues. With the concept of the tail emission, Monero addressed the problem posed by Bitcoin's declining currency reward schedule, which is necessary to avoid inflation and create scarcity but which eventually forces miners to charge potentially discriminating and highly contentious transaction fees.

Under Monero's arrangement, issuances of the system's XMR tokens steadily decrease over time, until they reach a point where they are frozen at 0.3 XMR a minute and stay that way forever. That amounts to a one percent inflation rate for the rest of Monero's life; but, according to developers, it offsets natural losses of currency from circulation as people lose control of their keys or hard drives.

As for Zcash, it went for a four-year halving schedule for rewards on 2.5-minute blocks that looked more or less like that of Litecoin but from a lower starting point of 12.5 ZEC, rather than the 50-coin start position for Bitcoin and Litecoin. The key difference was what Zcash developers called a "slow start" with only one ZEC per block for the first two days before it leapt to 12.5. The idea was to create a period in which small miners could gain access to coins before they became outcompeted. It also followed Litecoin's lead in developing its own RAM memory-heavy mining algorithm, creating something called *equihash* that led Wilcox and Jack Grigg, a Zcash developer, to argue on the cryptocurrency's website that it was "unlikely that anyone will be able to build cost-effective custom hardware (ASICs) for mining in the foreseeable future."[129]

Financial governance of Zcash and Monero

In following the Bitcoin and Litecoin model for PoW mining algorithms with no pre-mine or ICO, Zcash and Monero had to figure out how to finance development. Monero went for a build-it-and-they-will-come approach, hoping that the appeal of their privacy solution, a pet concern for many cryptographers, would draw volunteer developers to their project, who would invest in the currency and gain from its improvement. That's more or less how it has played out; Monero attained a market capitalization of $672 million by late July 2017 to rank ninth among all cryptoassets listed by *CoinMarketCap.com*.

Zcash has had a more volatile experience. The cryptocurrency soared on its second day of trading on 29 October 2016, at one stage surpassing $4,000 a coin, partly because the slow-start strategy created a coin shortage at the outset and partly because of buzz around the project and reputation of Wilcox. It soon dropped to below $100, where it more or less stayed for the following six months.

But in the spring of 2017, it enjoyed the massive pan-cryptoassets rally and by late July was up fourfold year-to-date, despite some criticism of the funding strategy that Wilcox employed, which was to incorporate a 20 percent payment—dubbed the "genius tax"—from every ZEC block reward to a special founder account during the first four years of the cryptocurrency's existence. This tax was ostensibly to cover the three years of development and to reward early investors who put $1 million into the Zcash company. As of late July 2017, the pool of distributed founders' funds was worth $75 million. Who gets access to those funds and to how much of them is unclear, but the company lists 55 Zcash addresses as recipients.

Opinions over the founder reward have varied markedly, with some applauding the transparency and the creation of a clear funding mechanism for developers—arguably the most important participants in any network. But others see it as excessive, with one critic even proposing that miners adopt a self-injected code alteration in the form of a "forked" Zcash copy currency that lets them keep all of the ZEC reward and stops the siphoning of 20 percent to founders.[130]

However, the proposal has had no real traction, presumably because adopters of the new coin would lose access to the marketing and support of the existing Zcash Company and, most importantly, the developer community would refuse to work on the new coin. Miners likely recognized that they'd lose more than they'd gain in such a deal. The result is a reminder that whereas miners provide a commoditized service, the work that specialized, top-notch cryptodevelopers do is hard to secure, particularly in a boom period for cryptocurrencies.

Here, too, the personality of the lead developer matters. Zooko Wilcox, who swapped his given name of Bryce for Zooko after an experiment with pseudonyms on a cryptographers' mailing list, has had a storied career in the field. He worked on some important innovations in cryptocurrencies before Bitcoin, including David Chaum's DigiCash in the 1990s, and is known for "Zooko's Triangle," which describes the challenges of creating secure, decentralized, and human-meaningful names for participants in a network. Given his deep interest in both security and privacy, Wilcox devised what he called a "ceremony" with other trusted crypto experts from North America to devise jointly, in almost obsessive secrecy, a random seed number from which Zcash would be born. This event was documented—and became the subject of a *Radiolab* episode on National Public Radio—so as to prove the integrity of the project's genesis.[131]

Wilcox intended to instill the notion in future users' minds that this otherwise incorruptible system of encrypted privacy enhancement had not been corrupted during its brief moment of vulnerability at birth. Whether or not this elaborate ceremony has succeeded in breeding confidence, it has likely bred an air of mysticism around the cryptography itself, which factors into the value of the token.

CRYPTOCOMMODITIES

Cryptocommodities refer to tokens that are necessary components of applications built on the blockchain platform to which they belong. This includes the native tokens of permissionless blockchains—those that have no authorizing body granting access permissions to users or miners—and, typically, the platforms that facilitate smart contracts and a variety of Dapps beyond digital money and payments.

Smart contracts are pieces of shared software code that contain agreed-upon business logic whose event-contingent terms and conditions are executed automatically and securely by a decentralized computing network. For example, if the price of a certain stock fell below a certain price, a digitally executed contract would instruct payments to go from one investor to another. When these agreements are written to an immutable blockchain, parties to the contract can now trust that no other party can intervene in the automatic execution of their rights and obligations.

If we think of computer programs, as many engineers do, as contracts—as codified agreements based on "if X, then Y" constructs—then this structure effectively creates a global, unstoppable, decentralized meta-computer whose processing power is shared across the network. In this context, we can think of a cryptocommodity as a kind of fuel that runs this global computer. Extending this metaphor, the developers of Ethereum, the dominant smart-contract blockchain, used the term, "gas" to describe the flow of payments its native token, *ether*, required for transactions across its network.

Ethereum: Turing complete

In 2013 at the age of 19, Russian-Canadian engineer Vitalik Buterin conceived of Ethereum's blockchain as a tool for developers to build Dapps, which engage decentralized nodes to ensure that their programs—synonymous with smart contracts, in this case—execute independently of any centralized entity.

To achieve this, Buterin gave Ethereum its own built-in "Turing complete" language, a condition that added far greater programming capacity than Bitcoin's protocol ever had. That structure and a number of other features turned Ethereum into a go-to platform for writing smart contracts and Dapps. Some engineers complain that the flexibility of Ethereum's programming capabilities makes the system insecure. A number of high-profile attacks, including that which siphoned $55 million from the DAO, a decentralized investment vehicle, have underscored this vulnerability.

On the flip side, the array of possibilities that Ethereum's programming capacity offers has attracted a massive community of enthusiastic developers trying out all sorts of new ideas. As of May 2017, there had been 90,000 downloads of Ethereum's developer suite of tools, according to co-founder Joseph Lubin.[132]

While most are still in "proof-of-concept" phase, the number of Dapps now operating on top of Ethereum is expanding rapidly. As of late July 2017, the tracking website "State of the Dapps" listed 601, though many experiments fall outside the purview of the Ethercasts team that runs that site.[133] A good many of these applications include tokens, all testaments to the critical role Ethereum has played in the development of the ICO market and the token economy.

Early on, Ethereum developers came up with the ERC-20 standard interface for issuing digital assets and tokens over the platform. The vast majority and most prominent of the token sales in 2016 and 2017 were issued with that standard. That linked Ethereum's value intrinsically to the ICO ecosystem of value. Investors would need to buy ether (ETH), Ethereum's native token, to obtain the needed secondary token—such as Brave's BAT—and so the former's price got a boost from the surging token market.

Unique protocol features of Ethereum

Miners of the Ethereum network do more than just validate currency transactions and maintain the Ethereum ledger; they receive ether for providing the processing power that executes the imbedded logic of each smart contract. Together, the computers behind the miners form what's often referred to as the "Ethereum Virtual Machine" (EVM). To keep those miners honest, Ethereum initially adopted a PoW consensus algorithm modeled on Bitcoin's. However, in a bid to avoid centralization of mining power, it followed the lead of Litecoin and other Bitcoin successors in adding more memory-heavy computation to that algorithm to make it more ASIC-resistant.

Not content simply to moderate the PoW competition, the Ethereum founders said from the outset that they intend to migrate the platform to a *proof-of-stake* (PoS) model. In theory, PoS would not have the environmental impact that PoW has had—a major motivation for its adoption. In essence, a PoS algorithm keeps miners honest because their capacity to confirm transactions, participate in the network, and earn ether depends on how big a stake they hold in that same token.

To mount a 51 percent attack consistently, a malicious actor would first have to acquire more than half of the ether in circulation and put it all at risk. In practice, however, the Ethereum developers have struggled to define a clear road map and timetable for migrating from PoW to PoS—known as the Caspar project—in part because of doubts raised about the latter's reliability. The main criticism of PoS stems from the "nothing-at-stake" problem: because malicious miners have no electricity demand to meet, they could mine multiple blocks simultaneously, at virtually zero cost, to up their chances of adding a fraudulent block to the blockchain.

New improvements to PoS, including the delegated proof-of-stake algorithm that both EOS and Tezos use (described below), might resolve the nothing-at-stake problem and mitigate the tendency toward concentrated wealth that the basic version implies. But Ethereum's cautious developers, now charged with protecting an ecosystem worth $30 billion, have been deliberately slow to introduce a PoS update. Some wonder whether, with so much money at stake, they'll ever be able to make the shift.

Financial governance of Ethereum

Unlike Bitcoin, which began with Satoshi Nakamoto's mining the genesis block at the same time that he invited others to participate, the early issuance of ether tokens in 2014 involved both a crowdsale and a distribution to the founders. Raising around $18 million worth of bitcoin—at the time, one of the biggest crowdfunding exercises in history—Ethereum set the stage for the ICO records of 2017. The incoming funds were held by the Ethereum Foundation, a nonprofit organization incorporated in Switzerland and charged with a transparent process for distributing the money.

After an early crisis, when the falling price of bitcoin almost depleted the foundation's coffers, the entire enterprise's fortunes have since recovered, with many of the founders becoming very wealthy. In addition to those early distributed ether, the protocol follows an ongoing schedule of issuing fresh ether to miners. Unlike Bitcoin, however, Ethereum has not clarified if and when the supply of fresh tokens will ever end. This feature can make investors nervous, especially those who are looking for the digital scarcity function that's guaranteed by Bitcoin's hard limit of 21 million coins over 130 years. But the difference underscores the point that ether is not a currency intended purely as a store of value or medium of exchange. It is a cryptocommodity.

The outsized role of Ethereum's founding developers in guiding protocol development is perhaps the platform's most contentious aspect for investors. Whereas the lead Bitcoin developers find it extremely difficult to introduce even worthwhile protocol changes, Ethereum's founders loom large over policy decisions.

For example, during the DAO crisis in mid-2016, the team decided that the best way to recover the $55 million in stolen funds was to institute a hard fork that rendered the DAO smart contract transactions invalid from a certain point on. It was a dramatic decision. Critics described it as a breach of the vital blockchain principle of immutability. The Ethereum founders argued that they'd put their decision to a democratic process and won, since a large majority of the miners voted with their feet by mining blocks off the newly forked chain.

However, a group of developers and miners was so incensed that it continued to mine from the old, pre-forked blocks, creating something it called Ethereum Classic, denoted by the code ETC as a competitor to ETH. To this day, the maverick ETC version continues to trade alongside ETH—and some immutability-concerned developers are using it for Dapp and smart contract development, though the 2017 surge in the price of ETH has left ETC far behind.

Tezos: Born of the commons

Tezos (TEZ), founded by the husband-and-wife team of Arthur and Kathleen Breitman, is a smart-contract-enabling blockchain intended to be more dynamic and less costly to maintain and govern than Ethereum and other systems for Dapps. Tezos briefly ranked as the biggest crowdsale in history after it raised $232 million worth of bitcoin and ether in just 12 days in early July 2017. (A month later, Filecoin beat that by raising $252 million.) The interest in Tezos stemmed from the notion that it might resolve some of the biggest problems facing cryptocurrencies—primarily in decentralized governance and scalability. Billionaire venture capitalist Tim Draper's public support for the ICO didn't hurt, either.

Unique protocol features of Tezos

"The core observation that led to [Tezos'] development was the recognition of blockchain protocols as a commons," said Kathleen Breitman, Tezos CEO. "Typically, commons suffer from two issues in economic theory: 1. Maintenance, or the question of who will fix issues in the code and, 2. Governance, or the question of who decides upon the direction of development."[134] To deal with those challenges, CTO Arthur Breitman said, the Tezos team created a "self-amending blockchain." He modeled it on the game Nomic, invented by philosopher Peter Suber, in which the rules of the game include mechanisms for the players to change those rules. On that basis, Tezos starts with a seed protocol but, from that point on, the governance takes shape as the changing pool of tokenholders and validators vote on what rules to impose.

The consensus algorithm is based on a proof-of-stake, staged voting system by which holders of Tezos tokens delegate authority to certain participants to encourage updates to the protocol without getting bogged down in the slanging matches and gridlock that afflicted the Bitcoin community. Updates also go through a rigorous testing process, which smart contracts must pass before they are implemented across the entire blockchain. Stakeholders can put the governance itself to this tiered voting and testing process, which means the mechanisms and rules by which updates are incorporated can also change—with something akin to a constitutional amendment. It's called "on-chain governance."

Critics, including Ethereum founder Vitalik Buterin, said the system is too unpredictable and worry that dynamic changes to the protocol could introduce instability, which could undermine the core blockchain goal of immutability—the very criticism of Ethereum's hard fork.[135] But, from the Tezos side, we could argue that rigid adherence to preexisting rules overly constrains systems like Bitcoin. There may be an optimal balance between a more a flexible approach to protocol changes and strict protections against rushed modifications that might undermine immutability.

What is clear is that governance within the two dominant, permissionless, public blockchains is less than perfect. The bruising, unending Bitcoin block-size debate showed that the community had no viable mechanism for processing compromise and fostering organized decision-making; and the DAO experience did not bolster any sense of democracy in the Ethereum ecosystem. "Governance happens behind closed doors and few have a seat at the table," said Arthur Breitman.[136] "While coin votes do sometimes happen, they are typically an afterthought and do not proceed from a predictable set of governance rules." Buterin, on the other hand, maintains that "extra-protocol" governance such as the decision to hard-fork Ethereum is a crucial backstop tool to prevent hard-coding some kind of harmful process, as with the DAO, into the protocol itself.

Only time will tell whether the Breitmans' blockchain governance model is superior to Bitcoin, Ethereum, or whatever other forks of those two might emerge in the future. Even so, it does seem that the outcome of Tezos' bet could be an important determinant of future blockchain design.

Financial governance of Tezos

The tokens that define Tezos' financial governance are also integral to its dynamic protocol governance system. Ownership of the Tezos token, known as the Tez, confers a right to users to stake their coins—locking them up as a part of a commitment to mine blocks—and to vote for delegates to validate the blockchain and make decisions on new rules and protocol upgrades. Owners can use "Tezzies" not only to compensate miners for validation work but also to reward developers for software upgrades if and when they get incorporated into the live protocol.

Within the context of Tezos' self-amending governance approach and as one of the first proposals for an amendment to the systems rules, the founders are promoting the idea of a *futarchy*, based on economist Robin Hanson's proposal of the same name for a system in which "democracy would continue to say what we want, but betting markets would now say how to get it."[137] The idea has earned the slogan, "vote values, bet beliefs."

Under the Tezos futarchy, users could stake their Tez on delegated votes on matters of "value" and then place bets on which code alterations are most likely to achieve those value results, creating a kind of wisdom-of-the-crowd market mechanism for predicting optimal outcomes. The original 2014 Tezos white paper included this example:

> Stakeholders would first vote on a trusted datafeed representing the satisfaction of a value. This might be, for example, the exchange rate of coins against a basket of international currencies. An internal prediction market would be formed to estimate the change in this indicator conditional on various code amendments being adopted ... . In the end, the amendment deemed most likely to improve the indicator would be automatically adopted.[138]

These methods emphasize how a community can use the economics of tokens to incentivize its members to push for the betterment of the underlying platform, the commons of the blockchain itself.

Tezos' unexpected ICO influx of $232 million created a whole other set of questions around financial governance. CEO Kathleen

Breitman told Paul Vigna of *The Wall Street Journal* that, six months earlier, she'd "had a dream that we raised $30 million." She'd then thought to herself, "That's impossible."[139] Like other cryptoasset platforms that raise money through token sales, Tezos set up a Switzerland-based foundation to manage the funds and distribution. Shortly after the ICO closed, the foundation took charge of $220 million of ether and bitcoin and announced that it would invest the funds slowly in a "conservative," diversified portfolio of cash, stocks, bonds, and precious metals to "ensure that our organization is resilient in good times, and bad times."[140]

With both the Bitcoin and Ethereum foundations badly hurt during the 2014–2105 downturn in the bitcoin prices, Tezos' decision to create a noncorrelated pool of funds was mostly viewed as sensible. However, it also emphasized the distortions created by massive open-ended fundraising exercises like Tezos'. What to do with all that money? Tezos decided to dedicate $50 million of it to a venture capital fund.[141] This prompted some mocking analysis from ICO skeptics, who saw irony in token-raised funds plowing back into VCs, but the Tezos Foundation had a clear strategy behind the move. Calling "innovation and growth of the ecosystem" its "top priority," the foundation said the funds would explicitly target start-ups working with applications that work on top of the Tezos platform.

If Tezos is to compete with Ethereum as a smart contract and Dapp development system, then it needs to foster a vibrant ecosystem of creators and developers. Traditional VC funding may be the most effective way to achieve this. Still, who will oversee and manage the investment strategy? Who will do due diligence and sit on the start-ups' boards? These sorts of questions buttressed critics' portrayal of Tezos as a software company that has accidentally become a fund management company. It's why some people are arguing that successful ICO issuers should either be paying dividends or buying back—and "burning" or neutralizing—the recovered tokens to boost their value. That's what blockchain fund management platform ICONOMI did with its tokens.[142] Whether such actions are red flags for securities regulators remains to be seen.

EOS: Parallelization

Launched around the same time as Tezos, EOS is the brainchild of Daniel Larimer, one of the most prolific, innovative but also controversial developers to emerge in the era of post-currency applications for blockchains. Larimer's first project, BitShares, was a decentralized exchange on which stable-currency tokens such as the dollar-pegged BitUSD could trade. Despite concerns that its name, bearing the word, *shares*, would attract action from the SEC, BitShares has survived.

More importantly, its delegated proof-of-stake blockchain architecture, labeled *Graphene*, has stayed on as the foundation for other Larimer projects. One of those was Steemit, a decentralized social media platform in which users can upvote articles in a similar fashion to Reddit's voting system but with Steem tokens included as rewards.

After surging in June 2016 to become one of the most well-capitalized cryptoassets on the market, Steem's prices plunged amid concerns about the system's perverse incentives to boost pro-Steemit articles in favor of the founders' stakes. But the system has since stabilized and now claims an average of more than 20,000 daily users.[143] Steemit is still a fringe product, but its survival has some hoping that its decentralized model will pose a challenge to the centralized behemoths of social media such as Facebook and Twitter.

EOS, however, has even bigger objectives. It takes the Graphene model to a wider goal: the creation of a global virtual machine for enterprise users that is both fully decentralized and scalable to a level currently unimaginable for Bitcoin and Ethereum. EOS tackles the fundamental challenge of how to ensure that a fully decentralized, permissionless blockchain can process a massive amount of transactions very quickly—how to move beyond Bitcoin's seven transactions a second to something the whole world can use.

Unique protocol features of EOS

EOS.io's software creates what its development team describes as an "operating system-like construct" that "provides accounts, authentication, databases, asynchronous communication and the scheduling of applications across hundreds of CPU cores or clusters"—all across a decentralized network of computers.[144] This setup is designed as a suite of tools for companies to easily create decentralized applications without having to engage engineers in the cumbersome process of development and coding. It's a bit how Microsoft's Windows or Apple's MacOS come bundled with add-ons like browsers and office tools. By contrast, Ethereum is more application agnostic, providing a flat platform upon which any Dapp can be built.

Most importantly, the EOS team claims that the underlying architecture "scales to millions of transactions per second, eliminates user fees, and allows for quick and easy deployment of decentralized applications."[145] Behind that bold assertion is an approach known as *parallelization*, which frees computers from having to do multiple tasks in sequence before moving to the next one. The company claims to have stress-tested the system in simulations, but in reality there's simply no way to know whether something as complex as a global ledger of smart contracts that runs on a fully decentralized validation model can work at that level. If it can, of course, it could be a game changer, especially if block.one's marketing efforts, aimed at enterprise clients, pays off.

Ever since Bitcoin's broader implications were made apparent to them, thought leaders have imagined the transformative economic power of a fully functional "Internet of Value," a permissionless system for individuals and businesses to create and transfer value without intermediaries, an open-access system of innovation. Scalability, symbolized by Bitcoin's meager seven-seconds-per-transaction capability, has long been seen as the barrier to that imagined possibility. Even if EOS doesn't work, it shows how, much like the pioneers of the Internet, a set of adventurous developers is constantly attacking those scalability barriers in search of the bigger vision and, in doing so, are bringing us closer to breaking through them.

Financial governance of EOS

With the engagement of famed cryptographer Ian Grigg and a host of early professional investors, Hong Kong–based block.one, the start-up behind EOS, launched a token sale that took in $185 million in the first five days of its offering. That was the third-largest intake in history as of this writing. Block.one had a strong opportunity to raise even more as the crowdsale was to continue over the course of a year, offering a billion tokens in total. With the price per token, which uses the same three-letter EOS symbol as the blockchain, quoted at $1.36 on *CoinMarketCap.com* at the time of writing, some observers are predicting a total fundraise in excess of $1 billion.[146]

The EOS token was sold as an ERC-20 token, an asset issued over Ethereum. However, on 1 June 2018, an independent EOS blockchain will begin, which means that all registered ERC-20 EOS tokens will convert to a native token on that chain, which happens to include some dynamic governance procedures similar to Tezos. In a move that has some investors a little unnerved, EOS advised tokenholders to register with EOS or risk losing them at that time.

Like many ICOs, EOS' included heavy disclaimers such as the tokens "do not have any rights, uses, purpose, attributes, functionalities or features, express or implied, including, without limitation, any uses, purpose, attributes, functionalities or features on the EOS Platform," and so forth. It's an especially conservative legal strategy, since the SEC could construe any promise of value as a security offering, and investors clearly were able to see past it on the belief that EOS will one day build a valuable ecosystem regardless of what it can or cannot promise.

Yet, even with this explicit disclaimer, block.one found itself the victim of a regulation-by-stealth move in August 2017 when Hong Kong–based crypto exchange Bitfinex barred American investors from trading EOS tokens on its platforms. Bitfinex was clearly spooked by the SEC's statement on the DAO tokens, which reminded exchanges to register with the SEC if they allowed trading in any tokens deemed securities. The move had no discernible effect on EOS' price, perhaps a mark of the global nature of trading in this technology right now. However, some saw the Bitfinex move as a warning of the subtle ways in which the SEC can extend its regulatory reach across an industry while retaining its discretionary power.

CRYPTOTOKENS

Cryptotokens, the third category of cryptoassets, are directly associated with a particular economic purpose, usually defined by their role in governing a community of users of a particular decentralized application or Dapp. It's here that the most adventurous thinking around programmable money, incentive structures, and economic design is happening. It's also where the modern-day gold rush of ICO mania is most vividly playing out.

The vast majority of these tokens are assets issued on top of another blockchain. By far the biggest category is that of the aforementioned ERC-20 tokens issued on top of Ethereum. There are now hundreds of ERC-20 tokens trading within the Ethereum ecosystem with new ICOs coming to market daily. Consider the four offerings that the ICO Alert website listed on 17 August 2017, for the five days to 22 August:

- Decentraland, "a decentralized marketplace to turn virtual commodities into real commodities"

- Imperium, "no-fee sports betting platform built on Ethereum"

- Latoken, "tokenizing fractions of assets such as real estate and art"

- Snapup, "a platform to shop for premium products."[147]

So long as these tokens continue to attract both primary and secondary market investment, a positive feedback loop of value creation will boost the value of ether along with the tokens. But if the market goes south, a vicious circle of wealth destruction might also eventuate.

The sheer breadth of ideas covered by these tokens—many of them half-baked, a few truly brilliant, nearly all unproven—leaves us no chance of representing all of them here. Instead, we'll review a number of industry categories, each defined in terms of the particular commons whose management the system is seeking to improve.

The media commons

As we discussed in reference to Brave's BAT, there are clear signs of dysfunction in the online ad market, where publishers compete for the core resource of user attention in a bid to deliver it to advertisers. But the concept of an Internet media commons is more far-reaching than the advertising market. The idea that cyberspace should be a setting in which ideas can be openly and freely shared was intrinsic to the philosophy that shaped the early design, if not the eventual outcome, of the Internet.

Even though traditional TV and publishing entities, in migrating their businesses to online platforms, imposed a model of corporate control with digital rights management and aggressive litigation, the mantra that "information wants to be free" has lived on in the "freemium" pricing models of many publishers. However, protecting and maintaining this commons requires more deliberate effort to recognize the rights of those who create, as well as those of the audience, which gives away valuable data.

Initiatives such as the Creative Commons license, with which photographers and artists have attached usage rights and conditions to 1.2 billion of their digital images, have provided new tools for creators and self-publishers to assert ownership while encouraging free use.[148] But if we are to nurture and protect the Internet commons as a public good, then we could do more to better manage the rights and obligations of both users and creators.

The amount of information available is not the problem; it's the quality of it. Nothing has brought this home more than the problem of fake news, which people using social media distribution strategies can now produce and distribute at much lower cost than it takes labor-intensive news organizations to gather, verify, produce, and distribute their news. In essence, the problem has come down to one of incentives misalignment: people are not properly incentivized to produce, share, and support reliable information. The commons is suffering as a result.

Here a new wave of crypto-inspired innovators is betting that tokens can be game changers. A range of strategies is emerging. Some, like elements of Brave's BATs model, are focused on incentivizing honesty in the reporting of traffic data to avoid advertising fraud. Others are grappling with the problems of fake news and disinformation by giving users and publishers skin in the game that drives them toward more honest assessments of the quality of content. There are also efforts to tokenize the business of creation itself, so that artists and writers can be more fairly recognized for their work, and even monetize it.

In the first category, a significant competitor to Brave is adChain, launched by MetaXchain. The system has two main elements. One is the adChain registry, which keeps a blockchain-proven record of domains deemed to be honestly reporting traffic. The other is a pool of adTokens (ADT), used to incentivize people to vote on the worthiness of domains added to that registry via a time-lock voting system. By locking up money when they vote, they submit a *proof-of-integrity* action that's not dissimilar to how Tezos and others use proof of stake to ensure confidence in blockchain validation.

One billion adTokens are in circulation, following a crowdsale on 26 June 2017 that reached its cap of $10 million in just 23 seconds.[149] The founders wanted to create what they call a "virtuous circle" in which adToken holders, with skin in the game, vote honestly on the quality of the reporting of different publishers' domains, which serves the needs of advertisers, who buy up tokens to pay publishers for ads, driving up the price and rewarding the tokenholders for acting honestly. Honest publishers also win because they can distinguish themselves from dishonest sites and attract a fairer share of the ad business.

Here's how Hunter Gebron, MetaXchain's director of strategic initiatives, metaphorically described what adChain represents: "If digital advertising were a giant city, one could say that adChain is laying down cleaner more efficient pipes underneath the city which provide residents cheaper and safer utilities ('residents' being advertisers and publishers)."[150] In this sense, the system is designed to incentivize the upkeep of a commons defined by a clean, honest record of publisher websites' traffic data.

How to incentivize honesty and integrity in the business of social media is also a challenge. There, the abuse of metrics such as "likes," "upvotes," and "retweets," including the deployment of specialized bots to replicate such processes, has elevated certain destructive content for the wrong reasons, creating disinformation, fake news, and political upheaval. This contentious industry is where Warsaw-based Userfeeds.io has turned its attention.

The company's bet is that if both users and publishers are going to engage in media curation, either formally or through their votes on the quality of content—with likes, upvotes, and so forth—then they should have skin in the game if they are to be more inclined to make honest, thoughtful assessments. Userfeeds wants to do this by turning people's holdings of tokens into provable measures of reputation that they put at stake whenever they make some judgment on a piece of content.

The strategy is an attempt, said Maciej Olpinski, Userfeeds' founder, to grapple with the fact that, "in the current environment, producing toxic information that is viral is essentially a free option on attention ... a situation where information is free or almost free to produce but has a potential to generate lots of attention dollars if it spreads virally." This asymmetry, he said, benefits everyone except the "attention suppliers," that is, users. The big social media platforms collect user data, and the content creators rack up eyeballs and generate traffic. Sure, users may experience instant gratification on social media, but it comes with long-term opportunity costs. Olpinski presented an alternative:

> What if we could bring symmetry to online relationships where every time someone wants your attention they'd have to prove what incentives they have, and they've had to sacrifice something to make you pay attention to them? The concept of digital tokens on platforms like Ethereum, allows us to design systems where tokens can be used for signaling relevance of information to communities owning these tokens.[151]

Userfeeds' use of tokens differs from many of the ICOs. The start-up has not issued its own token per se. Rather, the platform is designed to allow users to pledge existing tokens such as ether to assert their reputation and show their integrity. But it also has the prospect of having curators issue their own, unique reputation tokens that others could buy into as a way to support their work and encourage good-quality newsfeeds and content curation.

Blockchain developers are also intently working on applications that use the blockchain to immutably register unique creative works and, with that, to empower creators to take more direct control over the rights to their works and, potentially, to monetize them through smart contracts and digital currency. These same engineers are also talking a lot about tokenization, but the concept hasn't yet been well formed.

Po.et, a service for registering authorship data with original content, was launched with the support of a number of Bitcoin veterans, including David Bailey, CEO of *Bitcoin Magazine* publisher BTC Media, and former Bitcoin core developer Jeff Garzik, and raised $10 million in an ICO. Other than its role as a fundraising vehicle, it's not clear whether or how the Po.et token will incentivize participants in the publishing industry to build out the commons.

A more pointed proposal was the CCCoin, from Mediachain, which has created a blockchain-ready registry filled with the authorship metadata from 100 million Creative Commons–licensed creative works. As conceived, artists and writers would generate CCCoins for themselves when they register their CC-licensed photos, images, or other works.

Pondering who would then buy those tokens to support their value, Mediachain founder Jesse Walden posited that philanthropic organizations that wanted to support an open Internet commons and incentivize artists to make their content public via the Creative Commons process would find Mediachain effective.[152] Development of CCCoin stalled, however, after the music-streaming company Spotify acquired Mediachain.[153] In fact, the name "CCCoin" has since been adopted by a platform that has developed a token for charities to raise and distribute funds.

An identity commons

One of the more high-profile token sales of 2017 was that of blockchain identity verification platform Civic, whose mobile app–based system stores its customers' various certified markers of identity—birth certificate data, verified bank account information, certified health records, and so forth—in an immutable blockchain registry.

Civic said the system is so good at detecting changes to the blockchain-secured data that it can provide real-time monitoring alerts if anyone tries to fraudulently use a customer's identity—and it offers free insurance of up to $1 million to insure against the legal costs of identity theft. With digital identity solutions viewed by many as a potential killer app for blockchain technology, interest in Civic has been strong: its sale of a billion CVC tokens attracted strong demand on 22 June 2017.

A billion CVC tokens were sold, representing a third of the total supply. Sensing that early demand was strong and sticking steadfastly to a $33 million hard-cap fundraising limit, the Civic team, led by serial entrepreneur and prominent cryptocurrency commentator Vinny Lingham, decided to introduce a randomized rationing system to avoid letting the biggest, fastest "whales" dominate the ICO. The goal was to spread ownership more widely.

Civic wants to ensure the widest distribution possible because the value of its identity system is a direct function of network effects. Identity systems are a bit like currencies; they are effective only to the extent that everyone accepts them. It's why Civic is looking to grow its ecosystem as aggressively as possible. In this context, the token becomes a value-generating incentive tool for expanding the ecosystem. Customers can be rewarded with tokens for uploading certain information to the system and attesters can be paid in tokens for validating people's various claims of certification and identity.

"The bigger the network grows, the more utility in the token—because the number of tokens are fixed (no inflation in the total supply, although they will be released over time)," said Lingham. "As the size of the network and transaction volumes within it grows, this will create demand for the tokens."[154] It's another bet on a positive feedback loop that serves the wider community's interest.

The honesty commons

Online prediction markets, in which people bet on the outcome of events, are nothing new. Ireland's Paddy Power site has been delivering up betting odds on the outcome of elections and other aspects of daily life since 1988. But blockchain technology takes these systems to a new level for two reasons:

- In the decentralized structure of a blockchain, no one can be suspected of manipulating the algorithm; and

- They let anyone set up their own prediction market and, instead of relying on the judgment of the site owner, generate a crowd-sourced system for adjudicating the outcomes upon which payouts are based.

With those features in place, advocates say these systems are a powerful way to tap the wisdom of the crowd, which can guide policy decisions.

What could make these systems revolutionary is the introduction of tokens, designed to reward honest adjudicators. With Augur, the first blockchain-based prediction market, the token is called a "Rep," short for reputation. The idea is that adjudicators will bet in the markets in which they are casting judgment, wagering their Reps as skin-in-the-game proof of their honesty. If the facts turn out differently, then not only will they lose money but also their reputation will decline. But if they are consistently correct, the opposite happens: a virtuous circle of reputation and profit that, in theory, encourages honesty.

Writing in a *WIRED* article, "Forget Bitcoin. The Blockchain Could Reveal What's True Today and Tomorrow," Cade Metz posited that tokenized blockchain prediction markets could help society assess truth in news reporting. "If, say, Trump's national security adviser steps down and Augur's Rep-funded 'reporters' verify his resignation, that fact gets burned into a blockchain," Metz wrote.

Any application can then make use of this digital fact, from Wikipedia to Facebook to Google search results. In an age when fake news bounces around Facebook's echo chambers and presidential tweets see no difference between online hoaxes and the careful reporting of *The New York Times*, the possibility of creating a digital market for facts becomes a powerful idea.[155]

With prediction markets now envisaged for blockchain governance solutions such as Tezos', interest in these tokens has surged. Augur's token has been around since 2015, starting out at a valuation of $1.47, according to *CoinMarketCap.com*. But other than a brief spike above $12 in March 2016, it tended to hold to levels below $5 for the first 15 months of its existence. Come the spring of 2017, however, Augur's Rep took off, peaking at $36.30 in early June. It later sold off again over the summer, but at the time of writing (Sept. 2017) was still trading around $20. This enthusiasm was even more evident in the outcome of the Gnosis ICO, mentioned above, which, by some measures of its market valuation, turned the Augur competitor into an almost instant unicorn.

These numbers offer a valuable reminder of the pure speculative nature of this market. Prediction markets, if they work, could have enormous value for society. We don't yet know whether they will work or if malicious actors might find ways to collude and game Augur's Rep market to distort outcomes of different bets, inserting a lasting, immutable record of falsehood into the permanent blockchain—creating something worse than fake news. Still, the prospect of creating a market in truth is exciting.

The decentralized computing commons

"There is no cloud. It's just someone else's computer." So goes the statement on a popular Silicon Valley T-shirt. In truth, the phrase underplays the sophistication of the computing resource management that "cloud" providers carry out within giant arrays of data-center-based servers. However, it does tell an important truth about centralization within the outsourcing business that controls much of the world's file storage and processing.

What if we abandoned the centralized model by which IBM, Amazon, Google, Apple, Dropbox, and Oracle charge us five-star markup rates for their hard drive-space and forged a "sharing economy" model, an Airbnb of hard-drive rentals? What if anyone with extra space and RAM to spare could offer it to anyone who needed it and get paid for it?

In theory, since there is much unused capacity on everyone's desktops, this sharing model should drive down the price of storage and hosting significantly. That's what several blockchain start-ups are offering, and they've discovered that some kind of token is vital for a market to form around this service. With offerings like Siacoin (SC), Maidsafe's Maidsafecoin (MAID), or Storj (STORJ), creators of decentralized computing networks have found that tokens can create a marketplace between those who supply excess computing resources and those who need it.

In a similar vein, there is filecoin, the token created and sold by Protocol Labs, creator of the InterPlanetary File System, or IPFS. Filecoin's $252 million haul in early August 2017 is generally described, as of this writing, as the biggest crowdsale in history. The purpose behind filecoin is to reward, and therefore incentivize, computer owners to provide their hard-drive space for creating a new, decentralized world wide web.

Applying some of the ownerless file-sharing principles of services like BitTorrent, IPFS offers a radically different approach to hosting the files that make up websites than the traditional hosting service model. Under IPFS, multiple copies of the various component files that comprise a website—the text files, JPGs, MP4s, and so forth—are spread across multiple computers and retrieved via the fastest route available whenever someone accesses that site. The arrangement creates redundancies, backups that protect against fails, all within a structure in which no one can control the documents that comprise the web.

The environmental commons

The biggest commons of them all is facing the most overwhelming tragedy of the lot. Our planet is relentlessly succumbing to the impact of climate change. To some it will seem like clutching at straws to argue that cryptocurrencies and tokens could help us address such a monumental problem. After all, bitcoin, the most impactful cryptocurrency, inspires the deployment of massive electricity-gobbling mining farms around the world.

But critics should view this not from the perspective of the practical solutions needed to reduce the world's carbon emissions—a shift to renewable energy, greater efficiency in production processes, and so forth—but in terms of how token economics might help us deal with the politics of climate change. Once again, it comes down to the capacity to align incentives around a common goal. Might tokens encourage people to work collaboratively on warding off this most serious threat to life on earth?

Environmental degradation falls into the classic economic problem of *externalities*: that our economic system is incapable of putting a price on the costs that one person's environmental damage imposes on everyone else. Using traditional economics, we have no way to apportion fairly that cost to a polluting industry, without doing so via some political act of taxation, fines, or other regulation. Yet in many cases, those who are doing the harm recognize and are motivated to work toward mitigating it. But without collaboration, their competitors may free-ride on their generosity. That risk is often too big to bear from a market strategy perspective. This is where hope lies in what some people are calling *crypto-impact economics*, an effort to hard-code into tokens the objectives of fighting environment degradation.

Some examples are worth highlighting. A team that included Erick Miller, a serial entrepreneur and CEO of token investment platform CoinCircle, UCLA finance professor Bhagwan Chowdhry, and World Economic Forum oceans conservationist Gregory Stone came up with two special value tokens: the Ocean Health Coin and the Climate Coin. They proposed to issue those tokens to key stakeholders, a mix of companies, governments, consumers, nongovernmental organizations (NGOs), and charities, who can use them to pay for a range of functions to do with managing carbon credits and achieving emission and pollution reductions. The World Economic Forum would control a reserve of tokens to manage the value of the global float of coins.

The meat of the proposal involves a plan to destroy irrevocably some of the coins in reserve whenever international scientific bodies confirm that improvements in pollution and carbon emission targets have occurred. That act of destroying, through a cryptographic function, certain tokens will increase its scarcity and thus its value. The point: holders are motivated to act in the interests of improving the planet now, not tomorrow.

The other is an idea floated by the team from LO3 Energy: an exergy token. *Exergy* refers to the amount of useful work performed per unit of energy generated.[156] It is in many respects a more useful measure of how communities generate and use energy than the standard measures of generation and consumption in joules or kilowatt hours because it takes into account the loss of energy in transmission—as much as 30 percent in some places—and the efficiency of the devices we use.

In the Internet of Things age, where all our devices will be smart enough to make transactions with each other and can turn themselves on or off depending on our preferences, exergy is likely to become a critical concern for everyone. As solar generation and storage technologies become more affordable and more and more generation capacity moves to people's homes, an exergy management system will be vital for communities at large, as grid managers must optimize the timing of energy generation and distribution, engaging both household "prosumers" and traditional, wholesale providers in a complicated load management process.

LO3 Energy believes the exergy token will be a vital piece of the solution: the token, whose price-per-energy unit will float, will become a critical market-signaling device. At the household level, it will allow people to automate decisions on which devices to run at what time inside their homes; and at the regional level, it will allow grid managers to calibrate the right mix of wholesale and retail power.

As a source of revenue for anyone who generates electricity, the exergy token will also provide price signals and incentives for households to invest in solar energy. The token will depend on trusted computing and certified solar equipment to prove and verify in a blockchain recording system that the source of a particular amount of electricity is renewable. That quality should also turn the token into a sought-after investment for cap-and-trade and other carbon-offset markets.

The current design of global capitalism, where money is not just a means of exchange but a fetishized marker of value that we're incentivized to accumulate in demonstration of our power, is directly responsible for the stress being imposed on our planet's resources. Surely, we owe it to the generations to whom we are handing it to redesign that system in a bid to save life on earth while we can. The opportunity to do that may come from programmable money—money that is not itself an end-goal commodity but rather what it was always meant to be: a tool for exchanging and collaboratively generating value.

BUT IS IT LEGAL? IS IT SAFE?

The SEC's July 2017 statement declaring that the DAO tokens were securities, followed by China's more aggressive move to outright ban ICOs—was a reminder that a regulatory crackdown remains a distinct possibility for the token industry. More than that, though, these developments got people thinking about possible triggers to deflate what looks to many, many people like a bubble. A correction in prices, and quite likely a severe one, seems inevitable in the token market. Whether SEC indictments or a price plunge comes first, there's a real prospect that the current "virtuous circle" of rising speculative investment driving up the value of all tokens could turn into a vicious version of the same self-perpetuating cycle.

These issues also shine a light on what's needed for this market to mature, to bring greater protection for investors and a more effective way to value cryptoassets, so that the unbridled financial speculation of the moment can migrate to a more orderly framework. That way society can focus on the real promise of this technology—its capacity to redefine economic management, to incentivize collaboration and efficient resource usage—rather than on the gold-rush mania of the ICOs. Here we review some of the areas of reform that are needed for this market to function in a way that is constructive for society.

Tailor compliance solutions

Despite the pro-forma disclaimers included in virtually every ICO white paper stating that the token confers no ownership rights or promise of value and (for good measure) that US citizens should not buy it, it's likely that many ICOs will be judged to be securities by regulators. In the case of the SEC, it will come down to the *Howey* test, which has determined that any offering that involves an investment in a common enterprise and an expectation that profits will flow from the efforts of the promoter constitutes a security.[157]

Anyone offering something that meets those criteria to the public needs to register with the SEC, requiring a prospectus and a host of other costly and cumbersome disclosures and procedures. There seems to be a wide gulf between certain lawyers and traditional securities experts who believe the majority of the tokens will pass the *Howey* test and be subjected to fines or worse and the confidence of many token issuers, who declare that they've had sound legal advice that their particular offering is in the clear. That gulf is, in itself, a source of uncertainty.

A safer route, to avoid this uncertainty, would be to sell only to accredited investors, which broadly means professional investment institutions such as venture capital firms and hedge funds or individuals with a liquid net worth of more than $1 million and income of more than $200,000 a year.

There are two problems with this:

- It loses the democratizing benefits of public offerings.

- It's harder for the token to achieve the network effects that wide distribution would allow.

There may be a compromise, however: the new concept of a simple agreement for future tokens or SAFT. Modeled on a contract known as a SAFE (simple agreement for future equity) that professional investors sometimes enter into with companies that are yet to issue equity, SAFTs can be sold to accredited investors as a bridging mechanism. The idea is that they convert to tokens that can be accessed by users and the public once the network has been built out.

"The issuers then use the funds they raise to develop the platform's network," said Marco Santori formerly of Cooley LLP, which used the idea for Filecoin's successful offering. "Only then, once the network is functional, and tokens are functioning as a real product, can they be sold to the public."[158] The idea is not only to stay out of legal harm but also to avoid what some see as a moral hazard risk of the current fundraising approach, where developers bring in far more money than they need and are potentially disincentivized to work hard to develop the product.

There are also mechanisms emerging for small investors to get exposure via professional investors. The Crypto Company, founded by entrepreneur and poker champion Rafe Furst, which bills itself as "the responsible gateway to digital currencies", could provide one route to this.[159] It's modeled on Crowdfunder, of which Furst is a co-founder and which lets retail investors take stakes in venture capital deals.

If this industry is to deliver on its promise to democratize finance, it will need a host of other products that give small investors an entry point, such as exchange-traded funds. But after the SEC rejected two bitcoin exchange-traded funds (ETFs) in 2017—those of Winklevoss Capital and SolidX—the near-term prospects of a cryptotoken ETF aren't strong. The SEC's rejections highlighted unreliable liquidity in bitcoin exchanges and the prevalence of trading within unregulated settings, which the Commission saw as impeding the ETF sponsors' ability to stand behind the prices it quotes to investors. The lesson, then, is that the entire cryptoasset industry, including tokens, has an interest in promoting transparent, reliable, and regulated exchanges.

Note also that token platforms, as well as the Dapps they support, constitute inherently global, borderless technologies. That has important implications for regulators looking to control them. As we've seen elsewhere in the cryptocurrency and blockchain field, developers will simply move to the most accommodating jurisdictions when one country's rules are too onerous, creating a global pattern of regulatory arbitrage and region-to-region distortions. For the most part, any tokens judged to be exempt from securities filing requirements should be left free from formal regulation—in keeping with the widely observed principle of not regulating software, which is what these products essentially are.

This is not to say that this global industry doesn't need some kind of governance or, as Don and Alex Tapscott describe it in a recent report for the World Economic Forum, a "self-organizing, bottom-up, and multistakeholder" system of "stewardship."[160] As token technologies and the ecosystem around them develops, engineering standards, modes of dispute resolution, advocacy representation, and other forms of collective action will need to emerge, ideally without the interference of governments. To achieve this, token issuers, investors, exchanges, industry users, and any other stakeholders in this emerging industry need to engage with each other, as well as with regulators, to carve out a robust framework for ongoing development that's not burdened by legal constraints.

Vet the founders

Investor analysis in the ICO market badly needs sophistication. Some offerings come to market with no prewritten codebase for their Dapp protocol and little more than a vaguely worded white paper explaining the idea. Yet these vaporware products, as cynics sometimes label them, can still fundraise seven figures. Even when there is comprehensive software development to point to, there's a serious shortage of vetting done—in part because blockchain technology is quite complicated, but also because there's little in the way of institutional analysis services to aid investors who are operating in the dark.

One warning of the danger came when researchers at MIT Digital Currency Initiative found serious bugs in the proprietary hashing algorithm used by IOTA, a bold new blockchain solution for Internet of Things transactions whose token is one of the most valuable listings. IOTA has struck deals with major companies such as Bosch and has a large global community of developers testing its tangle protocol for sending and confirming transactions between devices.

Yet IOTA ignored this major flaw, by which the developers had broken a cardinal rule of "rolling their own crypto" rather using existing, tested algorithms, until the MIT team tested it.[161] It's likely that bugs are riddled through many of the Dapp protocols that support the tokens people have invested in. We need a more sophisticated vetting process.

Here, too, institutional solutions are emerging. One comes from CoinList, a service created by Juan Benet's Protocol Labs, the developer of IPFS and Filecoin, and Naval Ravikant's AngelList. It offers a platform for token issuers to reach a network of investors but is promising to be highly selective about which tokens it supports, which is leading to expectations that CoinList-issued tokens will carry a de facto stamp of approval.[162] Notably, CoinList is also favoring the SAFT option developed by Cooley LLP, which was the case with Filecoin, the highly successful first CoinList offering. That means it is for now limiting the ICOs it supports to those that sell exclusively to accredited investors.

We also need some kind of ratings system, akin to that of regular bond markets, but tailored to the decentralized architecture of cryptoassets. Given the cryptocommunity's aversion to centralized models and trusted third parties, few have an appetite for giving the kind of power to ratings agencies that Moody's, S&P, and Fitch have accumulated and for which they were criticized in the wake of the global financial crisis. Still, specialized services offering objective ratings are emerging and may help investors cut through the noise of constant marketing pitches.

ICORating is a listing of past, current, and upcoming ICOs, some of which get assigned unique ratings, based on what the service describes as a "thorough independent audit by ICORating experts." Its ratings range through "Negative," "Risky," "Stable," and "Positive" with "+" or "-" modifiers. The ratings' components consist of a "risk score," a "hype score," and an "investment potential" score. Separately, ICORating gives outright "scam" labels to certain egregiously managed ICOs. The service provides fairly comprehensive reports, explaining the rationale for its ratings, which may boost the perception of objectivity.

But in an industry that's inherently wary of third-party certifiers, the complaint of "who's auditing the auditors" will likely arise toward ratings services like these. Expect pressure for blockchain-based audit logs that might enhance the transparency of the ratings process. Drawing from some of the ideas within the token industry, such as prediction markets and reputation tokens, there may be an option to create market-based bounty systems for smart coders and auditors to freelance their analysis within decentralized ratings systems.

More broadly, there's also a need for an independent, informed press within this industry, as well as for objective research and analysis by third-party observers. Currently, the number of journalists with the right knowledge and skill set to cover the token industry is woefully small relative to the number of ICOs coming to market. But with major business publications like *Forbes* and *The Wall Street Journal* recently creating full-time cryptocurrency and blockchain beats, the landscape is slowly changing. Meanwhile, newsletter services like the *Token Report*, launched by Galen Moore and early Bitcoin pioneer Peter Vessenes, are also starting to emerge, responding to demand from the emerging professional investor class with stakes in the token market.

Professionalize the token industry

Aside from the desire to widen the community of investors beyond Silicon Valley, the influx of VC and hedge-fund money into the ICO and token issuance market could be a positive, stabilizing effect. Big-name VC firms such as Andreessen Horowitz, Sequoia Capital, Union Square Ventures, and Bessemer Venture Partners had put a total of $245 million into two hedge funds geared to this market as of late summer 2017. One of those, MetaStable Capital, was founded in 2014 by AngelList CEO Naval Ravikant, among others. The other, Polychain, which started in 2015 with a $200 million funding round, was launched by Olaf Carlson-Wee, who was bitcoin wallet and exchange provider Coinbase's first hire in February 2013.[163]

Separately, specialized blockchain venture outfits such as Dan Morehead's Pantera Capital and Blockchain Capital, backed by brothers Bart and Brad Stephens, have set up funds dedicated to tokens. As mentioned, Tim Draper of Draper Fisher Jurvetson has also been an active investor in ICOs, as has tech billionaire Mark Cuban. More recently, some 15 different hedge funds have said they are going to be dedicated to investing in cryptoassets, according to *Forbes*.[164] The presence of these seasoned investors should bring some stability to the market—so long as these funds aren't wiped out by a big correction in the market.

Beyond their presence, though, the market needs the discipline that these investors should bring. As of now, there are very few standards that issuers are expected to abide by—given the pseudonymous nature of cryptocurrency addresses, there is widespread suspicion that many secretly support their own tokens during the ICO to prop up the price. But it's now clear how investors, professional or otherwise, can exert pressure through tokens. The nature of token investment is

that they don't get any say in governance—these are not shares; there is no prospect of a VC tokenholder getting a seat on the managing start-up's board.

The flipside is that these professional investors may feel less committed to a buy-and-hold strategy and won't have the same conduit for providing advice and leadership to the platform developers. It will be up to the issuers to keep them and the wider investor community happy through good-faith actions. If these professional investors can be convinced to hold for the long term, everyone in the wider ecosystem of token development should benefit.

Similarly, the growing engagement of big law firms in the token industry should also help promote more sophisticated structures, a commitment to staying within the law, and, hopefully, foster a deeper sense of fiduciary duty to tokenholders among platform developers. In addition to the aforementioned Cooley, the bigger firms taking a position in this area include Perkins Coie, BakerHostetler, Debevoise & Plimpton, MME, and Sullivan & Worcester.

CONCLUSIONS AND RECOMMENDATIONS

Whenever a lot of people quickly make a great deal of money in a new enterprise, the dollars and cents can become a distraction. It's inevitable that headlines will focus on nine-figure crowdfunding exercises that are over in a matter of minutes. In this chapter, we've tried to avoid that temptation and focus on the real economic potential for tokens themselves. We've framed that potential in terms of solving the Tragedy of Commons problem and believe that this potential captures the prospect of a global impact far greater and more important than the fortunes that are being made and that could soon be lost.

If everyone with a stake in the development of this technology, including start-up companies, their customers, investors, and regulators, is to formulate the best response to it, some deep thinking about that potential—whether it's realistic or not—is vital.

Yet it's also true that the problems associated with the money mania, the risk of scams and of the potential unwelcome attention from regulators, means that the most important work to be done right now lies in confidence-building measures to promote the industry's positive potential. So, while the money is distracting, figuring out how to govern is vital. All with a stake in this industry need to agitate for better internal *and* external governance of the emerging token economy.

1. The ICO industry needs a multifaceted regime of self-governance. Those with a stake in it, especially the now well-funded developers of major blockchain platforms such as Ethereum, Tezos, and EOS need to support various elements of that regime. These include a wider array of independent analysis services, objective ratings, and independent press outlets and newsletter services. In all cases, the industry has an opportunity to use blockchain transparency structures and reputation token incentive models to enhance confidence in the objectivity of the information—in other words, to put its money where its mouth is.

2. Meanwhile, issuers should establish best practices around raising and managing public funds. They should ask, "Should we cap token sales or distribute tokens more randomly?" They should also consider other policies for ensuring wide distribution and discouraging hoarding. Clearer standards on what founders should declare about their own token holdings would also be constructive.

3. Development talent is badly needed. The rising intake of money has only heightened the competition for engineering skills, meaning that hundreds of new token-based Dapps will find very thin pickings of engineers to maintain, update, and develop their protocols. Unlike JavaScript, which as far

back as 2009 was estimated to have attracted nine million developers with an ability in that programming language, the community of dedicated blockchain engineers numbered no more than 5,000 in April 2016, according to estimates by William Mougayar, though he also suggested that perhaps another 20,000 had "dabbled" in it.[165] That's far too small a pool from which to build the kind of economy-wide disruption that the token promoters are foreseeing.

4. The lesson from the Bitcoin split and the outperformance of original Bitcoin over Bitcoin Cash is that money will go to where the developers are, because that's where the best prospects of growth lie. To address this shortfall, we need education, standardization, and improvements in programming languages that are both easier to use yet robust and difficult to attack.

5. Regulators won't sit on the sidelines for long. The SEC's DAO announcement is a clear signal that it is prepared to call out at least some tokens as securities. Other countries might follow China's draconian response. Even if token issuers believe that their offerings belong to a new paradigm of investing and economics, the 71-year-old *Howey* test will continue to rule the SEC's thinking in this area. Various token sales will likely be judged a de facto investment in a promise of profit and will pay the price. This is not to say that the industry wouldn't be better off with clearer signals from the SEC and other regulators. For that, the industry could expand its advocacy work.

6. While the broader business of digital currencies and blockchains has been served by a number of advocacy organizations in Washington such as Coin Center and the Chamber of Digital Commerce, a targeted effort to engage the SEC and other regulators specifically in defining the framework for tokens is warranted.

7. Participants should take SEC chairman Jay Clayton up on the offer that he made in the Commission's statement about the DAO. "The SEC is studying the effects of distributed ledger and other innovative technologies and encourages

market participants to engage with us," Clayton said. "We seek to foster innovative and beneficial ways to raise capital, while ensuring—first and foremost—that investors and our markets are protected." This technology has the potential to change the functioning of capital markets like few others. It is imperative that both regulators and industry jointly develop clear thinking about how to let innovation and public confidence in it flourish.

With so much dysfunction in the global economy, so much waste, and a serious waning of confidence in the institutions that oversee the prevailing capitalist system, the token economy is an idea whose time has come.

We cannot ignore the large potential benefits of a system of programmable money that could steer resources to where they are most needed, minimizes waste, protects the environment, and encourages innovation and open access. But if we are to seize the opportunity to explore and develop a solution to these problems, we need a clear framework for development and governance.

CHAPTER 3

FINANCING OPEN BLOCKCHAIN ECOSYSTEMS

Toward Compliance and Innovation in Initial Coin Offerings

Fennie Wang, Primavera De Filippi, Alexis Collomb, and Klara Sok

FINANCING OPEN BLOCKCHAIN ECOSYSTEMS IN BRIEF

- Most ICOs will not be true ecosystem tokens and will therefore be well suited as securities token offerings using registration exemptions and trading through decentralized alternative trading systems.

- Open-source blockchain-based ecosystems may choose to rely on fundraising practices typical of start-ups and private enterprises for the preproduction phase. Once they have established some profit centers, they may choose the use of coin offerings to fund postproduction phases.

- Token issuers might choose to devise creative corporate forms combining nonprofit structures, which would oversee access to shared open-source resources, with for-profit structures, which would develop specific business or decentralized applications.

- The SEC's concerns as a public watchdog for consumer and investor protection are well founded. We need regulations that encourage innovation, minimize speculation, and ultimately enable the creation of ecosystems that are more productive, more resilient, and more just in their allocation of power and resources.

- Markets will need some level of speculative trading in tokens to provide liquidity. Questions remain around how best to square the market necessity for some speculative activity, regulatory concerns around secondary markets, and the functional requirements of an ecosystem token.

- Collaboration in governance is critical. Members of the blockchain community—entrepreneurs, technologists, researchers, academics, lawyers, and others—should remain open to working with regulators in devising a regulatory framework for the emergent token economy.

INTRODUCTION TO BLOCKCHAIN'S IMPACT ON FUNDRAISING

Blockchain technologies could significantly affect how we interact and communicate on the web. With Web 2.0, the second generation of the Internet, we saw the rise of social media and user-generated content. Web 2.0 begat such Internet giants as Amazon, Google, Facebook, Uber, and Airbnb—leading to an increasingly privatized Internet, controlled by a few large, monopolistic operators.

Today, Web 3.0—the third generation of the Internet—portends a more decentralized Internet, more akin to a public good. Anticipated as early as 2006, in a term popularized by John Markoff of *The New York Times*, Web 3.0 promises an intelligent semantic web that is open and distributed.[166] For many veterans in the space, it will be a return to the original promise of the Internet as a public utility and network open to all.

In the past three years, blockchain technology has begun to impact traditional fundraising practices such as VC investments and crowdfunding. New mechanisms for raising funds have emerged through the public sale of cryptocurrencies and blockchain-based tokens.

These practices—sometimes called ICOs or *token generation events* (TGEs)—have raised more than $3.6 billion, surpassing the amount of VC funding in the blockchain ecosystem.[167] See Figure 3-1 for a comparison of the top five ICOs year over year.[168]

FIGURE 3-1

AMOUNT (IN $ MILLIONS) RAISED BY THE TOP FIVE ICOS

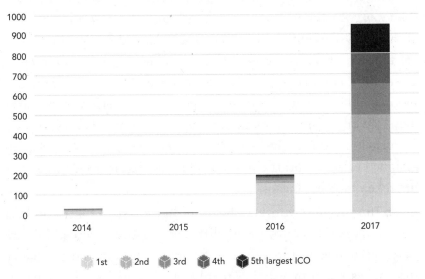

1st   2nd   3rd   4th   5th largest ICO

Source of data: CoinDesk *ICO tracker and* Business Insider.

While these token sales represent a new opportunity for projects or initiatives to raise the necessary capital to bootstrap themselves, they often operate in a regulatory gray area, especially with respect to securities law regulations. While the issuance of many blockchain-based tokens is likely to fall within the scope of securities laws, many grassroots projects or start-ups will have difficulty bearing the regulatory burden of these laws—with regard to the disclosure requirements, the asymmetries of information surrounding these investment tools, and the current lack of accountability or redress for retail investors. At the same time, access to traditional venture capital remains difficult for projects and entrepreneurs outside of major financial and technology capitals like Silicon Valley.

We start by distinguishing between blockchain-based systems that qualify as an *ecosystem* (e.g., Bitcoin, Ethereum) and those that qualify as a Dapp running on top of an ecosystem. We argue that the two approaches require the implementation of different token models and, consequently, different mechanisms to comply with relevant legal requirements.

There is a structural difference between the issuance of an *ecosystem token*, which represents a fundamental and *necessary* component of the ecosystem with which it is associated, and the issuance of an *app coin* (short for *application coin*) that may have some functionality similar to loyalty points or be used in lieu of cash payment to use services. The difficulty with such app coins is that, in many cases, they rely on a thin economic rationale, often merely serving as a disguise to fund the development of a blockchain-based application designed around a private profit center—acting, in effect, as a security token by other means.

In this chapter, we argue that only an ecosystem token can be a true *utility token*. We overview different practices adopted by various projects involved in a token sale, and investigate the regulatory approaches taken by existing regulatory authorities. We focus, in particular, on the SEC and how its thinking has evolved in the past year. We give specific attention to the interpretation of the *Howey* test for a finding of securities, and its potential application to the sale of blockchain-based tokens as a fundraising tool.

In the absence of regulatory clarity, blockchain-based projects and initiatives have to navigate murky waters. Some projects engage in a series of complicated techno-legal solutions in order to adapt their business practices and technological design to conform to the intent of existing regulations. These solutions try to take advantage of regulatory exemptions in various jurisdictions, with specific requirements that—if met—would allow securities issuers to reduce their regulatory obligations. Others continue to take the view that true utility tokens should be exempt altogether from securities laws, although it is becoming increasingly difficult to conduct such sales to the public.

In light of that, we analyze and evaluate the viability of existing solutions designed to comply with these different regulatory frameworks. The most common of these practices include the creation of nonprofit foundations acting as the umbrella organization that issues the tokens (e.g., the Swiss foundation model introduced by Ethereum) or the elaboration of specific contractual arrangements, such as the SAFT model, introduced by Filecoin. Yet, most of these solutions require extensive overhead while still bearing significant regulatory risks and uncertainty, and are often limited to specific exemptions under securities laws that do not enable token issuers to benefit from the full opportunities of a token sale.

We then suggest a series of creative solutions or best practices that could be implemented to launch successful token sales in compliance with existing regulatory frameworks, both in the United States and Europe. We stress the risk of existing marketing practices that create excessive expectations of profits. We also delineate ways to leverage the power of smart contracts to codify a number of technologically driven fail-safe mechanisms (or technical guarantees) so as to reduce the opportunities for speculation over the token's price. These include, for instance:

1. The issuance of nontransferable tokens to preclude the creation of a secondary market

2. The use of vesting schedules for token issuers and investors to avoid "pumps and dumps"

3. The introduction of a ceiling cap to prevent the price of tokens from rising over a specific threshold.

Finally, recognizing the inherent tension in using ecosystem tokens as financing instruments, we explore the use of more traditional financing arrangements (e.g., convertible notes) at the preproduction phase, for example, through the establishment of a for-profit entity that is arm's length with a nonprofit open-source software foundation.

Under this model, ICO funding would no longer constitute a replacement for a seed round, but is used to leverage the power of blockchain technology and public funding at later-stage rounds with a faster timeline than traditional initial public offerings.

INHERENT TENSION OF PRIVATELY FUNDING A PUBLIC GOOD

This section explores the use of blockchain-based tokens as a potential financing mechanism for the decentralized web, and analyzes the inherent tension in privately funding a public good. We refer here to *private funding* as funding coming from various private sources rather than from government, NGOs, or public institutions, which are more centralized funding sources. Private funding is more decentralized; however, it is currently caught up in the mental models of Web 2.0, where entities extract and monopolize private network value.

Equity is a classical instrument used to fund private enterprises, with the value of shares based on the expectation of revenues and profit in the private enterprise. As such, equity is an appropriate tool to fund private profit centers, such as the centralized online platforms from the Web 2.0 world, or even the various Dapps emerging in the Web 3.0 landscape.

However, when we move into the realm of new decentralized blockchain-based protocols or platforms that operate as a foundational layer of Web 3.0, equity alone might be an inadequate tool for funding these emergent ecosystems, which share many of the characteristics of a "public good." So what is the right funding instrument for these platforms?

The advent of the *token sale* or ICO was an attempt to resolve the tension inherent in the private funding of public goods. An ICO consists of the practice of offering blockchain-based tokens for sale to the public, and using the collected funds to support the development of a blockchain-based platform or Dapp—which, once deployed, will become publicly available to all tokenholders. Fundamentally, the idea is that if we are building a public good, then we should let the public who will benefit from this good fund it.

ECOSYSTEM TOKENS

The model is particularly well suited for open platforms or ecosystems that fundamentally require the existence of an ecosystem token, that is, a token native to a decentralized network or protocol, whose function is to coordinate and incentivize otherwise adverse and self-interested parties to contribute and grow the resources of a public commons. An ecosystem token essentially solves the problem of the "Tragedy of the Commons" that characterizes many common-pool resources.[169] The tragedy of the commons emerges from two conditions:

1. Participants individually benefit from the use of common-pool resources

2. The externalities of overuse or under-contribution are shared among all members of the community.

Hence, utility-maximizing actors are likely to act in a way that may lead to overexploitation or under-allocation of resources.[170] Ecosystem tokens, as a resource allocation and staking mechanism, could at least partially contribute to resolving these issues.[171]

Those who seek access of a common-pool resource must have a buy-in or stake in the commons to gain access to them. Accordingly, ecosystem tokens are often required for accessing network resources, used as a means to pay transaction fees between network nodes, or employed as other internal accounting and payment mechanisms. Participants who contribute to the ecosystem may also be rewarded in ecosystem tokens, for example, by running validator nodes or otherwise building network infrastructure or applications.

Decentralized blockchain-based protocols, at their core, need an economic incentive for validator nodes to confirm on-chain transactions and maintain network security that is tied to network value, rather than the profit value of specific applications that utilize a particular blockchain. The value of a true ecosystem token captures value across multiple profit centers in the network and all possible future profit centers, without necessarily taking on specific enterprise risk in any particular profit center.

This kind of economic incentive *does* require secondary market trading in order to decentralize its allocation and provide liquidity to validator nodes, allowing them to realize the value of their contributions to the network. Furthermore, using cryptocurrencies like ether and bitcoin would be inadequate as an incentive model. These cryptocurrencies have price movements that are entirely exogenous to, and independent of, the network value; a node validator wishing to earn ether or bitcoin would simply mine those blockchains instead. It would also be overly capital-intensive for new protocols to use ether and bitcoin as the reward mechanism.

Network utilization, including building the ecosystem and providing services and products that meet end-user demand, increases demand for access to the network and, consequently, the demand for ecosystem tokens. If all else is equal, then this increased demand results in an increase in the value of the tokens. Therefore, ecosystem tokens align individual incentives with those of the public commons. Individuals must, in effect, obtain tokens to access the network and participate (both individually and collectively) to build the value of the ecosystem—for instance, by contributing to the core network architecture and infrastructure, or by building Dapps that enhance the utility value of the ecosystem.

The long-term value of an ecosystem token fundamentally requires a number of stakeholders to build out the ecosystem with the open-source tools that the initial founders created, and contribute their own resources, creativity, and imagination. That is a key point that traditional VC investors fail to appreciate and Web 2.0 business models fail to capture.

Let's consider the Ethereum ecosystem. The Ethereum Foundation raised (only) $18 million in one of the first ICOs ever, completed through the sale of its own native cryptocurrency, ether, in September 2014. In the three subsequent years, independent projects around the world have raised more than $3.6 billion, all building on the Ethereum network and enriching the ecosystem. In classical finance parlance, this is called *leverage*.

DECENTRALIZED APPLICATION (DAPP) TOKENS

A Dapp token is fundamentally different from an ecosystem token. Even where the Dapp token has a utility function—it coordinates operations within a particular blockchain-based application—its economic function is fundamentally limited: Dapps do not build public, shared infrastructure as true network ecosystems do.

Profit centers focused on a particular product or vertical have long used equity as the main financing mechanism. Dapps have revenue and profit models, and users of Dapp services can pay with such existing options as fiat, cryptocurrencies, stablecoins, or even the ecosystem token of the underlying network or ecosystem upon which the Dapp is built. In many cases, it is hard to justify giving a Dapp its own unique utility or app coin distinct from ecosystem tokens.

Even where the Dapp utilizes an access or membership token (e.g., to access content), there is no economic reason for such a token to need secondary market liquidity, whereas an ecosystem token requires it as part of its economic design. In practice, the utility value of a Dapp token often seems forced, as a mechanism to avoid securities laws in public fundraising of what is essentially equity for a private profit center.

In the ICO landscape, the analysis currently focuses on the "nature" or "function" of these blockchain-based tokens—in particular, whether a certain token is categorized as a utility token, a tokenized security, or a cryptocurrency like bitcoin. A tokenized security would clearly be categorized as a security, subject to all applicable laws and regulations. However, there is a nuanced distinction within the utility token category. While utility tokens may cut across both ecosystem and Dapp tokens, these tokens are essential for the operation of a decentralized ecosystem and blockchain-based network, whereas they are not indispensable for the running of Dapps.

Because of the fundamental difference between ecosystem tokens and app coins, we believe that legal analysis should start from there, not from whether a token has a utility function. Taking the analysis to its logical conclusion, the reasons for a Dapp utility token are often very thin, if only to take advantage of the ICO hype, which regulators around the world are currently scrutinizing.

There is no economic or design reason why Dapps should not or could not be funded by traditional equity, which makes the utility case harder to justify. As SEC chairman Jay Clayton said, "Certain market professionals have attempted to highlight utility characteristics of their proposed initial coin offerings in an effort to claim that their proposed tokens or coins are not securities. Many of these assertions appear to elevate form over substance."[172]

What is worrisome is that, as a result of the regulatory crackdown due to many irresponsible and opportunistic ICOs, the original rationale for tokens as the essential funding mechanism of open-source ecosystems may get lost.

In the following sections, we examine the evolution of ICO practices, and the ensuing SEC guidance and enforcement action in the ICO space. We then provide a series of recommendations and insights on how compliant financing of open ecosystem projects might evolve that would both enhance the long-term viability of such projects and provide new value propositions to investors.

AN EVOLVING LANDSCAPE OF PRACTICES AND REGULATORY APPROACHES

HISTORICAL ANALYSIS

Bitcoin and Satoshi Nakamoto

The first instantiation of a blockchain-based system was Bitcoin, a peer-to-peer electronic cash system elaborated by a pseudonymous entity, Satoshi Nakamoto, in 2008, with its first transaction on 3 January 2009.[173] By design, Bitcoin is an open ecosystem, which we can regard as a quasi-public good in an economic sense.[174] As opposed to a centralized digital platform, Bitcoin does not have any private profit center and uses its native cryptocurrency, *bitcoin*, as a means of decreasing the risk of under-contribution and overexploitation.

This self-regulation derives from the mix of *transactions fees*, which users must pay in bitcoins, and mining rewards, whereby new bitcoins are issued to those who contribute computer power to maintain and secure the network.[175] Bitcoins thus acquire value because they are necessary to execute a transaction. Bitcoins can also be traded on secondary markets or exchanges where they can be bought or sold against fiat currency.

Ethereum and Vitalik Buterin

As Bitcoin started to gain traction, people like Vitalik Buterin realized that they could use the underlying blockchain technology for other types of applications beyond simple financial transactions. Buterin, a cryptocurrency researcher and programmer who had co-founded *Bitcoin Magazine*, first conceived of an open-source, decentralized, and blockchain-based computing platform in late 2013.[176] Whereas Bitcoin implements a very basic scripting language for transactions that is purposefully not Turing complete, Buterin's ambition was to create a platform with a Turing-complete programming language that enabled the execution of smart contracts for the creation of user-generated Dapps and their attendant app coins.[177]

He named this platform Ethereum.[178] The development of this new blockchain-based network was funded via an online crowdsale of ether (its native cryptocurrency) between July and August 2014.[179] As with bitcoin, ether can be regarded as an ecosystem token: people use the token to pay for the transactions fees (i.e., "gas") necessary to use the Ethereum infrastructure; and users can ether by contributing resources to the network—that is, through mining. Similarly to Bitcoin, the Ethereum ecosystem does not run any profit center. Yet, its governance differs slightly from Bitcoin's since Buterin maintains an active leadership role in the project, and the community can lean on the well-identified nonprofit Ethereum Foundation for the development and maintenance of the code.

In the past few years, Ethereum has evolved into one of the leading blockchain ecosystems, attracting a large crowd of developers, entrepreneurs, start-ups, established corporates, and various academic and research interests, all eager to explore, and potentially to leverage, its platform for building Dapps.

The DAO

One of the flagship initiatives of this new wave of innovation was the DAO, a distributed investment fund that collected all of its funds via a token sale launched in May 2016. Raising more than $150 million from about 11,000 investors in a few weeks, the DAO set a record at the time as the largest crowdfunding campaign in history.

One of the key features of the DAO was that it had no conventional management structure (i.e., it had no official management body or board of directors) and no formal organizational form. The DAO had no legal entity; it subsisted merely as a decentralized organization built on the Ethereum blockchain.

While the DAO never actually started operation, it is nonetheless relevant to analyze the function or utility of its tokens, called TheDAO.[180] The DAO was intended to become a significant player in the Ethereum ecosystem, enabling tokenholders to develop the ecosystem further by investing into various commercial and noncommercial endeavors that would contribute to the utility, and therefore the value, of the Ethereum network. Moreover, as an attempt at creating a decentralized organization, the DAO could itself be regarded to some extent as an open ecosystem: using TheDAO tokens, anyone could engage with or contribute to the DAO.

Even though the German company Slock.it developed the DAO's code, Slock.it was but one of many other contenders to receive funds from the DAO.[181] The DAO was intended to be fully autonomous, an independent endeavor that would take on a life of its own. It would be administered—collectively—by the investors themselves, transacting directly with the DAO open-source smart contract code. Therefore, after its launch, it would be the tokenholders—rather than Slock.it— who would control the operations of the DAO.

Yet, unlike bitcoin or ether, the utility of TheDAO token was not fundamental to the ecosystem. Much like a security, it was a transferable token endowing every holder a share of any future profits that the DAO would make from its investments. Moreover, tokenholders were entitled to participate in the governance of the DAO, whereas *curators* were responsible for whitelisting eligible projects, and a quorum of tokenholders would determine the allocation of the DAO's funds.[182]

In other words, just as shareholders can participate in the governance of a company by voting at annual shareholder meetings, TheDAO tokenholders could directly influence the DAO's final allocation decisions through their votes. The DAO was an investment fund whose investors did not delegate the task of selecting projects to an investment manager; rather, they determined the investment selection process themselves, according to their share of the total capital invested.[183] In a sense, the DAO operated similarly to an open-ended fund investing in securities, whereby shareholders can decide upon the fund's investments according to their share of total capital invested in the fund.

TheDAO tokens did have a particular utility: anyone willing to submit a project to the DAO had to spend TheDAO tokens. Yet, they could have achieved the same functionality by spending ether, had the DAO's original design included this option. The only incremental usage value of TheDAO token over ether was that it enabled its holders to vote in the DAO's investment submission and selection process.

FIGURE 3-2

TOP 10 ICOS (IN $ MILLIONS) OF 2017

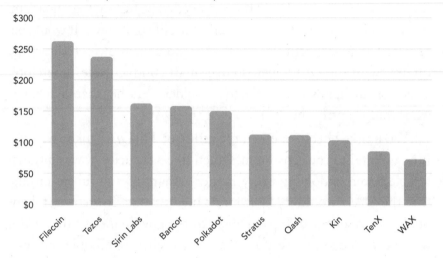

Source of data: Oscar Williams-Grut, "The 11 Biggest ICO Fundraises of 2017," Business Insider, 1 Jan. 2018.

Even though the DAO's management process differed from a standard corporate management process, the voting rights that TheDAO tokens conferred to their holders were somewhat similar to those of standard shareholders and the private interests they represent. It appears that TheDAO token existed not to support the operations of the DAO's ecosystem, but to ensure that token-holders could secure a return on investment proportional to their individual contributions.

The unexpected success of the DAO's crowdsale inspired a large number of blockchain-based projects and initiatives to launch their own token sales, some of which surpassed their founder's expectations. Filecoin ($257 million), Tezos ($232 million), IOTA ($434,000), and EOS ($185 million) are a few initiatives that used the ICO model instead of a VC scheme.[184]

Munchee

While those projects were directed toward the creation of an ecosystem, an increasing number of private companies are experimenting with these new fundraising mechanisms to raise funds for the development of blockchain-based applications or Dapps that do not operate as open ecosystems, but as private profit centers.

An emblematic example of this latter trend is Munchee, a San Francisco–based company that created a mobile app for users to review restaurants and comment on their food experiences. To improve its app, Munchee launched a token sale (with MUN tokens) in the fourth quarter of 2017, with a target to raise $15 million.

The MUN tokens enabled holders to buy goods and services on the app, such as advertisements, food purchases, and restaurant loyalty points, and to receive payments for their reviews based on their membership status, tiered according to their token holdings. Munchee referred to its token as a method of exchange inside of the Munchee ecosystem.[185]

However, the MUN token was not, in fact, an ecosystem token. The Munchee application operated as a private profit center: whatever users achieved with the MUN token, they could have easily done with ether, fiat, or even a centralized token system.

These four initiatives—Bitcoin, Ethereum, the DAO, and Munchee—illustrate the spectrum of possibilities, from a purely ecosystem token (e.g., bitcoin and ether), to a security token used in an open ecosystem (TheDAO), to a fully private token or app coin (MUN).

EVOLVING SEC STANDARDS

In this section, we provide a legal analysis of ICO tokens and look at the evolution of the SEC's approach, from its initial report on the DAO in July 2017 to its latest press release and enforcement action against Munchee in December 2017.

Report on the DAO

On 25 July 2017, the SEC issued an investigatory report, along with a press release cautioning the industry that the use of blockchain technology does not exempt token issuers or exchanges from the need to respect existing laws and regulations designed to protect investors and market integrity.[186] Specifically, the report stated that the sale of digital assets (or tokens) by decentralized blockchain-based organizations, such as the DAO, could very well qualify as a securities offering and thus be subject to the registration and disclosure requirements of federal securities laws.

While the report was meant to provide general guidance on the legal consideration of ICO practices, the SEC focused most of its legal analysis on the DAO. Although it determines whether a particular token qualifies as a security on a case-by-case basis, the SEC focused on the DAO to illustrate the application of securities laws to the issuance of blockchain-based tokens in the context of "virtual organizations" more generally.

Specifically, to determine whether TheDAO token qualified as a security, the SEC applied the *Howey* test, a test from a US Supreme Court case (*SEC v W.J. Howey Co.*, 328 US 293) used to determine whether an investment contract implicates US securities laws. As the Court in *Howey* determined, an investment contract requires (1) an investment of money (2) in a common enterprise (3) with a reasonable expectation of profits (4) to be derived from the entrepreneurial or managerial efforts of others. All elements must be met for a security to be found, thereby implicating securities laws and regulations.

In the case of the DAO, the SEC found that the Slock.it team took on sufficient managerial efforts such as writing the white paper, designing the protocol, writing much of the code, maintaining public forums and the website, and advertising the expertise of the Slock.it team and the DAO curators. The SEC noted that

> Investors in The DAO reasonably expected Slock.it and its co-founders, and The DAO's Curators, to provide significant managerial efforts after The DAO's launch. ... Slock.it and its co-founders did, in fact, actively oversee The DAO. They monitored The DAO closely and addressed issues as they arose, proposing a moratorium on all proposals until vulnerabilities in The DAO's code had been addressed and a security expert to monitor potential attacks on The DAO had been appointed. When the Attacker exploited a weakness in the code and removed investor funds, Slock.it and its co-founders stepped in to help resolve the situation.[187]

Furthermore, according to the SEC, TheDAO tokenholders' voting rights were limited and therefore not sufficient to displace the overarching reliance on the Slock.it management team: "Even if an investor's efforts help to make an enterprise profitable, those efforts do not necessarily equate with a promoter's significant managerial efforts or control over the enterprise."[188]

The necessity of public participation in growing the long-term value of an ecosystem token is why many lawyers thought the SEC analysis of the *Howey* test in the DAO report was weak on the final element, requiring the expectation of profits derived primarily *from the managerial efforts of others.*

Building an ecosystem is no passive investment, but requires community participation. However, the difficulty is that building an ecosystem takes time and requires significant effort from the initial promoters. Hence, the initial founders of a project must first build some of the ecosystem for others to come and participate. In the case of the DAO, a variety of people, including the Slock.it team, contributed to building up the value of that ecosystem (thereby also increasing the value of the token associated with that ecosystem). Yet, following the SEC report, it appears that, if an identifiable team is marketing a potential investment to the public and the public is entrusting confidence in that team to galvanize the community, then the team's efforts will necessarily fall within the "managerial efforts" of the *Howey* test.

Enforcement action against Munchee

A few months later, on 11 December 2017, SEC chairman Jay Clayton issued a statement on ICOs just as the SEC was taking action against Munchee for its ICO. Chairman Clayton attempted to strike a balanced message. On one hand, he said that the SEC saw ICOs as effective fundraising mechanisms and encouraged Main Street investors to be open to them. On the other hand, he warned that most ICOs (to date) would squarely qualify as securities but had not followed the necessary registration and disclosure requirements designed to protect Main Street investors. In his statement, Chairman Clayton noted that:

> I believe that initial coin offerings—whether they represent offerings of securities or not—can be effective ways for entrepreneurs and others to raise funding, including for innovative projects. ... We at the SEC are committed to promoting capital formation. The technology on which cryptocurrencies and ICOs are based may prove to be disruptive, transformative and efficiency enhancing. I am confident that developments in fintech will help facilitate capital formation and provide promising investment opportunities for institutional and Main Street investors alike. I encourage Main Street investors to be open to these opportunities, but to ask good questions, demand clear answers and apply good common sense when doing so.[189]

However, as both the *Munchee* enforcement order and Chairman Clayton's statement noted, simply calling a token a utility token is not sufficient to escape securities laws. Securities law analysis will take into account how the token is actually marketed, to whom the tokens are targeted, and whether purchasers of the token have a reasonable expectation of profits as a result of efforts and statements of the project promoters. As Chairman Clayton explained,

> [C]ertain market professionals have attempted to highlight utility characteristics of their proposed [ICOs] in an effort to claim that their proposed tokens or coins are not securities. Many of these assertions appear to elevate form over substance. Merely calling a token a "utility" token or structuring it to provide some utility does not prevent the token from being a security. Tokens and offerings that incorporate features and marketing efforts that emphasize the potential for profits based on the entrepreneurial or managerial efforts of others continue to contain the hallmarks of a security under US law.[190]

The accompanying *Munchee* enforcement order provides color and detail. The SEC did not appear to believe that the MUN token was a true utility token, despite its being described as an "ecosystem" (the SEC put ecosystem in quotation marks throughout its enforcement order, signaling its skepticism of the ecosystem argument). The MUN token appeared opportunistically retrofitted to an existing app merely as a funding mechanism that would purportedly escape the regulatory requirements of the SEC. Munchee indeed was *not* an ecosystem as we have defined it above, since its goal was not that of building an open network of open-source tools upon which others could build applications. Instead, Munchee was purely a traditional social media–type application for food reviews, now incorporating an internal token as a payment and loyalty reward mechanism.

The SEC noted that the MUN token did not have immediate use, that it was marketed only to crypto speculators and profiteers, not to Munchee app users, and that the Munchee team used language describing how the value of MUN, as a utility token, would increase because of the demand and the efforts of the Munchee team to build the Munchee ecosystem.

The SEC provides some valuable guidance as to how tokens may be sold in a way that would be consistent with a utility token, despite the token not being immediately usable:

> Munchee and its agents targeted the marketing of the MUN tokens offering to people with an interest in tokens or other digital assets that have in recent years created profits for early investors in ICOs. This marketing did not use the Munchee App or otherwise specifically target current users of the Munchee App to promote how purchasing MUN tokens might let them qualify for higher tiers and bigger payments on future reviews. Nor did Munchee advertise the offering of MUN tokens in restaurant industry media to reach restaurant owners and promote how MUN tokens might let them advertise in the future. Instead, Munchee and its agents promoted the MUN token offering in forums aimed at people interested in investing in Bitcoin and other digital assets, including on BitcoinTalk.org, a message board where people discuss investing in digital assets.[191]

As the SEC intimates, Munchee could still have sold the MUN tokens to its existing and future customer base for *future utility* of the MUN tokens. But because the tokens were promoted exclusively to crypto investors interested in the profit-making aspect of ICOs and cryptocurrencies, the marketing effort and sales strategy undermined Munchee's argument that the token was integral to the function and internal economy of the app itself. Rather, the sales channels deployed were evidence of Munchee's true intent to sell these tokens as purely investment vehicles. In short, the MUN token was a security token dressed up as a utility token.

While the SEC noted that the MUN tokens had no immediate utility, careful reading of the enforcement letter shows that actual utility of a token is not dispositive of the securities law question either way. Selling for *future* utility to the appropriate audience using language that eschews any expectation of value appreciation may pass muster. Conversely, selling a utility token with immediate usability through sales channels and marketing language targeting investor profit expectations and value appreciation will run afoul of the *Howey* test and be viewed as a securities offering. The SEC stated:

> Even if MUN tokens had a practical use at the time of the offering, it would not preclude the token from being a security. Determining whether a transaction involves a security does not turn on labelling—such as characterizing an ICO as involving a "utility token"—but instead requires an assessment of "the economic realities underlying a transaction." *Forman*, 421 US at 849.[192]

Rather than solely focusing on the utility aspect of a token, the SEC enforcement letter and Chairman Clayton's press release made clear that the marketing language and sales strategy is an important factor in the securities law analysis in determining those "economic realities." Chairman Clayton noted:

> It is especially troubling when the promoters of these offerings emphasize the secondary market trading potential of these tokens. Prospective purchasers are being sold on the potential for tokens to increase in value—with the ability to lock in those increases by reselling the tokens on a secondary market—or to otherwise profit from the tokens based on the efforts of others. These are key hallmarks of a security and a securities offering.[193]

Furthermore, in the *Munchee* enforcement letter, the SEC noted that Munchee had used language describing the economic mechanism by which the team expected the MUN token would appreciate in value. Such language, therefore, created a reasonable expectation of profit in the token purchasers. It quoted the following language that a founder had used in a podcast:

> So [users] will create more quality content to attract more restaurants onto the platform. So the more restaurants we have, the more quality content Munchee has, the value of the MUN token will go up—it's like an underlying incentive for users to actually contribute and actually build the community.[194]

In addition, the SEC also noted that Munchee planned to burn tokens in order to regulate the token supply and therefore the token value.

While we do not disagree with the ultimate decision of the SEC to cease and desist the MUN token sale, which we believe was clearly a security offering, we find somewhat puzzling the language around value appreciation that the SEC has chosen to highlight as evidence supporting a securities classification. Most economic transactions do not implicate securities laws. *All* economic transactions involve some assessment about value, whether the goods or services are fairly priced, and whether that good or asset will rise in value because it is currently undervalued relative to the purchasers' views of factors affecting that asset's values, and so forth.

Let's examine investing in real estate, which may include buying shares of a corporation in a cooperative structure. Real estate investments generally do not implicate securities laws. Real estate certainly has a utility value. It is a place where people live, work, play, and develop. But many people also purchase real estate in hopes of future value appreciation. In fact, for most ordinary people, their homes are their primary financial asset, from which they derive both utility (living in the home) and financial security (value appreciation). A developer may use proceeds from real estate sales to invest further in the development, thereby enhancing the value of the real estate units.

Others explicitly buy real estate as investment properties or for rental income, with clear analysis of rental pricing trends or historical housing appreciation trends as part of the sale process. Should the law forbid a real estate broker from discussing with prospective homebuyers what they believe the true "appraised" value of the home is relative to the market price, and therefore whether a particular house is a good buy that will likely increase in value because of such factors as positive demographic trends?

The language that the SEC has singled out in the case of *Munchee*, when applied in the context of a true ecosystem (not Munchee's), is the economic mechanism by which ecosystem tokens incentivize public contribution to a public resource: individuals contribute positively to the ecosystem because they are rewarded for doing so.

The greater the community participation and end-user uptake, the greater the demand for the ecosystem token, which increases its value, if all else remains equal. Describing this economic mechanism alone, in our view, should not require the supervision of securities laws. It is no different from a real estate agent's explaining to a prospective buyer that home values are affected by such factors as demographics, gross domestic product, crime, quality of local school district, gentrification, and so forth. Simply describing the factors that affect value in a particular economic transaction should not categorize an ecosystem token, on its face, as a security.

On the other hand, the public should be protected when project promoters make or endorse statements such as "199% GAINS on MUN token at ICO price! Sign up for PRE-SALE NOW!" or "Pretty much, if you get into it early enough, you'll probably most likely get a return on it" or "a $1,000 investment could create a $94,000 return."[195] *Specific* statements about profit appreciation of a particular asset should be the crux of the focus, rather than general statements describing the economic theory on how a particular asset may appreciate to align incentives.

Marking all such discussions—regardless of their nature—as evidence of a securities offering will likely have the negative public policy effect of chilling relevant discussions about the inherent characteristics of a networked ecosystem. Given the nascent field of tokens and token economics, hampering public discussions by entrepreneurs and market participants would be harmful to analyzing, challenging, and testing these new theories and models.

Nonetheless, despite remaining open to ICOs and the use of tokens as a fundraising tool, the SEC appears to have narrowed its view on the securities law question. When the SEC first issued its report classifying TheDAO token as a security, many practitioners such as former SEC attorney Nick Morgan thought the SEC analysis of the *Howey* test was weakest on the last element, requiring the expectation of profits derived from the managerial efforts of others. In this area, a legal fight might possibly be won.[196] This element centered on the conclusion that the DAO, despite being a decentralized fund mechanism, was not sufficiently independent of the managerial efforts of the Slock.it team; therefore, the DAO investors were primarily passive investors relying on Slock.it to fulfill its expectations of profit.

With the latest SEC guidance in the *Munchee* enforcement letter, the last prong of the *Howey* test—whether the expectation of profits are to be derived from the entrepreneurial or managerial efforts of others—appears to be increasingly moot, especially for preproduction projects. That prong goes hand in hand with finding a reasonable expectation of profit.

As with the DAO report, the SEC in *Munchee* noted that Munchee highlighted the credentials of its team, creating reasonable reliance on Munchee's promise to alter the app and foster a valuable "ecosystem" of food reviewers and restaurants that use MUN tokens as loyalty rewards. As such, the expectation of profit would depend on Munchee's ability to create that "ecosystem" and to manage the token supply by burning tokens, thereby increasing their value.[197]

Distilling the latest guidance, what becomes clear is that a utility token is a *necessary but insufficient condition* to escape SEC jurisdiction. Whether a utility token has immediate versus future usability is neither necessary nor sufficient to escape the securities law question. We purposefully use the word *usability* here to distinguish between "theoretical utility" and "actual functionality." A utility token is functional by design, whereas its immediate usability in a platform or network is a function of how far along the development process is.

Usability of a token, as the SEC has stated, is not dispositive of (i.e., does not settle) the securities law question. Rather, how a token is marketed and sold, including the customer channels, may suffice in determining the application of securities law, including whether a token is truly a utility token. For example, marketing language and strategies that would create a purchaser's reasonable expectation of profit are sufficient to bring a token offering within the bounds of securities regulations, irrespective of the token's utility with immediate usability.

From an advocacy perspective, we would argue to the SEC or to a judge (i.e., judicial review of SEC administrative lawmaking) that the marketing and sales strategies of a token sale are important (and perhaps decisive) *indicia* of whether a token is truly a utility token or a security masquerading as one. Nonetheless, we believe that the marketing analysis alone is not an element or requirement of the securities law analysis under the *Howey* test.

RECONTEXTUALIZING *HOWEY* IN LIGHT OF ECOSYSTEM TOKENS AND APP COINS

Step 1: Functional analysis of the token

Because of the latest SEC guidance, and respecting the adage of "substance over form," we reiterate our view that the securities law analysis of a token must start with a functional analysis:

- What is the nature of the project or the application being built?
- What is the economic design and rationale for the token?

- Are there compelling reasons for the token's existence and design?
- Is fundraising the token's primary function?

Yet, we believe that, to determine whether a token will qualify as a security, we must also look at the type of platform to which the token belongs.

- Is this platform an open-source ecosystem or network that enables many businesses and use cases to be built around it, where the token represents an essential feature and economic mechanism to coordinate and develop shared open-source resources?
- Or is it one particular business application or Dapp, with the token serving as an internal economic mechanism (e.g., loyalty points) that is not intrinsically connected with the inner operations of the platform, but is being used merely in lieu of traditional membership fees, revenues, or transaction fees?

Such a distinction between ecosystem tokens and Dapp tokens (or app coins) is useful in determining the extent to which, when assessing the future profitability of the tokens, investors considered the "effort of others" as one significant criterion of analysis. With a Dapp, there is no fundamental economic need for investors to be involved in development and operations. Investors play a rather passive role, mostly relying on the efforts of the Dapp team to develop, maintain, and promote the system.

In an ecosystem, tokens play a function intrinsic to the operation of the underlying blockchain-based platform. Hence, these tokens will always have a utility, as they are used to solve the Tragedy of the Commons related to the overexploitation or underutilization of common resources. Moreover, because the value of these tokens is inherently connected with the value of the ecosystem, their value will increase as more stakeholders participate or contribute to the ecosystem.

In this context, the token appreciation also depends on the "effort of others," but "others" refers here to a much wider community of stakeholders, including the investors, who all contribute to furthering the ecosystem in such different ways as contributing to the open-source code, promoting the platform, developing the community, or even creating or developing other Dapps on top of that ecosystem.

In light of this, we think it useful to recontextualize the applicability of the *Howey* test depending on the type of tokens under assessment. When the *Howey* test was established in 1946, it could not anticipate the existence of open-source projects, let alone blockchain-based ecosystems. We should be mindful of that when applying the test to an entirely new context. In particular, we argue that the fourth item of the *Howey* test, concerning the "effort of others," should be interpreted differently according to whether the test is being applied to an open ecosystem or to the private profit center of a Dapp.

Indeed, an open and decentralized ecosystem will always rely on the "effort of others," because the ecosystem is built through the contributions of all actors in that ecosystem. We argue that in the Web 3.0 context, the last element of the *Howey* test should be interpreted as *significant* or *material permanent* reliance on the efforts of others—where "others" refer to an identifiable management team or organizational body without which the ecosystem would no longer and could no longer effectively operate. Thus, we may need a "fragmentation" or "granularity" test to determine whether the fourth prong of the *Howey* test is indeed satisfied:

- Is there a group of community members that is significantly more involved than others and produces the lion's share of effort?
- Will the removal of that team from the community jeopardize the whole project?

If the answers to both of these questions are positive, there likely exists a standard core "management" team whose activities are crucial to the success of the system. Yet, the same is not true if the efforts of a small team remain "atomic" relative to the rest of the community. That a particular group is influential and core to the community should not be the dispositive factor; rather, the question should be whether the project's survival or success fundamentally depends on the operations of this group over a long period.

Accordingly, token sales intended to raise funds for the development of an ecosystem—what we might refer to as an *ecosystem coin offering* (ECO)—should not necessarily be subject to securities laws because of the efforts of others or the mere possibility of token value appreciation, unless other reasons justify the application of the *Howey* test.

Of course, we are not saying that an ecosystem token will never be regarded as an investment security. Some behaviors might trigger the security flag, such as the blatant marketing of the investment value of the token by a core and identifiable team, as with Slock.it's marketing of the DAO.

Ultimately, the SEC will have to rely on the "smell test": does it smell like a security offering? It is a "totality of the circumstances" type of analysis. No one particular feature, in isolation, will likely sway the analysis. Ultimately, only a few projects will likely qualify as true ecosystems like Bitcoin or Ethereum, and most projects will simply remain in gray areas of the law.[198]

Step 2: Marketing and timing of a token sale

A true utility token, as we have argued, is always a utility token by design, irrespective of its usability at any point in the development of the underlying protocol. Utility is a necessary but insufficient condition to fall outside securities law. As the SEC has clarified, the securities law question depends not simply on the usability of a token, but also on its marketing:

- To whom, how, and when is the entity selling its tokens?
- Did marketing language give purchasers a reasonable expectation of profit?

The timing of the token sale relative to the development of the project has critical implications since it affects the marketing and sales strategy, as well as the degree to which potential purchasers rely on the efforts of others to make profits. Claiming that a token is not a security is easier when selling it to a potential customer or user base rather than to a purely investor base, because customers will be able to use the token on a running network.

So far, projects have been using ICOs only to raise funds at preproduction phases; that's why this usage has been the scope of the SEC's analysis. In preproduction phases, the difference between an ecosystem token and an app coin is theoretical: in practice, both an ecosystem and Dapp project are likely to be nascent, with small managerial teams controlling and writing a limited codebase. Therefore, ecosystem tokens are at risk of classification as securities, given the practical difficulties of selling to future customers and users before there is a ready platform.

For the regulator not versed in parsing technical white papers, there will be little difference between an ecosystem and a Dapp; most of the analysis will focus on the mechanism of sale the promises made, and whether such practices and promises warrant action from the SEC to protect the public. The SEC is mandated to consider this important public policy point: a token purchaser has significantly greater risk without the protections that securities laws offer an investor in more traditional financing.

For these early-stage projects, the SEC found that token purchasers relied significantly on the managerial efforts of the project promoters. The SEC has not been moved by the argument that token purchasers had to put in their efforts to increase the value of the token (as was the case of the DAO). In early-stage projects, arguing against the applicability of the fourth prong of the *Howey* test ("the effort of others") will be difficult because it could always be argued that purchasers predominantly rely on the efforts of the project promoters to seed the ecosystem and galvanize the community.

Therefore, interesting questions remain for ecosystem projects that are much further along when they seek funding through a public token sale. For example:

- What facts and circumstances will change the analysis of whether purchasers relied on the managerial efforts of others?
- Will it be relevant to the SEC if

  o Forking the code becomes a real possibility or has already happened?

  o Anyone can join as a node validator or miner?

  o The public is actively using, adapting, and consuming open-source code and building on top of the ecosystem without any kind of centralized control?

  o The voting and governance mechanism is robust enough to overcome the criticism the SEC noted in its DAO report?

As before, the analysis will come down to a smell test and whether public policy warrants the SEC to take action against an offering. If the overall smell of the offering is that of a security, as in the case with the DAO, then the SEC may deem the purchasers' efforts insufficient to overcome the reliance on the managerial efforts of the promoters.

LEGAL FICTIONS AND CREATIVE STRUCTURING: A REVIEW OF PRACTICAL SOLUTIONS

In this section, we review and assess various legal solutions that projects have deployed to anticipate various regulatory issues, including the Swiss nonprofit foundation model, the SAFT, convertible notes, and securities registration exemptions.

THE FOUNDATION MODEL

The Swiss environment and its regulatory facilities appeared attractive for establishing new blockchain ventures. The Swiss foundation model, in particular, was first used to manage the proceeds of initial crowdfunding transactions aimed at funding the development of new blockchain-based networks or applications. In 2014, Ethereum was the first blockchain project to establish its foundation (*Stiftung Ethereum*) in the Swiss canton of Zug. Soon followed by other blockchain-based projects, the Ethereum Foundation laid the cornerstone of "Crypto Valley," self-described as "one of the world's leading blockchain and cryptographic technology ecosystems."[199]

Until mid-2017, Zug was the jurisdiction of choice, and the Swiss foundation (*Stiftung*) the organizational structure of choice, for crypto projects looking to fundraise in a (hopefully) legally compliant manner. Zug was attractive for its low cantonal taxes and business-friendly reputation. The Swiss organizational structure would frame fundraising as donations to a foundation, the mission of which was that of an open-source software foundation in the vein of the Linux and Mozilla foundations, both based in California with tax-exempt status.[200] To our knowledge, none of these Swiss foundations has received actual tax-exempt status to date, which would enable donations to be tax-deductible in Switzerland.

The idea was, if the funds raised were framed as charitable donations (despite the lack of legally recognized charitable status) rather than investments, then they would not be in violation of securities laws globally. Yet, given the requirements of the *Howey* test and the long-arm jurisdiction of US regulators such as the SEC, Swiss lawyers recommended blocking US persons and US IP addresses from participating in ICOs as an extra precaution.

Furthermore, because the Swiss foundation was strictly regulated with a purpose that could not be changed without approval from the Swiss Federal Foundation Supervisory Authority (*Die Eidgenössische Stiftungsaufsicht* [ESA])—the federal regulatory body overseeing charitable foundations in Switzerland—it was argued that the Swiss foundation was actually a good governance structure to oversee the use of funds to develop blockchain projects. As defined in the Swiss Civil Code, Swiss foundations are "established by the endowment of assets for a particular purpose."[201] For instance, the official purpose of the Ethereum Foundation is:

> to promote and support Ethereum platform and base layer research, development and education to bring decentralized protocols and tools to the world that empower developers to produce next generation [Dapps], and together build a more globally accessible, more free, and more trustworthy Internet.[202]

Subsequent crypto foundations have been using similar language in describing their official and legal purpose.

However, as increasingly large sums of funding came through the Swiss foundations, regulators and politicians in Switzerland have increased their scrutiny. Swiss foundations were originally meant to function more like family trusts or endowments, rather than global fundraising instruments or cutting-edge technology projects. According to our discussions with several law firms in Switzerland, FINMA (the Swiss Financial Market Supervisory Authority, which is equivalent to the SEC but has a broader mandate including commodities and banking) is now requiring all projects to receive a no-action letter prior to public fundraising.

FINMA's primary concern is that the sale of tokens constitutes public deposit-taking, which would thereby require the organization conducting the sale to have a banking license. Furthermore, token sale contributions greater than 500 Swiss francs will need full KYC video verification and be subject to full ongoing AML obligations (e.g., filing suspicious activity reports, or SARs).[203]

FINMA recently released specific guidelines describing how it intends to apply financial market regulations to ICOs. The guidelines distinguish among

- Payment tokens that are not treated as securities but must comply with anti-money laundering regulations;

- Utility tokens that provide access to a particular application or service and would not qualify as securities to the extent that they are already functional at the point of issue, provided that they have no additional features with an investment purpose;

- Asset tokens that represent participations in physical assets, companies, or other revenue streams and that would clearly qualify as securities under Swiss law.

In theory, this is legally distinct from the SEC's approach—where actual utility is not necessarily dispositive. Yet in practice, we expect both approaches to converge, as utility tokens with investment features will qualify as securities according to both the SEC and the FINMA. Besides, under both regimes, utility tokens sold before they are actually "functional" will likely be held as securities with investment purposes. Questions of fact remain as to how functional a token must be to draw the line between a security token and utility token—that is, how much actual utility is sufficient for a token to qualify as a utility token?

In addition, cantonal authorities in Zug are also concerned that while hundreds of millions of Swiss francs have been technically raised in Zug, the canton of Zug has hardly seen any benefit, as most of these proceeds have been subject to very little tax. At the same time, very few jobs have been created in the area (although it has been a boon to lawyers and consultants), bringing in technical expertise and developing a true ecosystem of knowledge and talent. Most of these foundations have a foundation council, as required by law, with a statutory local Swiss resident council member, usually a professional council member, to satisfy their local presence requirements. The core teams of these projects remain located elsewhere outside of Switzerland. It is likely that Swiss authorities will also scrutinize local presence requirements and tax treatments.

As a result of the change in regulatory landscape, it has become increasingly difficult for a crypto foundation (or any other legal structure) to open bank accounts in Switzerland, as compliance departments in banks may take a more conservative approach than regulators. Many have stopped taking on crypto clients altogether.

As other jurisdictions globally compete for business, the attractiveness of the Swiss foundation model remains to be seen in 2018. Many jurisdictions are now working on reforming their own regulatory frameworks to accommodate blockchain-based projects and token sales.

THE SAFT MODEL: SIMPLE AGREEMENT FOR FUTURE TOKENS

The SAFT model, popularized by Filecoin and Cooley LLP, is an investment contract that limits participation to "accredited investors" to benefit from a SEC exemption (Regulation D, or Reg D for short). While the SAFT qualifies as a security and is targeted only toward accredited investors, it provides investors with the right to a particular number of tokens as soon as the relevant platform is up and running.

The SAFT model is based on the idea that, before a platform is built, utility tokens issued through an ICO might qualify as a security despite their future utility. Only after the platform is operative will these utility tokens actually acquire the necessary usability not to qualify as a security anymore. Consider the Ethereum crowdsale: when ether was sold in 2014, before the Ethereum network was even built, these tokens had no usability and thus probably qualified as a security. Today, however, these tokens definitely have acquired a tangible utility because their holders can use them to pay for transactions on the Ethereum network.

To reduce the securities law risk of selling the tokens prior to the platform's operability, the SAFT model creates a two-step process:

- The first is the issuance of an investment contract to accredited investors who can bear the risk of the project's potential failure.

- The second is the issuance of utility tokens (once the platform is operative) to these early investors who will then be able to sell these tokens on a secondary market to those eager to use the platform.

More precisely, the SAFT white paper states:

> The SAFT is an investment contract. A SAFT transaction contemplates an initial sale of a SAFT by developers to accredited investors. The SAFT obligates investors to immediately fund the developers. In exchange, the developers use the funds to develop genuinely functional network, with genuinely functional utility tokens, and then deliver those tokens to the investors once functional. The investors may then resell the tokens to the public, presumably for a profit, and so may the developers.[204]

The SAFT creators recognize that their creation is a security that must comply with securities laws. However, they maintain that the tokens themselves are fully functional and ready for consumers to use; therefore, they ought to comply with federal and state consumer protection laws. In other words, regulators needn't deem the tokens securities: "Sellers of already functional tokens have likely already expended the 'essential' managerial efforts that might otherwise satisfy the *Howey* test."[205]

Given the latest guidance from the SEC and our analysis above, we take the position that the SAFT model is wholly untenable. The SAFT model requires two conditions to be true:

- The SEC will recognize a legal distinction between the investment contract to presell the tokens and the public sale or issuance of tokens at a later date.

- Tokens will indeed be considered non-securities utility tokens or commodities because of their actual usability.

We have already analyzed that the second condition is untrue, based on the *Munchee* enforcement letter. This alone is sufficient to render the SAFT moot, as both conditions must be true for the SAFT to work.

Given the SEC's primary emphasis on evaluating the "economic realities of the transaction" rather than the form of a transaction, the

SEC will very likely agree with the Cardozo Blockchain Project's analysis that, by declaring the SAFT itself a security (hence, subject to Reg D exemption), the entire transaction (including the object of such transaction, i.e., the utility tokens) is a securities transaction with an expectation of profit. The Cardozo report noted:

> Artificially dividing the overall investment scheme into multiple events does not change the fact that accredited investors purchase tokens (albeit through SAFTs) for investment purposes, and likely will not prevent a court from considering these realities when assessing whether these tokens are securities.[206]

Accordingly, to the extent that these tokens had been marketed as an investment vehicle at the time of contracting the SAFT, they are and will remain a security even if they subsequently acquire an effective utility within an ecosystem or a Dapp.

Furthermore, from a public policy perspective, the SEC is wary of presale pricing structures that give significant discounts to early investors, as is often the case with SAFTs, because these early investors have incentive to flip their tokens to the public for an immediate return. This incentive undermines the argument that the SEC would recognize a legal distinction between the sale contract and the eventual issuance of a utility token.

Even if the token had immediate usability, the SAFT contract would incentivize flipping the tokens in a manner consistent with securities trading and speculation, to the detriment of public buyers— irrespective of whether the public was buying these tokens for their utility. In fact, the injury would be much worse and the public policy concerns greater, if the public was purchasing tokens based on utility considerations and was negatively impacted by the speculative trading of these tokens.

Moreover, once an issuer has filed for an exemption, as a matter of law, it has declared the instrument a security. The SAFT model is particularly problematic because it requires issuers to file with the SEC under Rule 506(b) or 506(c) of Reg D. This exemption was designed to reduce the burden of security issuance by providing general exemptions from registration requirements—with the caveat that securities filed under Reg D can only be sold to accredited investors.

If the artificial separation between the SAFT and the tokens sold through the SAFT is not recognized as a legitimate one, and if these tokens qualify themselves as securities, then tokens sold through a SAFT contract will be treated permanently as an exempted security with all attendant restrictions. In other words, *once a security, always a security*: even if these tokens eventually acquire usability, they will remain subject to trading restrictions. Only accredited investors will be able to trade them, despite their actual utility within a particular platform.

Hence, true utility tokens cannot be exempt securities tradeable only among other accredited investors, because only accredited investors would be able to use the underlying network. That would defeat the purpose of these tokens.

A variation on the theme of the SAFT is the *simple agreement for future tokens or equity* (SAFTE) introduced by the blockchain start-up Colony. Instead of relying on the SAFT elaborated by Cooley LLP, the Colony team drafted an agreement that gave investors equity, should there be no ICO.[207] Like the SAFT, the SAFTE is also based on Y Combinator's SAFE (discount, no cap), which is a simple agreement for future equity "with a negotiated discount rate … off the price per share of the standard preferred stock … applied to the conversion of the SAFE into shares of SAFE preferred stock."[208] Colony's SAFTE stipulated that the funds raised from early investors could be converted either into equity (at a particular discount) at the first liquidity event or into tokens (at the same discount) at the token generation event—whichever came first.

Although it adds an equity fallback option, should an ICO not occur, the SAFTE is fundamentally no different from the SAFT in form and substance: it shares the fundamental securities law problem around the presale of tokens. As with a SAFT, issuers presell tokens classified as a security through the Reg D exemption. Expecting the SEC to accept a legal distinction between an *investment contract* that presells the tokens and the sale of the *actual tokens* once they have acquired "utility" requires the same leap in logic.

Investors taking equity as an acceptable alternative to receiving tokens may constitute evidence that the investors view the tokens as an investment instrument equivalent to equity, a classic security. Hence, the economic realities of the token sale are in fact that of a securities offering, irrespective of whether the token has actual utility.

We could imagine convertible loans where conversion is voluntary and offers investors not only equity or token conversion alternatives but also a third possibility: redemption and accrued interests in such a qualifying event as a successful token issuance.[209] However, this type of product—where entities acquire tokens through convertibility of an existing financial instrument—would likely entail the same regulatory risks as the SAFT and SAFTE. In other words, a strict interpretation of "once a security, always a security" could still apply.

SECURITIES REGISTRATION EXEMPTIONS

Section 5 of the Securities Act of 1933 requires any offer or sale of securities to be registered with the SEC or meet an exemption requirement. Numerous exemptions are available, primarily under Reg D Rule 506, which provides two distinct exemptions: 506(b) and 506(c). Both of these exemptions enable an issuer to raise an unlimited amount of money primarily from accredited investors, who satisfy either of these conditions:

- Annual income of $200,000 in each of the two prior years
- Net worth of at least $1 million excluding the value of the person's primary residence.

Under 506(b), issuers may not advertise the offering publicly but can sell to up to 35 nonaccredited investors, and given reasonable belief, may rely on the investor's self-accreditation. Under 506(c), issuers may advertise publicly but only to accredited investors, and the burden of proving accredited status falls upon the issuer.[210]

The SAFT model in particular has encouraged filing under the 506(c) exemption, as it would enable crowdfunding to accredited investors. Traditional financings that have availed themselves of the Reg D exemptions have chosen 506(b). Rule 506(c) is a more recent addition under the JOBS Act in response to the rise of crowdfunding platforms, enabling general solicitation for investors through the Internet, social media, and advertisements.[211] Up until now, uptake of 506(c) has remained slow, primarily because of legal uncertainty around the burden of verification of accredited status, such as review and verification of financial filings, although third-party services have emerged to verify status.

Securities issued pursuant to Reg D are restricted securities: the default rule of securities offerings is that they must be registered. Reg D exemptions are privy only to the issuer, not to a reseller. Resellers typically would be considered underwriters, requiring licensing. Rule 144, "Selling Restricted and Control Securities," provides a safe-harbor exemption for the resale of restricted securities on a public market without being an underwriter.[212]

Under Rule 144, a non-reporting company would need to hold a Reg D restricted security typical of ICOs for at least one year. Certain information about the private company should be available publicly, including the nature of its business, the identity of its officers and directors, and its financial statements. The primary obligation for complying with Rule 144 or seeking other exemptions for reselling falls on the reseller of restricted securities; however, the SEC expects issuers to establish adequate internal controls to prevent breach of federal securities laws by their officers, directors, and employees.

Moreover, any company with more than 500 nonaccredited share-holders or 2,000 total shareholders will be deemed a full "reporting company" under the Securities Exchange Act of 1934, effectively a public company with all attendant disclosure and reporting obligations.

The reporting company obligation under the Exchange Act also limits the attractiveness of crowdsales under Regulation A+, "Amendments for Small and Additional Issues Exemptions under the Securities Act (Regulation A)," which enables issuers to solicit the public without limitation to accredited investors.[213] Furthermore, Reg A+ requires disclosure documents and financial statements that must be approved by the SEC. To our knowledge, to date there have been no ICOs issued under Reg A+.[214]

We believe that, as most ICOs are for Dapps, the increasing practice will be to issue ICOs as security tokens using the various exemptions, particularly under Rule 506(c), which allows for public solicitation, but of accredited investors only. Like Reg A+, Rule 506(c) would be subject to the 2,000-shareholder threshold before being deemed a full reporting company.

However, in theory, a Rule 506(c) offering would raise more funds than a Reg A+ because there are no limitations on the offering size (up to $50 million under Reg A+ Tier II, and up to $25 million under Reg A+ Tier I) and no investment limits. (Under Reg A+ Tier I, there are no investment limits. Under Reg A+ Tier II, investors can invest a maximum of the greater of 10 percent of their net worth or 10 percent of their net income, which may be self-reported.)

These security tokens will require specialized trading systems, including regulated exchanges and *alternative trading systems* (ATSs) that are non-exchange trading venues that match buy and sell orders. The SEC regulates ATSs under Regulation ATS, as broker-dealers rather than as exchanges, with fewer regulatory requirements compared to exchanges. We predict market adoption of block-chain-based decentralized alternative trading platforms that enable peer-to-peer exchanges of security tokens with transactions recorded to a distributed ledger.

Security tokens and ATSs may leverage smart contracts to encode automatic enforcement of Rule 144 and other reselling exemptions (e.g., an automatic one-year lock period). The equivalent term for an ATS under European regulation is a *multilateral trading facility* (MTF).

CREATIVE SOLUTIONS MOVING FORWARD

All token issuers, especially at the early stage of development, will need to consider their sales, marketing, and token design approaches very carefully. Those launching Dapps, in particular, will need to identify how to frame their token sales to raise funds without running afoul of securities laws.

We present here a series of solutions that might reduce the likelihood of tokens qualifying as securities. While token issuers have no control over the motivations of token buyers, they can intervene on a series of technical, contractual, or practical grounds to discourage buyers from engaging in pure speculation.

SELL ONLY TO STRATEGIC PARTNERS OR POTENTIAL PLATFORM USERS

The marketing of a token is a determining factor in the SEC's assessment of whether the token qualifies as a security. Hence, the audience to which the issuer markets the token will likely have a significant weight in the legal analysis. Selling tokens for their utility value to those who want to use them in an ecosystem or marketing them as investment vehicles to those who want to profit from their appreciation could ultimately affect the legal qualification of these tokens.

Following the SEC reasoning in *Munchee*, an issuer could make a case for selling utility tokens legitimately before the launch of the platform, provided that the sale targets its users and customers. The marketing language to these stakeholders and future customers should

describe the utility of the platform rather than the value appreciation of the token.

For ICOs launched at the preproduction phase, token issuers
could form partnerships with key stakeholders or future users of the
platform for pilot funding in exchange for tokens. The result would
be a financing model in the form of a service contract that does not
appear to go against securities laws but develops go-to-market pilots
that demonstrate the viability of the project.

At the same time, if a platform uses utility tokens as an internal coordinating mechanism, then we could argue that these tokens
should not even be visible to end users. For retail users, we could argue
that the tokens should be completely invisible, just as card payment
networks are invisible to a card user.

Good user-experience design would have end users purchase
access to a service using fiat currency, and the platform would then
convert the fiat into the native tokens behind the scenes—that is, end
users would not need to know or understand that there was a utility token in the back-end. That's why many of the Dapp token sales
seem forced; the token appears only to complicate the user experience without adding functionality besides raising funds.

Aside from legal considerations, from a business and ecosystem
development perspective, institutional or bulk token sales to institutional and strategic partners and to large and repeat users of the
platform would make more sense than selling tokens on a one-off
retail basis. Institutional or bulk sales of ecosystem tokens to Dapp
developers would also make sense.

DISCOURAGE THE ESTABLISHMENT
OF A SECONDARY MARKET

To avoid tokens qualifying as a security, token issuers should not
promise to undertake any efforts related to establishing a secondary market for these tokens or to engage, support, or promote the

establishment thereof. As SEC chairman Clayton stated, establishing a secondary market constitutes one of the "hallmarks of a security and a securities offering."[215]

Of course, even if token issuers do not actually participate in creating secondary markets for their tokens, someone else might. To avoid the risk of investors purchasing tokens solely for speculation, token issuers can intervene technically by preventing, for example, the transferability of the tokens issued through an ICO. If a token is not transferable, then few will likely purchase it with expectations of profit—thereby failing the *Howey* test—and the token will not qualify as a "transferable security" under EU law.[216]

Actual or future users of the platform will purchase tokens merely because of their utility value, not because of the potential profits they might derive by reselling them later. A nontransferable token would also reduce regulatory concerns around banking and money transfer laws, including ongoing AML/KYC obligations, as regulated by Financial Crimes Enforcement Network (FinCEN) under the US Department of Treasury.[217]

This approach, however, is unlikely to be popular and actually applied in practice, especially in the context of real ecosystem tokens such as the native cryptocurrencies of many blockchain-based networks. As we discussed, without liquidity through secondary markets, attracting node validators to a new network will be difficult, as the tokens compensate for their time and resources to maintaining network infrastructure.

A less drastic alternative would be to limit token transferability for a period (e.g., one year), which would be required under Rule 144 safe harbor to resell restricted Reg D securities. While such a time restriction would not necessarily disqualify these tokens as securities, it could nonetheless reduce the speculative dynamics inherent in the trading of these tokens and align the interests of the tokenholders with those of the project or ecosystem.

CAP THE TOKEN PRICE OR USE TOKEN BOUNDING MECHANISMS

Even if issuers decide not to prevent transferability of tokens issued through an ICO, they can still avoid excessive speculation by introducing an upper cap on token price. Indeed, if there is a secondary market, there is a risk that the price of the tokens will rise to a point at which accessing or using the platform becomes extremely expensive. Depending on the actual or potential appreciation of the tokens' value, people might decide to hoard them or resell them at a higher price rather than spending them on the platform. It is a self-defeating model: speculation on the value of a utility token actually reduces the usability of its associated platform.

One critical element of utility token design is its price stability, because prices of services and goods should be stable, unlike profit-bearing or speculative instruments. To counteract speculative dynamics, token issuers can set up a continuous ICO so that, at any point in time, people can purchase tokens through the ICO smart contract at a particular price (upper cap).

Whenever the market price of the token exceeds the upper cap, people will stop purchasing tokens on the market and will instead purchase them directly from the ICO smart contract at the cap price. As people buy tokens through the ICO smart contract and increase supply in the market, the market price will drop. Only when the market price falls below the upper cap will people buy these tokens on the market again.

Ethereum researcher Vlad Zamfir discussed token bounding mechanisms that implement a price floor and price ceiling, whereby—contrary to the Bitcoin economics of fixed supply—the token supply may fluctuate to keep within price boundaries. As Zamfir noted, "A constant ceiling removes all reasonable expectation of return that token purchasers may otherwise have. Any low-enough ceiling can prevent 'pumps-and-dumps' from pumping."[218]

Token designers can tailor price-control mechanisms to meet desired objectives. For instance, a perpetual ceiling mechanism could adjust annually for inflation or other relevant metrics. In the crypto world, such metrics as gas costs for running Ethereum smart contracts may be better suited for anchoring a pegging mechanism than some broad-based economic definition of inflation.

The perpetual enforcement of a periodically adjusted ceiling should be (theoretically) easy to do, since it requires automatically issuing new tokens at the ceiling price whenever there is demand. However, guaranteeing a floor level may not be possible in all circumstances. As Zamfir noted, "[T]he sale administrator can't raise the floor price if doing so would make it unable to purchase all of the tokens at the floor price."[219]

Even if a significant portion of the ICO proceeds was deposited in the ICO smart contract so that people could redeem tokens at the floor price, this reserve would have limited capacity; once it was used, the ecosystem would lack funds for development, and the token price would plummet on the secondary market. The point here is not to support a floor price, but to ensure price stability: speculative gain in token value that is decoupled from utility demand reduces the incentive for real projects to use the protocol for its intended purpose.

By skewing downward the distribution of expected returns (since a price ceiling could be fully guaranteed, but not always a floor price), such a control mechanism should send a positive signal regarding the token buyers' genuine intention: they would be investing because they really supported the development of such platforms and believed that such platforms were necessary "infrastructural" investments to build out the token economy as whole (e.g., Dapps and security tokens).

As the token market matures, ecosystem tokens will become anchor tokens that investors hold in their portfolios of tokens to diversify risk as they would use fiat currencies or closely related instruments, such as government bonds, to reduce beta risk in more traditional portfolios.

Thus far, token bounding design remains legally untested. In the SEC's view, will the introduction of a price floor, which could potentially sustain the token price above a certain level, engender expectations of profit? Will the introduction of a price ceiling be enough to remove any profit expectation?

In the *Munchee* case, the SEC considered the team's promise to burn tokens as a way to increase token value germane to the profit expectation analysis. The SEC found this language under "Token Burning Plan" in the Munchee white paper relevant:

> Munchee could potentially choose to [sic] burn (take out of circulation) a small fraction of MUN tokens everytime [sic] a restaurant pays Munchee as [sic] advertising fee. This ... could potentially increase the appreciation of the remaining MUN tokens as the total supply in circulation reduces.[220]

Would the SEC's analysis have differed, had Munchee framed the token burning as downside risk mitigation rather than as value appreciation, to stabilize the token price for better functionality within the app rather than purely as a price-supporting mechanism no different from stock buybacks?

To limit the reasonable expectation of profit, we can imagine token designs with various price-ceiling mechanisms. However, as with all things in this evolving space, the analysis will come down to facts and circumstances. The SEC may consider such questions as:

- How tight is the price ceiling, and what are its drivers?
- Are the mechanisms truly deployed for price stability or for price appreciation?
- What enhanced functionality will token price stability provide in the platform?

Ultimately, the SEC will likely take a holistic approach to assessing the economics of token transactions—the smell test—to determine case by case whether a token qualifies as a security.

The necessity of price-stabilizing functions for true ecosystem tokens and the unclear position of the SEC on the subject highlight this inherent ontological problem: true ecosystem tokens are not quite classical securities, but function similarly to currencies. In fact, fiat currencies move resources and facilitate transactions within economic ecosystems that, much like Web 3.0 network ecosystems, have multiple profit centers sharing common infrastructure.

SEPARATE FUNDRAISING FROM TOKEN ECOSYSTEM GOVERNANCE

We return to our initial theme that there is an inherent tension in using an ecosystem token—meant to coordinate common resources—as a means of private fundraising. While there is merit to a true ecosystem token sold to core ecosystem stakeholders for maintaining and developing common resources, in early-stage fundraising, distinguishing between the development of a networked ecosystem and the deployment of a Dapp operating on top of that ecosystem might be difficult. In other words, the difference between funding a profit-capturing enterprise operating on public rails and funding the underlying public rails is often theoretical and unclear.

As a practical matter, these ecosystem projects will likely need a separate, arms-length, private enterprise for fundraising purposes that gives investors classical debt or equity financing instruments. This model would be analogous to what is generally found in the open-source ecosystem, which features a variety of nonprofit software foundations (e.g., the Linux Foundation), and for-profit companies commercializing particular products or services related to open-source software (e.g., the Red Hat company that distributes and commercializes an operative system leveraging the Linux kernel).

For ecosystem projects, funding from the private enterprise could be used to initially build the ecosystem infrastructure in exchange for tokens from a nonprofit organization that would be the steward of the open-source ecosystem. The exchange for tokens in this case would be a simple services agreement (e.g., tokens as compensation for open-source IP development), which would not run afoul of any securities law regulations. The private enterprise could focus on a particular vertical or business application of the ecosystem, or be a for-profit incubator for other Dapps in the ecosystem—thereby kick-starting the ecosystem development. The for-profit private enterprise may well be a social enterprise, electing to be a benefit corporation and/or be B Corp certified.

From a pragmatic perspective, the private enterprise could have access to a wide variety of investors, including crypto investors, but also more traditional professional investors whose funds do not have the legal mandate to accept tokens in lieu of equity. However, these traditional investors would get indirect exposure to tokens through the balance sheet of the private enterprise. In effect, the value of the ecosystem tokens represents the value of the private enterprise's contribution toward the open-source IP. Unlike traditional proprietary IP, which is often a start-up's core asset, the ecosystem tokens sitting on the balance sheet would, in theory, be marked to market with far greater liquidity and tradability, should a secondary market for them develop.

Eventually, such new creative financing instruments may emerge as

- Convertible notes typical of seed stage financing pre-valuation that may be extinguished with tokens rather than equity
- Equity interests that may be convertible to tokens
- Preferred interests that are redeemable for cash upon an ICO.

Through smart contracts, dynamic ledgers, and decentralized trading platforms and exchanges, it will become easier to manage perhaps more complex but also more dynamic capital structures that combine debt, equity, and tokens.

CONCLUSION

ICOs are changing the fundraising landscape, but at a different level than most people seem to think today. While currently a large majority of ICOs have been done at the preproduction phase (i.e., at the seed level), we argue that it is very difficult—both for an ecosystem token and for an app coin—to avoid securities laws and regulations if a token is sold before its associated blockchain-based platform or decentralized application is built.

An ecosystem token constitutes an inherent component of its blockchain-based system and might therefore have a greater chance of being regarded as a utility token. However, the current SEC guidance with respect to the *Howey* test seems to confirm the idea that selling a token with an actual or potential utility does not constitute, as such, a sufficient condition to preclude it from being sold as a security. We must also take into account how tokens are marketed to the public and why people are buying them.

Hence, unless issuers want to introduce specific technical guarantees that will reduce or eliminate speculative opportunities over the appreciation of their tokens (e.g., by making the tokens nontransferable or by creating a low-ceiling token price cap), they need to devise new approaches to ensure that the tokens being sold do not qualify as securities. While the SAFT (and the related SAFTE) is an interesting proposition for achieving that goal, the SEC will likely not accept its logic, post-*Munchee*.

There is an inherent conflict between the use of an ecosystem token as a coordinating mechanism and as a fundraising instrument similar to securities. Taking a pragmatic approach, open-source blockchain-based ecosystems will initially have to build some profit centers by relying on fundraising practices typical of private enterprises and start-ups. As such, these ecosystems may develop as the traditional Web 2.0 model did.

Decentralization is an evolution that, in practice, starts more centralized but, under the right governance and development, devolves over time into a truly decentralized ecosystem.

We believe that ICOs, especially for true ecosystem tokens, will have to move away from the preproduction phase (seed round) and instead be conducted at funding rounds in postproduction phases (series A, B, C, etc.), when there is a minimally viable network or product with a ready base of users and customers. Only after the platform has been deployed and an ecosystem has emerged around it, will the utility emerge and the value inherent in these tokens become apparent to all. Then the issuer will finally be able to sell tokens as true goods or commodities rather than as investment instruments.

To do so, token issuers might need to devise creative corporate forms combining nonprofit structures (overseeing access to shared open-source resources) with for-profit structures (perhaps as benefit corporations or B Corps) focused on the development of specific business applications or Dapps. Most ICOs will not be true ecosystem tokens and will therefore be well suited as securities token offerings using registration exemptions and trading through decentralized alternative trading systems.

Working toward the future, we hope the blockchain community—entrepreneurs, technologists, researchers, academics, lawyers, and others—can collaborate with regulators such as the SEC in devising a regulatory framework for the emergent token economy, including fundraisings such as ICOs and ongoing market oversight. Indeed, significant questions remain around how to think about and discuss token "economics," that is, the factors that should drive utility value, and whether token price bounding would allay some of the SEC's concerns.

Furthermore, even for true ecosystem tokens, markets will need some level of speculative trading in those tokens to provide liquidity. How does the market necessity for some speculative activity square with regulatory concerns around secondary markets, while respecting the functional requirements of an ecosystem token? As we try to create more decentralized economic models assisted by blockchain technology, how should we rethink what it means to rely on the "efforts of others," from the *Howey* test perspective?

The SEC's concerns as a public watchdog for consumer and investor protection are well founded. We hope to devise regulations that encourage innovation, minimize speculation, and ultimately enable blockchain technologies to fulfill the promise of Web 3.0—ecosystems that are more productive, more resilient, and more just in their allocation of power and resources.

CHAPTER 4

REINVENTING INTERNATIONAL CLEARING AND SETTLEMENT

How Distributed Ledger Technology Could
Transform Our Global Payment System

Bob Tapscott

 ## THE GLOBAL PAYMENT SYSTEM IN BRIEF

- The global payment system is the lifeblood of world commerce. In the Internet era, the sluggish pace, high cost, and opacity of international funds transfers, both corporate and consumer, are a source of frustration. Money seems to hang in limbo between institutions for days. Clearing a check from France to the United Kingdom within a bank that has a large presence in both countries can take six to eight weeks![221]

- Transfers are typically based on messages sent through the Society for Worldwide Interbank Financial Telecommunication (SWIFT) network. Most banks will not respond to an international funds transfer request unless it arrives via the highly secure and trusted SWIFT network. Although SWIFT messages for the movement of funds are near instantaneous, legacy processes within the banks are not.

- Emerging blockchain technologies may diminish or even replace SWIFT and the systems it supports. *Distributed ledger technology* (DLT) introduces three possibilities for speeding transfers and lowering costs:

- DLT obviates the need for layer upon layer of complex systems talking to complex systems to manage risk, while adding fees for their services.
- DLT enables funds transfers between countries without any significant delay.
- In DLT, trust derives from mathematics, not from fallible humans and their systems.

- As international commerce has exploded, it has demanded a lower-cost system with fewer time-consuming intermediaries. Smartphone applications will become the ubiquitous payment mechanism for the unbanked. Near- and nonbank payment systems are flourishing with and without blockchain.

- This is a game changer. Consumers and corporations will know exactly when their funds will arrive and need not guess at the final currency converted amount. Payment systems for the poor without intermediaries charging high fees will stimulate greater commerce by removing friction and inefficiencies that impede greater economic purpose.

- There are two approaches in technology to implementing dramatically new systems: (1) revolutionary (the big bang) and (2) evolutionary (the invisible whisper). Almost always, a massive change implemented quickly, no matter how well planned, has negative and unintended consequences. Therefore, the transformation of trillions in international payments made daily over to DLT technology must be evolutionary.

INTRODUCTION TO GLOBAL PAYMENTS

HOW THE GLOBAL PAYMENT SYSTEM WORKS

A simple foreign exchange (FX) transaction between banks in two countries can involve many players. The traders (or their computers) agree on the amount, the exchange rate, and the future settlement date of the transaction, which (for simple spot contracts) is typically tomorrow or the day after.

For a simple case, the financial institutions involved need to ensure that the funds are on deposit and available through the central banks of those countries with the currencies involved on the date that the transaction settles. On that settlement date when both central bank clearing systems are up and running, an inter-central bank clearing system known as CLS, an acronym originally for *continuously linked settlement*, coordinates the near-simultaneous bidirectional transfer of funds.

If the banks involved do not have accounts at CLS, then they typically must go through banks that do. To those outside the system, it is about the movement of money. To those inside, it is the movement of debits and credits, with historical audit trails as secured and trusted records, through many dual-entry accounting systems. In truth, it is simply the movement of trusted and regulated bits. Yes, it is just bits.

The counterparties must trust (and accept the risk) of the banks at both ends, the clearing systems of the currencies in their respective countries, the correspondent banks, and for coordination CLS. With the possible introduction of DLT, many will trust the mathematics proven to secure token movements and their messages over the trust in the many institutions (and their costs) to maintain their systems properly. Why can those tokens not be dollars or euros? The answer is that they can be and, we will argue, soon will be.

WHY THE SYSTEM SOMETIMES DOESN'T WORK

Despite the significant efforts (and systems) to ensure that both sides of the transaction occur simultaneously, our assumptions sometimes fail us. Consider the largest petroleum deal in Canadian history. As negotiations were ending in Calgary, the press announced that the deal was signed. Based on this, East Coast bankers transferred billions of dollars from US banks to Citibank Canada's accounts. The East Coast bankers then went home.

However, the deal was not signed. When the few who were left still working at the US banks realized that they had transferred billions with no corresponding asset (an executed sales contracts), they had to convince Citibank Canada to transfer the billions back or notify the US Federal Reserve that they were technically insolvent. It was a long night.

Had they used a blockchain-based smart contract, whereby the terms and conditions of the contract and its execution of massive funds transfers were mathematically inseparable, there would have been no risk. Again, who needs risk management when we can entrust the movement of funds to irrefutable math? There are simple solutions to today's complexity. The original blockchain created an immutable and mathematically provable log of activity. It combined public and private key cryptography to verify identity and a consensus algorithm to verify transactions and prevent duplicate or fraudulent spend, all in a peer-to-peer network. There is no requirement for centralized control. Each feature is not revolutionary. All were available in the 20th century. The simple combination of them may well be.

A HISTORY OF PAYMENT SYSTEMS

Moving money between accounts within a single bank is easy. The bank simply credits one account and debits another. The consumer covers the cost of these transfers in monthly account fees. Moving money between banks in the same country is not quite so direct. The money is redirected through that country's central bank, be it the US Federal Reserve (the Fed), the Bank of England (BoE), the Bank of Canada (BoC), or the European Central Bank (ECB). Bank automation has sped up check clearing, but banks kept most of the benefit. New systems could eliminate paper entirely. By using less paper and more bits, the clearing systems have successfully processed the dramatic rise in payment volumes.

Decades ago, most countries allowed banks to hold and, for their own profits, use their customers' funds for many days on checks drawn between financial institutions before the funds were made available to the payee. Country by country, the rules have tightened. For example, the US Dodd-Frank Act of 2011 required banks to make the first $200 available the day after a deposit and, if applicable, pay interest.[222] In the Philippines, next-day availability of funds became law in 2017.[223]

In Canada 25 years ago, the major clearing banks would run their own check sorting machines that sorted the checks deposited according to the various banks of origin. Once a bank had completed this sorting and determined what each of the other banks owed it, it would debit those other banks' accounts at the Bank of Canada. The following morning, it would return the checks to the issuing banks to verify the amounts and the accounts of the debits made.

The systemic risk was obvious; a bank in trouble could simply take (in the middle of the night) billions from other banks accounts at the BoC, in effect putting them in trouble without evidence to warrant their withdrawals. Typically, if a bank does not have the funds available at the central bank, the government will act as the "lender of last resort." Governments do go to extraordinary efforts (including reserve requirements) to prevent this from ever happening, but it does.

In the last 20 years, most advanced capitalist countries have implemented RTGS (real time gross settlement) systems that require settlement multiple times a day. This lowers the size of each settlement to avoid systemic failures. The amount of money is massive. In Canada, the *larger value transfer system* (LVTS) run by the central bank settles about $140 billion a day.[224] The retail (smaller value) system run by Payments Canada clears about $24 billion a day.[225] In 2017, CHAPS (England's RTGS system) was clearing about £500 billion a day.[226] Given the massive volumes of money involved, no central bank wants to implement a new system until it is proven to be flawless.

In 2016, Canada launched a P2P payment system through a bank consortium called Interac where accounts can be tied to a cell-phone number or an e-mail address. Through Interac, consumers can make near-real-time payments to one another, without knowing each other's account numbers. Accepting the cell phone text message on a deposit releases the funds into the recipient's account. Although to the consumer, the payments are real time, the funds actually are transferred between the banks later in the day through the central clearing system.

Venmo in the United States offers a similar service, but without direct access to the clearing system, days can pass between the payment initiation and the funds actually arriving.[227] Credit card users pay a three percent fee, but it is free otherwise.

In the summer of 2017, the five largest US banks launched a national consumer payments network called Zelle.[228] The expectation is that two dozen smaller banks and credit unions will join over the next year. Like Interac in Canada, Zelle in the States will provide near-real-time P2P payments between consumers. To hasten its adoption, Zelle is presently a free service, though the accounts it accesses typically charge fees.

International checks issued today in one country and cashed in another can be messaged through at least two central banks, a central bank transaction coordinating intermediary such as CLS, and possibly the accounts of other intermediaries called correspondent banks (Figure 4-1). Why did this complexity evolve?

FIGURE 4-1

CURRENT INTERBANK CROSS-BORDER PAYMENT

Even today, international payments pass from intermediary to interme-diary in relay from sender to recipient.

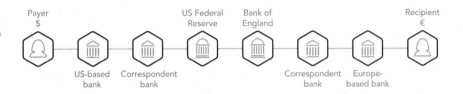

THE EAST INDIA TRADING COMPANY AND RONALD COASE

When we buy an apple at a market, we can see the apple and the vendor can see our cash. If one party cheats, it is easy to challenge the other. When we are 10,000 miles away, that approach is not possible. How does one establish long-distance trust? Very difficult. The other party is likely subject to laws that we are unaware of and vice versa. Clearly, for the exporter, it is imprudent to manufacture and ship without seeing the money. For the importer, it is equally imprudent to pay without seeing the goods. A conundrum.

Economist Ronald Coase presented his views on why the firm existed in a lecture in Dundee in 1932, when he was just 21 years old. He argued that the firm was created and still exists because going to market for the resources was more expensive than hiring those resources internally. More specifically, the firm exists to lower transaction costs. The search for resources, their coordination, contracting, and the establishing trust was easier inside the walls of the firm. He further argued that these transaction costs tended to grow as the enterprises grew. His insights were dismissed and ignored for decades, but he was eventually awarded a Nobel Prize in 1991.

Consistent with his argument, the first large-scale historical answer to the transoceanic trust problem was simply to trust oneself. Global companies arose that could buy products in India or China and ship them to their own warehouses in London or Rotterdam. One example was the Dutch East India Trading Company. It is the largest company in world history. In today's terms, it was about 10 times the size of Apple.[229]

Its English equivalent was also massive. Originally, its main product was shipping tea from India to England. Ultimately, it found the shipment of opium from Afghanistan to China more profitable. To ensure that its version of "trust" was not violated, the governor of India raised armies that were twice the size of England's. It was not the British government that seized India at the end of the 18th century, but an unregulated company that was run by an out-of-control governor and privateer (Robert Clive). Today he is regarded as a sociopath.[230]

With only 35 employees in its head office in England, the English East India Company was once a model of efficiency. That was until Clive, as a rogue operative, raised and deployed an army of 260,000 without the head office's concurrence. An army was not in the company's business plan.

As Ronald Coase explained, when the transaction costs of this massive overhead (the army necessary to enforce the company's version of trust) became too large the company became unsustainable. When the English government ultimately took control of this private army, some argue it was the birth of the British Empire.[231]

THE RISE OF THE MERCANTILE BANK, LETTERS OF CREDIT, AND THE ASSOCIATED PAIN

The next answer to the trust conundrum that emerged was the mercantile bank. It specializes and profits from managing and mitigating international trust issues between buyers and sellers that have no historical trusting relationship. Their major financial instrument to do so is called a *letter of credit* (LoC). This is a complex set of documents between four or often more parties that each trust one of the other parties that, in effect, link together for a transaction in a chain of trust.

If we don't trust the maker of goods, then someone we know may know someone else that they trust who trusts someone else who trusts another party, who trusts yet another someone that trusts the seller. It sounds completely unworkable, but for centuries these LoC were (and, largely, still are) the financial basis for international commerce. So, for example, one bank would pay for the goods (and accept the risk) when they were manufactured to spec and available for shipment. This bank was then paid by another bank (who would then accept the transit risk) when the goods arrived and were inspected at the dock for export. This bank would then be paid by yet another bank (who would then pay and accept the next phase in the transit risk) when the goods arrived at the importer's docks. This bank was then paid by another, the bank of the ultimate buyer, when the goods arrived as ordered and inspected on the delivery dock of the purchaser. The complexity of documenting and negotiating the lengthy terms and conditions of these deals for their successful execution is slow and expensive (Figure 4-2).

The advising bank assures the seller and their bank that the buyer's bank is legitimate. Intuitively, we would expect that the time consumption and the profits of so many intermediaries in a letter of credit would grind the wheels of international commerce to a standstill. In fact, it was the opposite. For centuries, letters of credit were the grease that made international commerce possible. Those that

FIGURE 4-2

HOW LETTERS OF CREDIT WORK

could negotiate these deals found them highly profitable, for the importer, exporter, and all the intermediaries.

However, these processes often failed in the negotiations of who exactly would accept what risk and when. To grease the international movement of goods, most exporter's governments will give an overriding guarantee to the guaranteeing banks through their import/export bank. Even with government backing, the "manufactured to spec" documents and the transfer of responsibilities with so many untrusting intermediate parties is a difficult but very profitable undertaking.

For a bank, anticipating the foreign payments of our customers is at best a guessing game that, depending on our effectiveness at playing that game both we and our customers can win or lose. Today, to meet the foreign currency requirements of its customers, banks are constantly moving funds from institution to institution and country to country in an attempt to achieve higher capital efficiency. Sometimes they succeed, sometimes not; regardless, it increases operational costs. Each leg in the payment process is serially processed, which adds settlement risk, delays, and time-consuming manual investigations for delayed or stopped payments because of improperly coded transfers or inadequate funding of a bank's nostro accounts in a foreign country.

Nostro ("ours with you") and *vostro* ("yours with us") accounts are where banks hold FX balances at other institutions in other countries to cover the possible foreign currency demands of their customers. For example, for a bank with branches in, say, 10 countries anticipating tomorrow's customer demand for foreign currency in an 11th country is difficult, if not impossible. Put in too much money, and funds are wasted. Put in too little, and a customer's payments may enter into an indefinite limbo. Today, international checks are temporarily held, trying to assess which are legitimate payments and which are not. This is time-consuming and, for many, results in a manually intensive reconciliation process.

All of this is a result of the lack of trust between financial institutions and their customers. Lack of trust is an overstatement, but limits on the extent of trust between banks are institutionalized. In the game of risk management, we can be right on whom to trust but still lose. Through financial markets, one can lose by trusting someone who trusts a third party that turns out not be trustworthy. This is the ultimate nightmare for all bankers. It is called *systemic risk*. For example, in 2008, those who trusted Goldman Sachs and then trusted AIG would have been in deep trouble without the Fed's massive intervention.[232]

What DLT will bring to the equation is the concept of money movement with (or without) banks that is 100 percent trustworthy. Clearly a game changer.

THE CREATION OF SWIFT AND ITS MESSAGING SERVICE

Up until the early 1970s, banks sent telexes for payment instructions between countries. Though the sums of money could be massive, the processes were manual and error-prone. The instructions were in unstructured sentences, typically in English. Sometimes the intent of these messages was lost in translation. Typed and sent over telephone lines, these *wire transfers* were easy to lose, easy to misinterpret, and easy to hack. Math was used to detect unauthorized changes to the message, but not as extensively as it should have been.

For example, one fraudster who knew that math was used to create a secret *message authentication code* (MAC) that verified the *from* and *to* counterparties and the *amount*, simply requested a small valid "wire transfer" message, intercepted it, and then changed the currency from Italian lire to US dollars before forwarding it on, knowing that it would be accepted as an authentic message. For a few-thousand-dollar investment (then many millions of lire), the fraudster's return was exponential. There had to be a better way. There needed to be standards. The introduction of computers to business in the early 1970s enabled a more secure approach.

In 1973, SWIFT was chartered in Brussels to oversee and automate these processes. By 1978, SWIFT went online with the basic third-party controls necessary to secure financial payment messages between the larger banks and to ensure that two people at the sending institution were involved in "making and then checking" the message before it was sent and that the MAC, the precursor to the digital signature, applied to all fields.

Each transfer was numbered in a sequence to ensure fraudulent insertion or deletion of messages was detected. Further standards were set for codes to indicate counterparties, currencies, dates, branches, intermediaries, and action codes for a basic set of financial services. SWIFT message types have evolved beyond payments to include treasury and securities messages.

The standard for the message formats and metadata is now ISO 20022 (pronounced ISO twenty-oh-two-two).[233] More specifically ISO 20022 is a harmonized set of *extensible markup language* (XML) financial messaging standards, across payments, trade, securities, card, and FX transactions. For changes to this standard, SWIFT is recognized as the ISO 20022 registration authority.[234]

FIGURE 4-3

THE UBIQUITY OF SWIFT

The Society for Worldwide Interbank Financial Telecommunication network is the world's leading provider of secure financial messaging services. It now has 11,000 members in more than 200 countries.

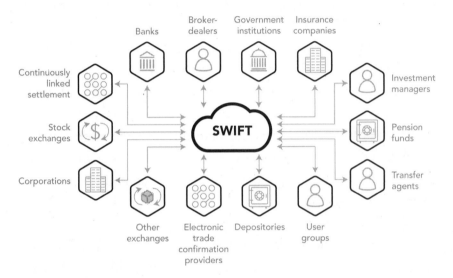

Source of data: SWIFT, swift.com/about-us, 5 Jan. 2018.

Today, SWIFT sets the ubiquitous message standard, reference model, and runs the system and network for international interbank payment instructions (Figure 4-3). SWIFT is a cooperative society under Belgian law owned by its 3,000 financial institution members. It is one of the world's most trusted systems, averaging more than 27 million transactions per day.[235] The service has expanded to include more than 200 message types, including instructions for customer payments and checks, financial institution transfers, treasury markets, foreign exchange and derivatives, collections and cash letters, securities markets, treasury markets, precious metals and syndications, and documentary credits.

It is important to note that money does not flow through the SWIFT network. It is simply a highly secured text messaging service for encoding, sending, receiving, and then authenticating standardized structured messages from one financial institution to another. The actual movement of money typically occurs through the national clearing and settlement centers of the central banks. The timing and coordination of the movement of funds through multiple central banks, and possibly other intermediary banks in the process, makes the system slow and complex.

Not surprisingly, people involved in the process want to be compensated for their efforts. These vary by institution, but typically commercial banks charge outgoing and incoming transfer fees, the combination of which will add up to somewhere between $50 and $100.[236] This does not take into consideration the profits that may be accrued from interest earned on the funds when redeployed for other purposes while they are temporarily under the various banks' control. On top of this, there is profit in the FX rate offered (Figure 4-4).

To illustrate, on 18 August 2017, at the TD Canada Trust site, we found that if we converted US$1,000 to Canadian dollars and then back again, we ended up with $948.06.[237] In other words, a typical bank would make 2.5 percent profit in each direction on the FX conversion of a $1,000 transfer between two major currencies. The less significant (and liquid) the currency, the greater would be the loss to the customer because of the wider margin between the buy and sell FX rates charged.

Difficult to measure are the resulting delays in business, and the possible loss of interest in a transaction as a result of the delays anticipated. TransferWise, Venstar, OFX, and other systems, although still based on fiat currencies, have discovered how to minimize the cost and the delays. Even before blockchain, the inherent inefficiencies and the profitable opportunities to disintermediate the legacy players and systems presented were compelling.

FIGURE 4-4

THE CORRESPONDING BANKING MODEL

In a $5,000 transfer from the United States to Europe, $211 goes to the banks. Half of this sum is the difference between the mid-market rate for US dollars–euro foreign exchange and the buy rate offered the customers. The rest constitutes fees paid to various financial institutions for their efforts.

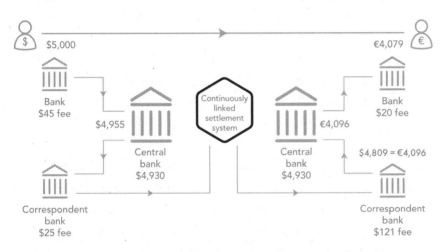

When SWIFT originally facilitated automated payments for institutions, it was primarily for large FX payments. In the 1980s, for a million-dollar cross-border payment, $50 to $100 in fees was considered acceptable. For a few personal transfers, there were always the inefficiencies of Western Union or the American Express office. However, with the birth of Internet commerce, when buying a $10 item online from China or sending money home to the third world, $50 in fees is clearly unacceptable. The slow pace of transfers (argued the Federal Reserve Faster Payments Task Force) impedes commerce or could be disastrous in a family emergency. SWIFT, the central banks, traditional banks, and fintech are aware of this as a big problem and the opportunity it offers.

Nevertheless, there is resistance to change. Many financial institutions have looked at the efficiencies gained through 40 years of automation efforts as an area for more profitability, not better customer service. They have invested billions in these systems so they are in no hurry to write them off or discount the fees and profits they bring.

For a bank to anticipate the FX requirements of its customers correctly on a real-time basis is next to impossible. In addition, not all banks are happy about the delays and fees associated with cross-border payments. For smaller banks, having another country's currency sitting idle in its nostro accounts overseas, in case of demand, is a necessary but undesirable and unprofitable deployment of funds. However, for the bigger banks that can act as foreign correspondents of smaller ones and that can reduce unanticipated demands by averaging over a much larger customer base, the profits are very real.

There is a lack of international standards or agreements on the speed of the movement of funds between countries. Expectations were once set based on paper-based manual systems. Inter-country regulations are typically far behind intra-country regulations. As such, there was little pressure for banks to pass on the advantages of automation to their customers. The banks looked at efficiencies gained through computerization as a source of profit, not customer service.

Intermediary institutions between the transferor and the transferee's institutions hold and use the transferred funds for as long as possible. Today a 30-day hold on an international funds transfer is still common.[238] Clearing and settlement systems to avoid settlement risk may queue the funds temporarily overnight. In situations with more than one clearing system, this queue can sometimes last two or three nights. For profitable use of the funds, the banks may hold the currency much longer. Nevertheless, the consumer, confronted with an opaque process, is told that the funds are "in transit." We can track a $50 international Amazon purchase from the point of shipment to the point of delivery, yet $100,000 can hang in limbo for many days.

Between countries' regulatory environments, there are few rules to protect the client, be they corporate or consumer.

Damien Vanderveken, head of research and development at SWIFT Lab and head of user experience at SWIFT, said that SWIFT is aware of the issues and has plans in place to address some of the frustrations: "If banks could manage their nostro account liquidity in real time, it would allow them to accurately gauge how much money is required in each account at any given point, ultimately enabling them to free up significant funds for other investments."[239]

Very true. Nostro accounts in one country, which may be accessible by any of the bank's deposit accounts from many countries, have always been the most difficult to reconcile and the easiest to defraud. By using DLT, we might be able to eliminate altogether the problems on nostro/vostro account reconciliation.

Some of these plans are now in place. Vanderveken explained that the SWIFT *global payment innovation* (gpi) plans to rejuvenate the correspondent banking model by enabling a tracker feature on international payments for transparency of fees and the possibility of same-day availability of funds.[240] No doubt competitive pressures on the banks may result in a change of behavior. Then again, the status quo is so profitable, there will be much resistance to change.

Fintech start-ups that move money between countries have put pressure on the established players to be more responsive, now squeezing margins. Even when services offer nearly instant, nearly free transfers, what customers gain in speed and fees, they often lose in the exchange rate without even knowing it. Blockchain solutions improving end-to-end fee and rate transparency have the ability to disrupt this market.

PAYMENT SYSTEMS TO MANAGE PAYMENT SYSTEMS

Launched in 2002, CLS is a system owned by the world's leading FX banks to address the differences in timing in settling the two halves of an FX transaction. More specifically, CLS is an international multicurrency clearing system designed to ensure that both sides of an FX contract are executed simultaneously, with certainty, and with the finality of payment in two different countries clearing systems. The CLS system settles payment instructions of underlying FX transactions in 18 currencies through accounts with 18 countries' central banks.[241] The technical coordination of that many banks' computers with each other in that many countries in that many time zones is not a trivial task.

The CLS system uses SWIFT messages to offer the largest FX cash settlement system in the world.[242] Each settlement member (typically a bank) holds a single multicurrency account with CLS. At the start and end of a normal settlement day, each settlement member and each central bank has a zero balance in its account. It is not a "lender of last resort." Settlement members may submit payment instructions relating to their own FX transactions as well as the FX transactions of their third-party customers directly to CLS. CLS maintains accounts with each of the central banks whose currencies settle through CLS. CLS, settlement members, and the national RTGS systems of many countries communicate via SWIFT messages.

CLS works by near simultaneously settling through the RTGS systems in the currencies and countries at times when both countries' central bank systems are open to send and receive payments. This enables concurrent settlement of the payments on both sides of an FX transaction, say, across the Atlantic.[243] If exchanging dollars for pounds, the movement of the two currencies (dollars in New York and pounds in London) is thus coordinated in the short time window when both systems' central bank clearing systems are concurrently accessible.

With an initial setup cost of over $300 million, CLS was criticized for its expensive structure.[244] The cost of the cure was far more (in historical terms at least) than the disease. To the bankers, this timing difference potential problem is known as *Herstatt risk*. In CLS' defense, during the crash of 2008, it accomplished its primary mission of keeping FX markets liquid, when many other markets froze.[245] Without CLS, it is probable that in the 2008 bank crisis, FX payments would have been frozen and the Great Recession could have been far worse.

However, setting up a clearing and settlement system to manage the movement of funds between clearing and settlement systems adds complexity to complexity. With the short overlapping time zones between the United States, Europe, and the Far East, the flow of funds is queued and slowed. But it does accomplish its objective of managing timing settlement risk.

Although CLS' membership includes the world's largest financial players, for smaller players the indirect routing of FX transactions between organizations results in days, if not weeks of delays. Let's not forget that every private party in these transactions takes fees.

To someone outside the banking industry, all these intermediary systems may seem insane. To those with knowledge about banking systems and their history, it is perfectly logical. For bankers, each leg of the meandering journey was designed to ensure greater trust and address specific risks. As we have noted, these steps take time and money. The customer is forced to accept the delays and the costs of the overhead, as arbitrary as they seem.

IN SEARCH OF A BETTER SYSTEM

The days of physical cash or gold being moved between countries' vaults at the US Fed for international payments is so early last century. Even letters of credit are exchanged with password-protected files, if not (more securely) digitally signed portable document format (PDF) files as trusted bits representing documents.

Even when sent over e-mail, this trust derives from many disciplines, rules, regulations, and controls for each step. Specifically, we trust our financial institutions to

- Meet their fiduciary responsibilities and cultivate the cascading trust an institution has in other institutions.

- Run their systems effectively, test those systems regularly, and apply change management processes to those systems.

- Maintain their firewalls, their virus protection software, their backups, independent and compensating controls, their reserve requirements, and the security of the network over which the messages are transmitted.

- Comply with standards and regulations, from Basel III to GAAP (generally accepted accounting principles).[246]

- Adhere to all of the above as overseen for compliance by competent management, verified by both internal and external auditors, and re-verified by government regulators against constantly changing regulations too often influenced by external lobbyists.

All of these functions have costs that these institutions force the customer to accept. We also know that each step has weaknesses that can result in failure.

Is this trust in governments, financial institutions, their people, systems, processes, auditors, and overseers actually earned? Many recent events have shaken this trust. In 2008 and 2009, $7.77 trillion in Fed loans and guarantees were fire-hosed into the banks to save them from their own folly.[247] That is roughly $40,000 for every man, woman, and child in the United States.

Later in 2015, Citigroup, Barclays, JPMorgan Chase, and RBS pleaded guilty to rigging FX currency rates and agreed to pay $5.6 billion in penalties.[248] US District Judge Stefan R. Underhill observed, "When the market is rigged, folks who play by the rules are suckers."[249] That almost condones cheating if not outright bank fraud.

In 2017 alone, Equifax exposed 145 million Americans' most secret financial information, in effect discrediting the entire credit scoring industry and exposing adult Americans to reputational harm and possibly fraud.[250] HSBC must pay $175 million for questionable FX practices, and Western Union had to pay $586 million for failure to stop wire fraud.[251] Wells Fargo paid a

$185 million settlement after it had opened as many as 2.1 million bank and card accounts in customers' names without permission.[252] The number of potentially affected customers has since grown to 3.5 million as Wells has expanded its probe of sales abuses. Egregious bank behavior and the resulting fines appear to many as just a cost of doing business.

As William K. Black hypothesized, the best way to rob a bank is to own one.[253] To add insult to injury, the US Congress passed a law to make it far more difficult, if not impossible, for those injured to sue the banks for their losses.[254] A major Wall Street win. Vice President Mike Pence cast the deciding vote.[255]

In the United States and other countries, trust in financial institutions and the government to regulate them properly is now at an all-time low, and representatives continue to erode that trust. In December 2017, the Republican Congress passed a $1.5 trillion tax cut that a survey of leading economists concluded would substantially increase the national debt.[256] Now the House and the Senate appear to be planning to repeal much of the Dodd-Frank Act, which was put in place to reduce the risk of the kinds of malfeasance that resulted in the near bank collapse and Great Recession of 2008.[257]

With the motto, "Bye, Bye Banks," TransferWise, a London-based fintech start-up, launched what it calls a "borderless" account. As of January 2018, it supports 28 different currencies, linked to local bank account numbers in the United Kingdom, United States, and Europe.[258] Its website explains how this "money without borders" business originated:

Taavet [Hinrikus] had worked for Skype in Estonia, so was paid in euros, but lived in London. Kristo [Käärmann] worked in London but had a mortgage in euros back in Estonia. They devised a simple scheme. Each month the pair checked that day's mid-market rate on Reuters to find a fair exchange rate.

> Kristo put pounds into Taavet's UK bank account, and Taavet topped up his friend's euro account with euros. Both got the currency they needed, and neither paid a cent in hidden bank charges.[259]

Hinrikus and Käärmann figured they weren't the only ones with this challenge, and so they turned this simple work-around into a billion-dollar business without blockchain.

It does not take emerging technologies to outsmart egregiously inefficient FX legacy systems. If we hold and net the payments, there is much money to be saved, and for the smarter intermediary, much money to be made. Companies that hold balances in many currencies, such as Facebook, Amazon, and Google, are aware of the opportunity.

Based on this model, TransferWise enables customers to receive and pay FX obligations without paying international transfer fees and off mid-market FX rates. Investors include Virgin's Richard Branson and PayPal co-founder Peter Thiel's Valar Ventures.[260]

TransferWise simply charges .05 percent off the mid-market rate. That does not sound like a lot until we realize that there are trillions of dollars in foreign exchange every day. Although its motto seems more threatening to financial institutions than SWIFT, its message is also directed at the heart of SWIFT. Its transfers bypass (to a large degree) the SWIFT, central bank, and CLS networks. By comparison, TD Bank in Canada charges from $30 to $80 for *its end* of an international funds transfer.[261] TransferWise is not alone; nanopay has similar aspirations.[262]

The heart of SWIFT is text messages transmitted as secure bits through telecommunication lines. Hypothetically, one could take a simple text messaging application such as WhatsApp (which encrypts text messages) as a transport medium; add some identity management, sequencing, message authentication codes; use ISO 20022 for financial message formats; and challenge the very existence of SWIFT. Today, payment services are trying to do that.

P2P payment systems are springing up everywhere from messaging services (Snapcash with Snapchat) to social networks (Facebook with Messenger, Google Wallet, Venmo/PayPal, and Square Cash). That's the same strategy as the Square Cash–powered Snapcash feature that Snapchat launched last November.

By integrating payments into its messaging service, Facebook is looking to edge out dedicated consumer payment competitors like Venmo/PayPal, Google Wallet, and Square Cash. Facebook said users log on to its website more frequently. Facebook has announced it is collaborating with TransferWise for international payments. Apple announced a launch of a text-message-based payments system.[263] EBay's PayPal is trying to undercut bank fees by offering PayPal's 2.9 percent plus $0.30 fee, whereas Facebook Messenger, whose income model is elsewhere, offers its Facebook Messenger Payment system for free.[264] Bankers, beware.

THE STRATEGIES OF EXISTING PLAYERS

SWIFT, central banks, and others around the world are designing next-step, if not next-generation, systems to address the current frustrations.

CANADA

Payments Canada envisions eight requirements for a modern payment system:

1. Faster payment options
2. Data-rich payments
3. Transaction transparency
4. Easier payments
5. Cross-border convenience
6. Activity-based oversight
7. Open and risk-based access
8. A platform for innovation

The Bank of Canada launched project Jaspar, which developed two DLT clearing and settlement system prototypes, first on Ethereum and then once again on R3's Corda. As a central bank, it equivocally concluded DLT "may not provide an overall net benefit" to central banks. It did, however, note that it might make more sense for an international clearing system that is decentralized by design. We agree.

US Federal Reserve

In the United States, the Fed commissioned a Faster Payments Task Force in June 2015 to look for ways of speeding up the payment process that are secure, equitable in access, and capable of settling transactions 24/7/365.[265] It stated that it wanted innovation that is market-based rather than mandated. The Fed wants to provide a formal framework for such innovation. It called for a road map to improve cross-border payments substantially. It said that slow cross-border payments and the opacity of costs, movement, and delivery time are impediments to economic growth.

The Fed defines its improvement goals as:

1. Speed: ubiquitous, safe, and cost-effective
2. Security: needs to remain strong
3. Efficiency: more electrons, less paper
4. International: for cross-border payments
5. Collaboration: involve a broad array of payment participants.

When we look at the Fed's desire for a payment system that is "safe, faster, ubiquitous, broadly secure, and efficient," it is hard not to think of the blockchain. Some proposals have blockchain as an immutable audit trail of all activities at the central bank, but money ends up in traditional bank accounts. Others like Ripple and TransferWise bypass SWIFT and to some degree manage the transfers themselves.

The Fed issued its payments study report in late July 2017. In it, the Fed admitted that "other countries have addressed these challenges through mandates and/or the development of a national faster payments system."[266] As the world's most important bank, the Fed has chosen not to mandate solutions but to encourage creativity. Of the 16 proposals to which the Fed gave serious consideration, and subsequently made public, 5 of them involved blockchain technology.

- ECCHO, Hub Culture, and Xalgorithms proposed DLTs as a real-time asset interchange ledger (RAIL) and a real-time asset interchange network (RAIN) that could one day make global payments on blockchain a reality.[267]

- The Kalypton Group described its proposal as "blockchain-like" without the limitations.[268]

- Ripple achieves high DLT throughput by direct end-to-end distributed ledger between financial participants without the need for a central ledger. Ripple's architecture and throughput indicate that they understand that the fewer the participants, the faster the throughput.

- WingCash went even further in suggesting that the Federal Reserve issue its own cryptocurrency.[269] It called for "ubiquitous receipt—where all payment service providers are capable of receiving faster payments and making those funds available to customers in real time."[270]

In January 2018, the total market capitalization of cryptocurrencies was $750 billion, which was roughly 20 percent of the US federal budget.[271]

European Central Bank

The ECB announced plans for a new instant payments and settlement system. It will enable businesses and consumers to send money in real time throughout the European Union. It will begin operation in 2018.

An ECB report suggests that DLT must be able to interoperate with non-DLT systems to be viable. It further argues, as does the Bank of England, that even though DLT is not mature enough to be considered a viable alternative to the market infrastructure offered by the Eurosystem, it certainly merits analysis and reflection.[272]

In August 2017, the Bank of England issued a similar report in encouraging future collaboration but said that DLT is not mature enough for real-time gross settlements. The Bank of England's requirement for interoperability gives great hints on how DLT will emerge in clearing and settlement.

Singapore

In early October 2017, the Monetary Authority of Singapore (MAS) and the Association of Banks in Singapore (ABS) announced a block-chain-based payment model for phase two of what they named Project Ubin. David Treat from Accenture told us that working with the monetary authority, they built side-by-side comparisons of systems in Hyperledger Fabric, R3 Corda, and Ethereum Quorum for interbank payments with real-time gross settlement. The same user interface was used to do direct architectural comparisons among the three. Treat said,

> One of the most interesting findings for me about that project was all three technical solutions met the requirements. They did it in three different manners, so they had different characteristics and implications as to how they approached privacy, and data segregation. But we basically showed that three different, competing, versions of the technology met the requirements.[273]

Will Singapore pick one as production-ready? We may soon see. As Treat put it,

> The state of play where we are right now, is that we're at the version one of all of these platforms. Reid Hoffman, the founder of LinkedIn, accurately stated, "If you are not embarrassed by the first version of your product, you've launched too late." The versions two are going to look dramatically different with significant improvements.[274]

Treat further indicated that regulators are enthralled with the obvious benefits of the new technologies and are unlikely to impede adoption.

Japan

In September, the Japanese Bankers Association (JBA) announced that it's working with Japan's largest IT equipment and services provider Fujitsu's cloud service-based blockchain platform as a test bed for its member banks. Through the JBA Fujitsu will provide its Collaborative Blockchain Platform to JBA members for applications such as for clearing and funds transfers.

JBA will work with others in testing and implementing these applications. Mizuho Bank and Fujitsu are also working on faster and more efficient ways of clearing and settling securities from the current T+3. Fujitsu has developed a variety of blockchain technologies including one for matching trade information for settlement processes, policy based transaction restrictions, and multiuser key management.

SWIFT

As the medium and the message standard for most international funds transfer, SWIFT manages three assets:

- A secured network, separate and distinct from the Internet
- A store, forward, and routing system between financial institutions

- An XML reference model with formats for message types defined by SWIFT as the registration authority for ISO 20022.

SWIFT's Vanderveken told us that SWIFT is well aware of the issues. He highlighted the SWIFT gpi to address many of the pain points in cross-border payments: gpi could enable the same-day use of funds, greater transparency of fees, and end-to-end tracking of payments including the stopping of payments where and when necessary. He also noted further data elements to enable faster and easier reconciliations. The speed of adaption of the banks to these features has yet to be determined.[275]

For nostro/vostro accounting, the SWIFT gpi initiative is giving end-to-end visibility to where a payment is in the process, from initiation through the correspondent banks and clearing houses. Where the daylight time zones of counterparties overlap it may even make near real-time payments a reality. Think of it as FedEx tracking where individuals can see where their transfer is as it moves from queue to queue.

On its pilot, SWIFT has stated, "DLTs are currently not mature enough for broad use on cross-border payments. [But] this technology may provide solutions for the associated account reconciliation."[276] Further, it stated that

> SWIFT will leverage its key assets to bring the technology in line with the financial industry's requirements, including strong governance, PKI [public key infrastructure] security scheme, BIC [bank identifier code] identify framework and liquidity standards expertise, with the goal to deliver a distinctive DLT proof of concept (POC) platform for the benefit of its community.[277]

On 13 October 2017, SWIFT published an interim report on the POC for real-time nostro reconciliation using a SWIFT-developed DLT sandbox. Thirty-three banks were involved. SWIFT concluded that it had identified issues that still need to be addressed to achieve industry-wide adoption.

SWIFT wisely is also participating in the new major ISO technical committees that met on standards critical to open blockchain-based payments, those being:

ISO/TC 307/SG 1 Reference architecture, taxonomy, and ontology

ISO/TC 307/SG 2 Use cases

ISO/TC 307/SG 3 Security and privacy

ISO/TC 307/SG 4 Identity

ISO/TC 307/SG 5 Smart contracts

Concurrently, SWIFT is demonstrating the benefits of DLTs by building a standard settlement instruction database for *over the counter* (OTC) derivatives markets in a reference data context in which there are no data confidentiality concerns. The POC may illuminate interoperability and backward compatibility with existing systems.

SWIFT is further working with the *central securities depositories* (CSDs) on standards for DLT management of securities. Participants include consulting firm E&Y, the Canadian Depository for Securities, the Moscow Exchange Group, South Africa's Strate, Russia's National Settlement Depository, Switzerland's SIX Securities Services, Nasdaq Nordic, and Chile's Depósito Central de Valores. This list will inevitably grow.

SWIFT also has a project for a bond life cycle POC. This is a sensible market because of its large size and the relative simplicity of issuance and maturity.

An obvious difference between old and new paradigms is identity. Damien Vanderveken told us that SWIFT is working on identity and access management.[278] The blockchain uses public keys for (arguably anonymous) identity; SWIFT uses X.509 certificates with its PKI for digital certificates and signatures. The goal is to assess how the two could coexist or interoperate and, we hope, achieve self-sovereign identity.

Many, if not most, SWIFT messages trigger or inform others about the movement of funds to the next intermediary or to the last provider.

DLT is capable of operating and storing, forwarding and ubiquitously routing tokens or cryptocurrency around the world to disintermediate many stakeholders and two-thirds of SWIFT's business model. What remains is setting standard message formats, which private company or other standards bodies could simply adopt. Ripple has done just that. In other words, we can foresee a funds transfer ecosystem on DLT without the SWIFT network.

Finally, SWIFT, as part of its gpi road map, launched a POC in 2017 to see whether DLT could assist in the reconciliation of nostro accounts more efficiently. For banks, getting the funds out of the customers' accounts in the original 10 countries and then clearing the payments (i.e., making these funds available) in the eleventh country are slow, risky, and difficult processes. SWIFT has smartly picked this high-risk problem but a low-risk area for its pilot. It is not about moving money; it is the reconciliation of money already moved.

Understanding the potential of DLT is not the same as radically transforming the payments business model.[279] SWIFT argued that "addressing automation problems in a multiparty network environment also requires business participants to define and agree on the meaning and content of shared data, business processes, roles, and responsibilities."[280] It fears that "attempting to impose standards too soon, before the capabilities and constraints of a technology are understood, risks creating standards that are quickly obsolete or irrelevant."[281] It noted that the current characteristics of DLTs, where everyone sees the same information (e.g., land title management) is clearly a plus, but everyone seeing everyone else's payment information is not.

Standards for identity that exist today (ISO standard 17442) that SWIFT uses are clearly not DLT public keys. That does not mean that there are not efforts to define new standards. The Decentralized Identity Foundation (including IBM and Hyperledger), Canadian banks, and many others are trying to do just that.[282]

SWIFT DLT efforts on nostro/vostro accounts will keep SWIFT current on emerging technologies. SWIFT needs to be extremely cautious and resistant to rapid change. However, this will not preclude less cautious competitors, particularly start-ups with little or nothing to lose, from vying to disintermediate them from existence. In 2017, most blockchain implementations are throughput bound. DLT for clearing and settlement will likely be implemented in far-lower risk environments and be proved to work, even with manageable teething problems. The race is on.

Although many start-ups aspire to replace the SWIFT network with a distributed ledger, we must remember that SWIFT's customers are also its members. We may expect a great deal of stickiness to the status quo to resist SWIFT's (or anyone else's) efforts on DLT. As a multi-member association, SWIFT was not designed for rapid change. The debate over how banks may clear and settle 10 years from now assumes that the growing numbers of other nonbank intermediaries won't make major inroads.

The messages' format and their metadata are standardized in ISO 20022, for which SWIFT is the registration authority. David Treat of Accenture believes that this is likely to be one of its enduring value adds. We're not so sure. In proposals to the US Faster Payments Task Force and start-ups all over the world, this standard is being extended. In a DLT-based system, identity management will be based on the keys for cryptographic hashing. Current business identifier codes through ISO 9362 need to be radically rewritten or retired.

No doubt through SWIFT's DLT efforts, they will learn much about the transfer, control, and safekeeping issues of DLTs. When current throughput, security, identity, and other limitations are overcome, it is not difficult to see how SWIFT could oversee a private blockchain that acts as an audit trail of international funds movement. For example, if the tokens in a SWIFT-managed DLT become the actual database of record for value, they might begin by obsoleting

CLS. It is also not difficult, if not more likely, to see others disinter-mediating SWIFT by doing something similar.

SWIFT brings to market three services: (1) the network, (2) secured messaging over it, and (3) well-defined formats and meta-data. We can achieve the first two more securely on DLT. The third is being morphed and extended for cryptography and smart contracts. No doubt, the diversion from standards, for such a critical process to world capitalism, will eventually converge back to a few standards. These may or may not come back to SWIFT. In the near future, innovation will abound, and the winners will capture a large share of the market.

Ripple

Extremely well funded through an ICO, Ripple has developed code for funds movement between two institutions reflected through synchronized ledgers at both ends. Through its ICO, it launched a cryptocurrency XRP. It aspires to transform the central-bank-ing-based hub-and-spoke payment models to a decentralized, if not distributed model. Ripple is an open-source chained ledger that supports multiple tokens and point-to-point synchronization to a single ledger. These tokens can represent anything from currencies to frequent buyer points to commodities.

Ripple is based upon a shared, distributed ledger that could replace much of today's clearing and settlement system with a spiderweb line architecture directly connecting all points, as opposed to the hub-and-spoke model used for clearing and settling today. It uses a synchronized ledger, which uses a consensus process that allows for payments, exchanges, and remittance in a distributed process at far-higher speeds.[283]

Ripple has announced that both American Express and Spanish bank Santander are positioned for, if not today using, Ripple for trans-atlantic payments via its blockchain, RippleNet.[284]

A well-circulated myth is that DLT's performance problems relate mostly to its block size and the current speed of computers. This is not the case. There is a common misperception that if we double the speed of a computer, then we halve its throughput time. For example, if our computer is running at 20 percent and waiting for I/O 80 percent of the time, doubling the speed of the computer will give us only a 10 percent increase in throughput (20%/2). Computers of all speeds (even quantum computers) wait for I/O at the same speed.

What slows down consensus-model DLT is the amount of time the computers are waiting for I/O that is the result of latency in the network as they communicate with each other. If we reduce the number of computers involved, then we eliminate much of the I/O problem. That is exactly what Ripple has done. By doing so, its asserted (and credible) throughput is orders of magnitude faster than the speed of either the Bitcoin or the Ethereum blockchain.

When we exchange relatively inactive currencies (e.g., Brazilian real for NZ dollars), we typically exchange them first through a more liquid currency (e.g., US dollar). Ripple hopes that we will someday use its cryptocurrency XRP instead. Extremely bold in ambition, XRP could replace the US dollar as the de facto intermediary currency.

Depository Trust & Clearing Corporation

The Depository Trust & Clearing Corporation (DTCC) is an industry-owned and governed financial market utility with more than 40 years of experience mitigating risk and driving operations and cost efficiencies for the financial industry. DTCC has a long history of driving innovation to strengthen the post-trade process. As a systemically important finance market utility, DTCC provides centralized depository and custodian services for equity and fixed income assets as well as centralized clearing and settlement services for trading in those assets.

Its leaders stated that DTCC operates some of the industry's most robust processing engines, with average volumes of over 100 million trade sides per day submitted in real time from 50 different trading markets, and as many as 25,000 transactions per second during peak processing.[285] DTCC has tested its system performance to handle well over 800 million trade sides, which is just over twice its historical peak volume. In 2016, its subsidiaries processed securities transaction valued at more than $1.5 quadrillion.[286]

In September 2017, the US settlement cycle was reduced to T+2 efficiency. DTCC oversaw this transition in coordination with the industry and employed existing technology to shorten the cycle. This move harmonizes with global markets, reduces risk and exposure, enhances market liquidity, and increases efficiencies.

The driver of this initiative was "client value—capital efficiency, risk reduction, and a globally harmonized settlement cycle."[287] The use of existing technology to shorten the settlement cycle exemplified how improvements to current processes don't always mandate the use of emerging technologies. According DTCC, the industry could use the existing technology to accelerate real-time settlement if it were inclined to do so.

In the DTCC's view, DLT is far past the proof-of-concept stage. DTCC is seriously considering DLT to enhance applications.[288] The tremendous efficiencies that the market has achieved reduce risk by netting DTCC's positions from a variety of trading activities across the day, indicating that a typical day may result in a 98 percent net.

DTCC leaders told us that their DLT efforts have gone beyond simple prototypes; but they are still challenged by the state of the technology in finding the right use cases, scalability, performance, resiliency, redundancy, approach to smart contracts, and, where applicable, cost benefits. DTCC has indicated that it does recognize that distributed ledger technologies can address limitations in the post-trade process by modernizing, streamlining, and simplifying the siloed design of the financial industry infrastructure with a "shared fabric of common information."[289]

According to DTCC, the short-term value proposition of DLT lies in addressing industry pain points in highly manual areas with relatively low volumes. Its current focus is to demonstrate ROI and client value by identifying opportunities through R&D investment, evaluating how existing technology can be better applied, and assessing how new technology can best be leveraged. DTCC explained:

> The technology is a means to an end—and the end is innovating what we do to create a stronger value proposition for our clients. Regardless of whether existing technology or emerging innovations are employed, client value guides the decision-making. Technology for the sake of technology is a losing proposition.[290]

Longer term, DTCC is assessing DLT's potential across a broad range of applications that include master data management, asset/securities issuance and servicing, confirmed asset trades, trade/contract validation, recording and matching for more complex asset types, netting and clearing, and collateral management and settlement. However, critical factors for moving forward include maturing the technology's capabilities for real-world financial transaction requirements, scalability, interoperability, and independent governance.

Given the transaction volumes in the US securities market that DTCC processes, it would need any distributed ledger to be equipped not only to handle the current peak transaction volumes, including validation and irreversible transaction finality, but also to manage significantly increased volumes. Current DLT implementations are orders of magnitude away from achieving this capacity.

Like most, DTCC expressed concerns on the maturity and throughput of today's technology but are watching it closely as it matures. The company stated:

> Currently, the technology doesn't have the scale or capacity to match the robust processing engines that underpin the clearance and settlement needs of the US markets today. In the future, any enterprise-ready distributed ledger solution for a mature, high-volume marketplace will need to achieve or surpass that processing power.[291]

To advance the technology, DTCC echoes industry calls for interoperability and integration of distributed ledgers and legacy infrastructure, in addition to the continued development of standards and protocols. The company remains a strong advocate for the development of independent governance to address challenges associated with implementation and operation of DLT solutions. According to its leaders, DTCC can play a key role in this function, serving as a neutral network operator and developing and enforcing the required standards and protocols.[292]

TransferWise

TransferWise's fee of 0.5 percent against a true mid-market FX rate seems like such a small sum that it is unlikely to make much profit, until we realize that it's a $5 trillion-per-day marketplace.[293] TransferWise's small fee could convert to tens of billions of dollars per day. When DLT technology fully matures, developing the software that could manage payments internationally would cost a few million dollars, possibly less. It is open source, and well suited for this application.

Putting together an ICO based on a credible value proposition is not difficult. Given the possible reward and the low barriers to entry, the number of market entrants will be large. Expect every major software company, and every major financial institution, to get involved in at least one effort for payments, of which international payments is the biggest prize. There will also be many aspiring start-ups. If they are smart, every major company with a competent technology arm will participate in one effort or another. The upside is enormous.

Although the barriers to developing such a system are low, getting the buy-in from market, regulatory, and existing financial players will be what defines the winner. David Treat's and our experience with central banks and the regulators are unusual in that they are to some degree driving this change.

The simplicity and the benefits of a DLT solution to them are obvious. Credibility, and establishing great relationships with a critical momentum of financial services players (which we know SWIFT already has), may cost far more that developing the technology. Given the elegance, security, and economic advantages of a DLT-based system, regulators and central governments are embracing DLT solutions and perhaps may even lead this charge. There will be many others, such as nanopay and Ingenico Group.[294]

ANALYSIS: CREATING A BETTER SYSTEM ON THE BLOCKCHAIN

It will soon be widely accepted that the inherent mathematics proven to secure token movements and their messages through a synchronized DLT, is better, faster, and cheaper than the serialization of messages between multiple legacy institutions, their people, and their systems. Even doubters may come to appreciate the dramatic reduction in delays and costs as overwhelming arguments to put international funds transfers onto a blockchain.

In the 20th century, for children, there was that teaching moment of why they should keep their allowance in a savings account to accrue interest. Low interest rates and a tsunami of 21st-century service fees have made that argument moot. The dire predictions of Bill Gross (the Bond King) and many economists that deficits and quantitative easing would produce higher interest rates and run-away inflation have not materialized.[295]

Instead, a combination of automation and outsourcing has increased productivity without corresponding wage growth. This is producing record profits while keeping inflation well in check. What is still surprising is how concerned the Fed chair and others are about inflation that is "still stubbornly muted."[296]

Bankers have trouble thinking outside the bank. An obvious but radical approach would be to develop a system that eliminates or radically reduces the dependency on the central banks and banks. The system would store currency values in distributed ledgers, as blockchain does for tokens. To many bankers, this is unthinkable. We must remember these values are just bits—trusted, regulated, and secured bits. There are far simpler ways to secure and trust different bits than a flotilla of banks, correspondent banks, central banks, CLS, regulators, auditors, and more. We could dramatically improve centralized clearing and settlement systems, even eliminate them, by providing the same functionality through a third-party DLT (Figure 4-5).

A blockchain system mathematically ensures that the counterparties are indeed who they claim to be. It ensures finality of payment, and unlike any dual-entry bookkeeping system, the contract intrinsically records and duplicates both ends of the contract in the same block. The simultaneity of both sides of the payment requires none of the massive complexity of systems upon systems we see today. DLT requires no central trusted authorities (read SWIFT and central banks), no time zone queue management (read CLS), and avoids the risks of failure in the central hub of a hub-and-spoke architecture. It can be distributed.

Distributed ledgers obviate the role of central banks to verify ownership and clear transactions. They can be open, permissionless, and public and allow anonymous actors to participate in the network or they can be closed, permissioned, and private and allow previously identified participants only.

We would no longer think of CLS updates in near-simultaneous time in two central bank systems, in the restricted time zones that they

FIGURE 4-5

CENTRALIZED CLEARINGHOUSES VERSUS
DISTRIBUTED LEDGERS

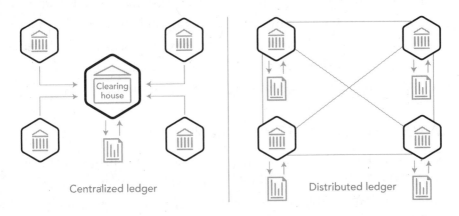

Centralized ledger   Distributed ledger

are open. The debits and the credits on both sides of the FX transaction can be inferred from that single contract block in the ledger, and the constructs of accounting can remain. When both sides of the FX transactions are in a blockchain ledger (as well as separate accounting systems), some refer to it as triple-entry accounting.[297] Thinking outside of the accounting box and through blockchain, we can create single entry bookkeeping. More specifically, it would occur when the entries for both banks in both currencies take the form of a transfer between wallet addresses in the same distributed, international FX public ledger, creating an immutable and interlocking system of accounting records.

One blockchain entry will in effect drive two bookkeeping debits and credits in two different banks' general ledgers with no central bank involvement. The system's design could be much simpler. From a SWIFT perspective, much of the functionality is already in the blockchain. For example, for large funds transfers, most financial institutions require two (or even more) signatures to authorize the large payments. *Multiple signature* on the pay side and *pay to script hash* on the receiving side do exactly that by requiring multiple private keys in order to transact. Implementations may vary but we could argue this is even more secure than SWIFT.

It would deliver what customers want: a real-time system for international funds transfers without delays or exorbitant fees. Combine smart contracts with the Internet of Things, and one could do much, at far lower cost, to have real-world events (such as those included in letters of credit) trigger the movement of funds. There would be a public, irrefutable ledger of the movement of funds.

A NEW ROLE FOR GOVERNMENT?

It is revolutionary. To start with, on international payments, we could derive the debits and credits in different banks in different countries and systems from a blockchain. Since we'd know that our asset in the blockchain was mathematically guaranteed to be our counterparty's liability, we'd no longer need all the reconciliations, compensating controls, and internal and external audits to ensure the integrity of the transactions. The audit function could focus on internal controls as opposed to the verification of assets. A true game changer.

These new architectures are based on emerging technologies that allow for the rapid integration of smart contracts and intellectual property beyond the traditional payments industry. If we define cryptocurrencies as "a digital currency in which encryption techniques are used to regulate the generation of units of currency and verify the transfer of funds, operating independently of a central bank," the answer is a definite partially.[298]

Most economists believe that capitalism would collapse without the government exercising some control over fiscal (government borrowing and spending) and monetary (interest rate) policy. Starting in the economic collapse of 2008, western governments injected trillions of dollars into the world's economy through what is called *quantitative easing*, where the left hand of the government (the Fed, the Bank of England, the Bank of Canada) prints money to lend to the right hand of the government (the Treasury) by buying its treasury bills.

Libertarians argue, "The Federal Reserve System should be abolished; that the Board of Governors of the Federal Reserve should be put on Social Security; and that Social Security should be abolished."[299] To those, a cryptocurrency outside of the control of governments, plus free market reign, does have a certain appeal.

To others, a cryptocurrency whose supply is controlled by a government may seem like a contradiction. As we witnessed in Venezuela, poor fiscal policy (printing money) can ruin an economy. In response, Venezuelan president Nicolás Maduro Moros announced the launch of a cryptocurrency, the petro, backed by oil reserves.[300]

In countries where there is no credible record of responsible economic policy, the arbitrary but transparent process of value creation (as with bitcoins on a blockchain) may reduce mistrust, meaning we may someday see a proof-of-work cryptocurrency as a national currency. Although it may forgo that country's ability to use traditional techniques to manage its economy, it would allow that country to escape the arbitrary attacks on its currency by FX traders from behemoth money-center banks.

Christine Lagarde, managing director of the International Monetary Fund, said, "Think of countries with weak institutions and unstable national currencies. Instead of adopting the currency of another country—such as the US dollar—some of these economies might see a growing use of virtual currencies. Call it dollarization 2.0."[301]

The Bretton Woods accord established the US dollar as the global currency, putting the US government in an extraordinary position of power, capable of denying access to the global system to, for example, Chinese banks that do business with North Korea. We should consider the adoption of a cryptocurrency à la XRP or bitcoin a serious possibility and disruptor to this world order.[302]

A NEW ROLE FOR SWIFT?

"Should the Blockchain replace SWIFT?" Chris Skinner asked in an issue of *American Banker.* He argued that a blockchain-based system could transform or replace the SWIFT network, which would boost the security, expediency, and accuracy of the system.[303] Partially true, we would still need metadata standards from some international body. That will depend on when and how SWIFT leadership embraces or ignores the new possibilities.

If it innovates, then SWIFT as the hub of international funds transfer could maintain its trust-based relationships with its financial partners. The limitations of the current blockchain and SWIFT's innovation with DLT and nostro/vostro accounts, although far from transformational, will position it to better understand the strengths and limitations of the technology. This experience will help SWIFT to guide if not herd the emergence of DLTs for FX. There are many issues outstanding before the world embraces cryptocurrencies. SWIFT likely has a better understanding of these issues than anyone.

If consumers could put their money into DLT, with locally denominated cryptocurrency, accessible from their phone, and with the level of trust that the blockchain has now earned, why would they continue using a fee-laden account at a bank? For digital fiat or cryptocurrencies to be widely accepted, they need twelve characteristics. They must

1. Be easily divisible
2. Be easy to transfer
3. Have strong governance and adequate data controls
4. Be portable and readily accessible
5. Be reliable and highly available
6. Accrue predictable interest
7. Be stable in value
8. Comply with regulatory requirements
9. Be standardized (there is likely no room for dozens of cryptocurrencies)
10. Have an identity framework that cannot be lost

11. Be scalable

12. Be retrievable if passwords (or wallet words) are lost

Satoshi Nakamoto designed the first five characteristics in bitcoin, and the fifth may soon move from inspiration to reality. There are institutions such as Magnr willing to pay interest on bitcoin deposits, and so item six is now true.[304] The seventh, for today, is wildly elusive with massive fluctuations in the value of cryptocurrencies. Today, cryptocurrency market value sites that one visits (such as *CoinMarketCap.com* or Smith + Crown) have a different exchange rate value. To mitigate the risk of these massive swings in value, brokers that buy and sell cryptocurrencies through de facto currencies can take markups of 10+ percent.[305]

However, this will soon change.[306] On 31 October 2017, CME Group Inc. announced that it would begin trading futures in the fourth quarter of 2017. When it does, the buy and sell rate gap should decrease dramatically.[307] It will also allow people the ability to buy bitcoin without the complexity of wallets and wallet words. In other words, today, for international payments, there is not yet a clear advantage in going through bitcoin as opposed to traditional FX systems.

"Citizens may one day prefer virtual currencies, since they potentially offer the same cost and convenience as cash—no settlement risks, no clearing delays, no central registration, no intermediary to check accounts and identities," said Christine Lagarde at a Bank of England conference in London.[308] She shared her view of cryptocurrencies:

> For now, virtual currencies such as bitcoin pose little or no challenge to the existing order of fiat currencies and central banks. Why? Because they are too volatile, too risky, too energy intensive, and because the underlying technologies are not yet scalable. Many are too opaque for regulators; and some have been hacked.

But many of these are technological challenges that could be addressed over time. Not so long ago, some experts argued that personal computers would never be adopted, and that tablets would only be used as expensive coffee trays. So I think it may not be wise to dismiss virtual currencies.[309]

The ease of transferring value as tokens with anonymity is what made bitcoin the de facto currency of the illicit Silk Road site. It is also of great interest to rogue regimes facing international sanctions. North Korea is believed to be behind the WannaCry virus that infected hundreds of thousands of computers around the world and extorted an estimated $81 million.[310]

Although the Bitcoin ledger is secure, the wallets and exchanges clearly are not. For example, over $70 million of bitcoin was hacked and stolen from the NiceHash marketplace in Slovenia.[311] The second successful hack on the Youbit exchange platform in South Korea put it out of business.[312] Today, cryptocurrencies stored in hardware wallets appear secure, assuming that they are not lost, stolen, or burnt, or do not malfunction.

Cryptocurrencies are of great interest to anyone who wishes to hide assets. Identity management is an issue still under much discussion. Knowing one's customers is a prerequisite to honoring sanctions and avoiding money laundering. We could debate whether, in the long view, the "full faith and credit" of a government can compete with the mathematical integrity of a cryptocurrency. They need not be mutually exclusive. They could even be merged. In response to the US Faster Payments Task Force, WingCash created a "national digital currency platform proposed for use by the Federal Reserve that extends the US dollar into the digital realm."[313] This seems inevitable.

Today, millennials (born 1977 to 1995) and centennials (born after 1995) think of a camera as simply part of their phone. Soon they will likely consider it a wallet containing their fiat and cryptocurrencies. Governments and financial institutions have eroded

their trust. So, on what could we base a new currency? Some want to return to the gold standard and others want to move to an energy standard. Some argue for energy as a base of a new common currency.[314] This seems unlikely.

A cryptocurrency—where the government controls the generation and units of currency—is mathematically and economically viable. Instead of proof of work or proof of stake, it would be based on proof-of-authority consensus, where the central banks are the authority. With such a definition, a central bank could slowly transform its fiat currency into a cryptocurrency. Some see a world without central banks. But they perform so many management functions, that this seems improbable.

The unsure part of the definition for national cryptocurrencies is the regulation of the generation of new units. With bitcoin, a predetermined mathematical algorithm sets the rate. The upper limit of bitcoins that can be mined is fixed.

For countries where there is no credible record of responsible economic policy, the arbitrary and transparent process of value creation (as with blockchain) may install a cryptocurrency as a national currency.

CONCLUSIONS AND RECOMMENDATIONS

As international commerce has exploded, it has demanded a lower-cost, more transparent, and timely payment system. The current system does not meet today's requirements and will soon be replaced.

- Smartphone applications will become the ubiquitous payment mechanism for the unbanked. Near- and nonbank payment systems are flourishing, with and without using blockchain, in crypto and fiat currencies. This is a game changer. Payment systems for the poor without intermediaries charging high fees will stimulate greater commerce. Digital technology that promotes financial inclusion can increase GDP by as much as nine percent, or more, for some economies in Southeast Asia, according to a new report, *Accelerating Financial Inclusion in Southeast Asia with Digital Finance*.[315] For less banked markets, arguably the impact should be greater.

- As revolutionary as it is, the transformation of international payments to DLT technology will be evolutionary for continuity and to manage risk. No major financial institution is going to convert to a new DLT-based system until its necessary characteristics as defined above by the BoC, the BoE, the Fed, and others are proven beyond doubt.

- For decades, for international payments SWIFT was supreme. But SWIFT risks being disintermediated if it does not transform itself. It could start by working with the 18 institutions in CLS to disintermediate CLS. Changing the interface to its 11,000 members from a messaging paradigm to a ledger paradigm will be a slow process. Both SWIFT and the US Faster Payments Task Force are correct to say introducing new standards is premature. This is a time for technological and social innovation.

- At least two and ideally far more of the major players in international payments could build DLT accessed by multiple organizations as a back-end log or irrefutable audit trail of which payment activities have occurred. If it fails, it is only a back-end log, not the freezing of markets.

- As the technology matures, they can test its throughput, security, veracity, flexibility, privacy, and other features necessary to conclude that it may be trusted as a database of record, before the regulatory changes that are required to define the bits in this DLT as representing currency.

- After many months, if not many years, of building confidence and trust, contracts can be drawn and regulations changed to allow DLT to become the database of record (after all, it is just bits). These organizations can lead the charge (while profiting) from re-architecting national and then international payments system.

- By having point-to-point replication, Ripple with its distributed—not centralized—architecture has mitigated the speed issues associated with distributed consensus models. It is in production today for nostro/vostro accounts, with the direct connection immediately indicating erroneous account numbers, as opposed to SWIFT's messaging model.

- Both Ripple's XRP and Stellar's Lumens (XLM) aspire to become the world's de facto currency. Whether this is wishful thinking or an achievable goal has yet to be seen. By limiting the number of distributed players in its distributed ledger technology to two, Ripple can produce throughput levels far in excess of its more distributed competitors. However, Stellar's market capitalization jumped from $194 million to $516 million (a whopping 265 percent) on simply stating that aspiration (with IBM).

- There seem to be two evolutionary paths for DLT to be implemented for world payments. One is coexistence of the older and the newer technology, as is the Bank of England's desire, so as not to disrupt existing money flows while moving to the new paradigm.

- The other evolutionary path is targeted implementation illustrated by Ripple and Ethereum, with DLT (or DLT-like) software aggressively entering smaller markets and then, once proven, moving to larger ones. Moving from national payments (with the permission and direction of one central bank) is far easier than negotiating the politics of transborder payments. The small scale of the city-state of Singapore, coupled with the throughput limitations of existing blockchain, makes it an ideal place for a manageable implementation.

- Blockchain-based solutions are in their infancy, and the hack of the DAO program and resulting fork of the Ethereum blockchain, has proven some need for caution.[316] It showed us that those with a solid understanding of DLT, with the best of intentions, can still make subtle implementation errors that compromise the system.

- The US Federal Reserve, in the second part of its Faster Payments Task Force's final report, "encourages competition among a variety of solutions, as opposed to endorsing a single approach."[317] This will ensure many competing implementations. The Fed wants real-time payments by 2020.

- There is the distinct possibility if not the inevitability that an international funds transfer design could run without an operator, let alone fees. This is so far outside current thinking that we believe a managed proof-of-authority DLT system is the likely first major step. The business case for an innovative fintech start-up or for a bank innovation group with simpler, faster, more responsive DLT solution seems likely.

- The absence of international rules or controls on payment processing has made it historically slow and expensive to change. This also creates billion-dollar opportunities for low-cost intermediaries. Hundreds of companies will enter the marketplace, and all but a few will fail.

- History may repeat itself. Forty years ago, the high end of computer management went to the big-league computer show in Las Vegas called Comdex. The people with the power over technology budgets saw the new state-of-the-art offerings. Later, a small and initially inconsequential Consumer Electronics Show grew and squashed the higher-end conference.

- The costs and risks of launching a low-risk consumer system are small, and once proven with or without regulator or SWIFT's approval, it may be perceived as the safe place for larger and then even larger international transfers. By proving itself in the consumer marketplace (without the risks of large-dollar interbank payments), it may well grow to become the 800-pound payments gorilla. In other words, there is a possibility, if not a probability, that existing institutions may be disintermediated by a consumer player.

The question of who will lead this new world order is unclear. Will it be SWIFT, R3, Ethereum, central banks, Visa, an existing megatech company like Facebook, or a new low-cost DLT-enabled start-up? Given the low costs of entry into this trillion-dollar-a-day marketplace, we expect the competition to be ferocious.

CHAPTER 5

CONSOLIDATING MULTIPLE LEDGERS WITH BLOCKCHAIN

A Single Digital Ledger for the Government of Canada Accounts

Anthony Williams

 ## CONSOLIDATING MULTIPLE LEDGERS IN BRIEF

- From global financial markets to healthcare delivery, blockchain technology is fundamentally changing how we collect, manage, and record information. It is simplifying complex ecosystems, creating trusted and secure repositories of data, and supporting complementary technologies, such as smart contracts and artificial intelligence.

- From Estonia to the United States, jurisdictions are deploying blockchain (aka DLT) to power innovations in business registration, identity management, e-voting, healthcare services, and international trade.

- This chapter explores the use of blockchain to consolidate the Government of Canada's multiple ledgers into a single distributed ledger that would increase the integrity of its accounts, boost the efficiency of auditing functions, and reduce its transaction costs.

- As transactions recorded onto the ledger would be instantly searchable and publishable, the blockchain-based ledger could also boost public transparency, fulfill and expedite the receiver general's auditing requirements, and improve the integrity of Canada's accounts.

OVERVIEW OF RECEIVER GENERAL LEDGER SYSTEM

The receiver general for Canada is responsible for managing the government-wide treasury, accounting, and reporting functions of the federal government. These activities include controlling all monies drawn from or deposited to the *consolidated revenue fund* and ensuring that all of these transactions are accounted for in the accounts of Canada—Canada's general ledger—and producing the public accounts of Canada.

To ensure that all transactions are reflected in the accounts of Canada, the receiver general implements a control framework, which sees government departments submit monthly, aggregated financial information (including all expenditures and revenues), which the receiver general reconciles against the general ledgers. The control framework is largely based on legacy applications that require human intervention, such as file uploads, verifications, and data refreshing. Some of these operations are highly time-sensitive, and any snag in the process can have severe repercussions.

What follows is a brief overview of the key components of the receiver general control framework, including the central financial management reporting system, the receiver general–general ledger, and the account balance concept.

CENTRAL FINANCIAL MANAGEMENT REPORTING SYSTEM

The Government of Canada uses a central *financial management reporting system* to maintain its accounts. This central reporting system compiles a general ledger from the certified trial balances submitted by government departments and agencies at the end of every month. These monthly departmental trial balances contain opening and closing balances for each unique combination of *government-wide coding*, a standardized input record layout needed to maintain Canada's accounts. The central system performs several key functions:

- Verifies account balances of the control accounts for all departments against the corresponding control accounts in receiver general–general ledger (RG-GL) and *payroll system–general ledger* (PS-GL)

- Ensures that all payroll-related transactions, payments, and money received by departments, including interdepartmental settlements, are accounted for in the books of Canada

- Validates codes submitted by departments in the chart of accounts

- Provides information to central agencies through an ad hoc reporting function.

RECEIVER GENERAL–GENERAL LEDGER

The RG-GL is maintained using the *common departmental financial system* (CDFS). The RG-GL maintains control account balances for all payments, interdepartmental settlement transactions, and deposits processed by the treasury systems for all departments. Every day, the RG-GL provides departments with an electronic file containing all payment and deposit transactions recorded against the control accounts.

ACCOUNT BALANCE CONCEPT

The control account balances maintained by the RG-GL and the PS-GL are a key component of the account balance concept. The RG-GL control account totals are based on data received from the treasury systems and internal journal vouchers for adjustments not processed through the treasury systems. The PS-GL control account totals are based on pay data received from Canada's Phoenix public service payroll system and from internal journal vouchers for adjustments not processed through Phoenix.

Departments are required to perform a periodic reconciliation between the control account balances in the *departmental financial management systems* (DFMS) and the daily control account totals received from the RG-GL and PS-GL. For example, departments receiving internal journal vouchers affecting their control accounts are required to manually upload the data into the related accounts in their DFMS and reconcile their DFMS account balances with the daily control account totals received from the RG-GL and PS-GL.

At month-end, the RG-GL and PS-GL send a *final control account balance* report to departments, which includes reports and data files containing control data and control account balances. Departments must reconcile the control account balances with the corresponding account balances recorded in their DFMS.

The receiver general uses the reconciled trial balances to produce the *monthly statement of financial operations* (MSFO) and the annual public accounts of Canada. If there are errors, omissions, or inappropriate coding in departmental trial balance data that will have a material impact on the results of the MSFO, the receiver general will make the appropriate changes and request that the departments adjust the following month.

PUBLIC SECTOR APPLICATIONS OF BLOCKCHAIN

A blockchain is an encoded digital ledger stored on multiple computers in a public or private network. It consists of data records, or "blocks," aggregated into time-stamped chains that cannot be changed or deleted by a single actor; instead, they are verified and managed through automation and shared governance protocols. As a result, blockchain provides an immutable, transparent record of the truth.

Use cases tend to focus on financial services. Government agencies could use blockchain not just for conducting financial transactions and collecting taxes but also for registering voters, identifying recipients of healthcare, financial support, and emergency aid; issuing passports and visas; registering patents and trademarks; recording marriage, birth, and death certificates; and maintaining the integrity of government records.

Governments are already exploring blockchain applications for land registry (Sweden), digitizing all public documents (Dubai), and bolstering cybersecurity for identity management and e-voting (Estonia). The US General Services Administration now uses blockchain to automate its public procurement process, and the State of Delaware introduced legislation to allow companies to incorporate using blockchain. This chapter explores the deployment of distributed ledger technology for public sector accounting; these use cases are all exercises in simplifying and improving data management in government.

IDENTITY MANAGEMENT IN ESTONIA

Formed as an independent nation in 1991—just as the public Internet was born—Estonia is a true digital native. Its lack of legacy infrastructure has freed it to build a digitally enabled society and economy from the ground up. Today, the normal services of government—legislation, voting, education, justice, healthcare, banking, taxes, policing, and so on—have been digitally enabled across one platform, wiring up the nation into the most ambitious project in technological statecraft on the planet.

Among the hallmarks of eEstonia is the blockchain-enabled Estonia ID card, a cryptographically secure digital identity card that unifies access to a mind-boggling array of services. Citizens can order prescriptions, vote, bank online, review school records, apply for state benefits, access medical and emergency services, file their taxes, submit planning applications, upload their will, apply to serve in the armed forces, travel within the European Union without a passport, and fulfill around 3,000 other functions with their

Estonia ID. Businesses owners can use the ID card to file their annual reports, issue shareholder documents, apply for licenses, and so on. Government officials can use the ID card to encrypt documents; review and approve permits, contracts, and applications; and submit information requests to law enforcement agencies.

The day-to-day efficiencies for citizens are considerable. Estonia's "once only" data policy dictates that no single piece of information about its citizens should be entered twice. Instead of having to "prepare" a loan application, applicants have their data—income, debt, savings—pulled from elsewhere in the system. There's nothing to fill out in doctors' waiting rooms, because physicians with permission can access their patients' medical histories. When a child is born in the hospital, his or her parents are automatically registered for family benefits. Citizens requiring long-term medication get a digital prescription slip on their medical record, which reduces queues at doctors' offices and hospitals.

According to the Organisation for Economic Co-operation and Development, "In 2016, around 68 percent of the adult population in Estonia used the Internet to send filled forms to the public authorities, which is almost twice the OECD average (35.6%)."[318] While citizens evidently like the convenience of online services, the savings for government are also significant. Digitizing processes reportedly saves the state two percent of its gross domestic product a year in salaries and expenses.

Confident that it could extend these benefits beyond its physical borders, Estonia launched a digital "e-residency" program in 2014, which allows nonresident foreigners to partake of some Estonian services as if they were living in the country. A €100 fee and a successful security check will get users an identity card, a cryptographic key, and a *personal information number* (PIN) to access e-services like business incorporation and banking. Estonia hopes its e-residency program will appeal to entrepreneurs and encourage international start-ups to put down virtual roots. Estonia has the lowest business tax rates in the European Union and has become known for liberal regulations around tech research. As of January 2018, 28,000 people had applied for e-residency (approx. 500 people apply each week), and e-residents own more than 3,200 companies.[319]

Estonia's eBusiness initiative has made it easy for both residents and e-residents to start and operate a business in the country: Estonia has one of the fastest growing start-up populations in the world, with 31 start-ups per 100,000 inhabitants, which is six times higher than the European average.[320] Once companies are up and running, they can connect their financial management APIs to the government online, automate reporting for annual tax filings, and reduce the administrative burden on businesses and the public sector.

Blockchain-enabled ledgers provide the underlying data management and security technology for much of Estonia's digital public services. The Estonian ID card, for example, records every piece of data with proof of time, identity, and authenticity—providing a verifiable guarantee that records have not been altered.[321] The *keyless signature infrastructure* (KSI) that Estonia's blockchain requires ensures the authenticity of the electronic data stored on its citizens: "No one—not hackers, not system administrators, and not even the government itself—can manipulate the data and get away with that."[322]

Leveraging the blockchain infrastructure means distributing storage of data, thus reducing the chance of major breaches of centralized databases. "Instead, the government's data platform, XRoad, links individual servers through end-to-end encrypted pathways, letting information reside locally," according to Nathan Heller of *The New Yorker*.[323] Hospitals, educational institutions, banks, and government agencies all maintain their own data sets. When a user requests data, the system delivers it via a series of locks, like a boat passing through a canal.[324]

A strict system of permissions and privacy safeguards ensures that citizens control who may see or not see their data. Teachers, for example, can enter student grades but cannot access a student's entire academic history. A file accessible to one medical specialist need not be accessible to other doctors if a patient deems it unnecessary. Few people are able to say exactly who has looked at their medical records. But Estonians can log into their records and see exactly what medical professionals have viewed and acted on. Citizens could challenge and justice departments could prosecute any government official who accessed a citizen's data without permission or a legally valid reason.

Estonia's advances are so well regarded that other governments are importing its innovative models for e-governance. Its experts have consulted on Georgia's efforts to set up its own digital registry. Estonia is also building data partnerships with Finland and sharing its methods elsewhere in Europe. "The vision is that I will go to Greece, to a doctor, and be able to get everything," Sandra Roosna told *The New Yorker*. She is a member of Estonia's eGovernance Academy and the author of the book *eGovernance in Practice*. "I think we need to give the European Union two years to do cross-border transactions and to recognize each other digitally," she said.[325] Nations as disparate as Moldova and Panama have adopted the Estonian platform. What started in a small Baltic state could soon provide the digital platform for e-governance across Europe.

US GSA AND FAST LANE

In fiscal year 2017, the US General Services Administration (GSA) procured over $15 billion in IT equipment, software, and services from more than 5,000 companies on behalf of federal, state, and local government buyers.[326] On average, the GSA took 110 days to onboard a scheduled contractor to deliver services—an exceedingly long time to wait for IT products in today's environment.

In recent years, GSA has worked to shave time off the procurement process using a new approach the agency calls FASt Lane, a mash-up of Federal Acquisition Services (FAS) and Integrated Technology Services (ITS). According to Jose Arrieta, director of the General Services Administration's Schedule 70 (IT products and services) operation, "The FASt Lane process can award contracts within 40 days, but only when the requirements are very clear."[327] In 2018, GSA initiated a blockchain-enabled pilot in an attempt to shave even more time off the process. The agency anticipates its POC will bring the FASt Lane review process down to fewer than 10 days.

Currently moving through both the design and proof-of-concept phases, GSA is looking to use blockchain to automate intelligently the most time- and labor-intensive aspects of the FASt Lane contract review process. The agency expects that automation will reduce the amount of human interaction required to review new proposal documents, improving the user experience and speeding the awarding of contracts and onboarding of companies.

A crucial element of GSA's POC was to change two steps of the vendor selection and onboarding process: the review of vendor-submitted financial statements and the preparation of prenegotiation letters. On the financial review, the traditional process involved a staffer extracting financial information from material the vendor provided and calculating the firm's financial viability. This alone could take up to a month. The blockchain POC accelerated that process so that, in most cases, an automated review is "nearly instantaneous," according to Steven Kelman, professor of public management at Harvard University. "Offers that pass are moved onto the next step in the workflow; those flagged for further review or rejected are routed to a human reviewer for further analysis."[328] Kelman elaborated:

> A prenegotiation letter, meanwhile, is a document listing issues for the GSA to raise in negotiations with a vendor. The blockchain … became the system of record for an entire offer, replacing multiple e-mails back and forth between the government and vendor, and back and forth with the contracting officer checking multiple systems. It has reduced preparation time from 15 to 30 days to fewer than 10 days.[329]

Automation will not only save time and money—possibly lowering the direct costs of analyzing a proposal by close to 80 percent, according to Arrieta—but it will free up staff for more valuable activities. "By automating these business processes, we can lessen the burden on our industry partners, and allow the contracting professionals to focus more on critical thinking tasks rather than the process tasks associated with interacting with multiple systems," said Arrieta.[330]

Accuracy and data integrity are further benefits of using blockchain to mediate transactions, especially when mediating (as GSA does) between thousands of IT vendors and thousands of local, state, and federal buyers. Blockchain provides a cheaper, more flexible, and more accurate platform for handling the procurement process than the traditional system, which required multiple databases. Arrieta said,

> In the old system, we had multiple databases with specific data elements and operations that can be performed on them. If one wished to introduce new data elements or new ways to analyze some data, we had to modify the databases. Multiple databases also create risks for errors in data transfer from one database to another.[331]

With the blockchain solution, vendors and purchasers enter their information once instead of logging onto multiple systems, and there is only one shared ledger and an open API connecting any user. According to Professor Kelman, "The applications that leverage the API for any given user's needs can be modified as appropriate without needing to modify the ledger itself. Also, having only one ledger eliminates errors that can creep in when transferring data from one database to another."[332]

Another big benefit of using blockchain is transparency. All of the government's interactions with vendors, such as requests for proposals, recommendations, and decisions, are recorded on the blockchain and viewable by permissioned parties. If an offer is rejected, for example, the information affecting that decision is available for protests and audits. Transparency also offers vendors access to the information in the ledger about them, so that they can detect and report any errors. "We're not going to share multiple industry partners' information with each other," said Arrieta. So-called permissioned blockchains allow distributed ledger managers discretion over who may view data. "But it's one transparent view that multiple stakeholders can see in real time, and it provides a trusted record of all of the interactions with one another."[333]

STATE OF DELAWARE'S BLOCKCHAIN INITIATIVE

Home to 1.2 million incorporated business entities, a well-established body of corporate law, and a sophisticated business court, the State of Delaware is widely regarded as the corporate capital of the United States, if not the world.[334] In 2016, 81 percent of all new US IPOs chose to incorporate in Delaware. The state remains the chosen home for more than half of all US publicly traded companies and 67 percent of Fortune 500 companies.[335]

On 1 August 2017, Delaware passed legislation that allowed corporations to use distributed databases and smart contracts to maintain a registry of stock issuances and transfers. State officials believe the blockchain ledger has enormous advantages—cost savings, error avoidance, accuracy of ownership records, and automation of administrative functions—for government and the companies registered in Delaware.

Under the old system, a corporate secretary or transfer agent maintained stock ledgers, manually updating them when shares changed hands. This paper-based system made tracking stock ownership burdensome, particularly as companies grow and change over time. Legal expert John Williams said, "It is a challenge to reconstruct the stockholders at any given point in time, including the exact number of shares held and any restrictions or agreements that apply to those shares, which impacts shareholder voting."[336]

The new Delaware legislation will allow existing corporations to convert their paper-based shares to distributed ledger shares, and new corporations will use electronic records from the outset. Corporate records will be easy to track and verify, allowing corporations to save significant time and money and avoid costly litigation.

How, specifically, will blockchain-based ledgers improve on current practice? The answer lies in the security, immutability, and efficiency of blockchain ledgers.

Currently, most corporate stock ledgers are stored on servers or "in the cloud" on a server network. This makes them vulnerable to hacking by outsiders and to manipulation/data entry error by insiders. Because this system results in a record that is less than fully dependable, companies are required to keep paper copies of documents to mitigate the risks.

In contrast, blockchain technology allows companies to store, manage, and share encrypted data on a distributed database. The system uses a vast network of encrypted servers, called nodes, to hold documents or digital signatures of encrypted documents. There is no central repository; instead, the digital assets are widely dispersed on a spiderweb of servers, and available only to those holding encryption keys.

The distributed ledger cannot be edited, even by an individual who holds all of the access keys. The stockholder record can be appended, but retroactive adjustments to the record cannot be made. This process generates a highly dependable audit trail that clearly—and indisputably—indicates how each stockholder acquired stock and from whom. That trail would be essential in a court of law, should a plaintiff dispute who the stockholders were at a given moment.

Eliminating paper records is a significant win, but users can gain potentially even greater efficiencies by speeding up incorporations, mergers, acquisitions, IPOs, and other sophisticated commercial transactions. Blockchain-based smart contracts, for example, will make it possible for parties to update, delete, and act upon records automatically when specific conditions are met, such as option expi-rations. Other possibilities include automatic updates to reflect name and address changes and amendments to collateral descriptions and secured parties.

Early adopters of blockchain stock ledgers include Medici Ventures and Overstock.com, and there are supporters in the legal community as well. "The technology is potentially incredibly power-ful," John Mark Zeberkiewicz told *Bloomberg BNA*. He's a partner at Delaware-based law firm Richards, Layton & Finger. "It can be used to create an immutable record of any number of transactions, not limited to the issue and transfer of shares, but theoretically any transaction that implicates or touches upon in any way the internal affairs of the corporation."[337]

SWEDEN'S LAND REGISTRY

The World Bank reported that, "despite [the] recognition that land rights are important, 70 percent of the world's population still lacks access to proper land titling or demarcation."[338] Even for countries with functioning land registries, keeping track of who owns what is difficult because the process is largely paper-based, people-driven, and therefore slow, costly, opaque, and vulnerable to human error and corruption. As tech reporter Joon Ian Wong put it, "Getting everyone to agree on every stage of a property transaction, and to record it permanently somewhere, is a feat of security, coordination, and trust."[339]

When it comes to putting national land registries on a block-chain, Sweden has made the greatest strides. Since June 2016, the Swedish Mapping, Cadastre, and Land Registration Authority (the *Lantmäteriet*, one of Sweden's oldest public institutions) has been testing how to record property transactions on a blockchain, in collab-oration with blockchain start-up ChromaWay, Landshypotek Bank, SBAB Bank, the mobile network operator Telia Company, and the consultancy Kairos Future. Early results were promising: they shaved some four months off the process and delivered a slew of other benefits, including greater user security, more transparent transactions, increased resilience of data in the land registry and the mortgage deed registry, increased liquidity of the real estate market, and better mortgage deed handling—for an estimated total benefit to Swedish society of over €100 million ($106 million).[340]

According to Wong, *Lantmäteriet* project owner Mats Snäll said, "Blockchain technology offers real digital trust. It's the only solution so far that handles digital originals, verifies both legal actions and processes, and secures transparency."[341] There are still legal and technical issues to resolve, from governance and process integration to the validity of digital signatures, before Sweden rolls the new system out to the public.

While Sweden is out in front, countries where land holdings have less certain ownership and fraud is more common will likely reap the greatest benefits of blockchain-based systems. Although blockchain does not eliminate the entry of incorrect data and the requirement for trusted inputs, countries with limited or no reliable land records will see blockchain registries as effective means of securing property ownership. According to the World Bank, a digital land registry could be the most cost-efficient and fastest way to increase gross domestic product in the medium term. It will serve as a foundation for better investments in land, enable the development of mortgage, credit, and insurance markets, and become an institution for trust in one of the most fundamental parts of an economy: land and real estate.

A SINGLE LEDGER FOR THE ACCOUNTS OF CANADA

According to Deloitte, "Organizations have traditionally recorded transactions in ledgers, kept under lock and key. Those ledgers are typically isolated to protect their accuracy and sanctity, and when conducting business, each organization maintains its own separate record, to verify information independently."[342] Most organizations—including the Government of Canada—maintain various trial balances, journal entries, sub-ledger extracts, account reconciliations, and supporting spreadsheet files in both electronic and manual formats.

In maintaining the accounts of Canada, the receiver general must consolidate the financial ledgers of 102 departments, each with its own financial system. In preparing summary trial balances, departments aggregate their detailed financial information to government-wide coding; the receiver general does not have visibility into the operations required to perform this amalgamation nor the actual detailed information itself. Mistakes and missing data are costly and labor-intensive to rectify. A lack of visibility into departmental data also limits public scrutiny and analysis of government spending and revenue streams.

With the proposed blockchain-enabled solution, Canada could consolidate multiple independent and isolated departmental ledgers into a single shared ledger that would retain a complete, indelible, and authoritative history of all transactions executed by the Government of Canada. Departments would no longer submit aggregate financial statements, as the blockchain would instantaneously encode each department's accounting entries into the single shared ledger managed by the receiver general.

Using a permissioned blockchain would ensure that the ledger is trusted and secure, while remaining easily accessible to key participants across the government. Such a system would eliminate layers of redundancy, increase the integrity and granularity of data, expedite auditing requirements, and enable the receiver general to refocus its energies on activities that would boost the efficacy and transparency of the government's accounting and reporting functions.

SOLUTION APPROACH

The proposed solution for the receiver general would take the form of a distributed blockchain ledger. Although the terms "distributed ledger" and "blockchain" are often treated as synonyms, blockchain is a specific type of distributed ledger, deployed in situations where parties to a transaction might not fully trust each other to agree on ledger updates, that is, one user might not accept the "truth" as reported by another user. Instead of using a third party or an offline reconciliation process, blockchain uses P2P protocols.

On a blockchain, nodes participating in the network arrange transactions in groups or batches called *blocks*. When parties broadcast their transactions to the network, various nodes on the network verify that the transaction data obey the rules and standards of that particular blockchain network and that the existing data have integrity. Once a majority of nodes agrees that the data are valid, all nodes in the network store the data as a new block in a chronological chain.

Cryptographic hash functions allow users to "hash" data in each block, which results in the persistence of a mathematical fingerprint representing the stored information. When a new block is assembled, the hashed value of the previous block is used to calculate the hashed value of the new block, creating a link between the blocks. Each block refers to the previous block, which forms a cryptographically linked chain—hence the name, *blockchain*. The chain's stored data and data references serve as a multilaterally accepted common repository for members of the blockchain network. Parties can update data only by appending new information to the ledger record.[343]

We can visualize blockchains as databases with sequential sets of validations not stored in central locations or managed by a few administrators. They are P2P networks that exist simultaneously on multiple nodes (computers): any interested or permissioned party can maintain a copy. They are distributed and redundant by design.

SOLUTION ARCHITECTURE

In the proposed solution, blockchain technology would enable departments to record and verify their transactions using a single shared ledger that would fulfill all of the accounting and auditing functions of the receiver general. Entries would be instantly hashed and time-stamped, creating an immutable record for each entry.

We can set up blockchains with varying degrees of access control. The creators of public blockchains, including Bitcoin, Ethereum, and most cryptocurrencies, designed them to be accessible by anyone with a computer and Internet access. These public blockchain platforms eliminate the need for intermediaries in any exchange value using P2P protocols.

Private blockchains, by contrast, essentially redefine the intermediary. Nodes in a private blockchain network require invitations and must be validated by the network administrator or a set of protocols that govern it. The access control mechanism may vary: existing participants could decide future entrants, a regulatory authority could issue licenses for participation, or a consortium could determine whom to include in the network.

Depending on the architecture of the blockchain, there can be varying tiers of access and participation within the network as well (Figure 5-1). Nodes that have access to read the ledger, for example, may not also receive permission to write to it or create new entries. Operators can allow only certain nodes to perform the verification process, and these trusted parties would be responsible for communicating newly verified transactions to the rest of the network. The responsibility for securing access to these nodes, including determining when and for whom to expand the set of trusted parties, rests with the blockchain system operator.

The receiver general could set up a permissioned distributed ledger and allow access to identical copies of the ledger to each federal department. Broadly speaking, the benefits of a private blockchain include faster transaction verification and network communication, the ability to fix errors and reverse transactions, and the ability to restrict access and reduce the likelihood of outsider attacks.

Using a permissioned network, the receiver general could assign differing roles to different departments (Table 5-1). Hyperledger

Fabric, for example, allows different classes of network participants: network proprietors, owners, members, users, and auditors.

FIGURE 5-1

POTENTIAL ARCHITECTURE OF GOVERNMENT BLOCKCHAIN

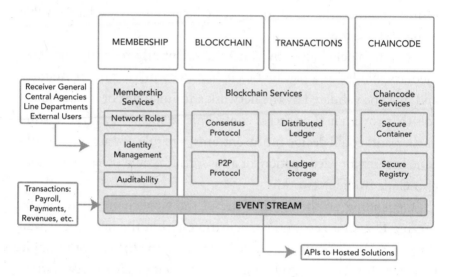

Source: "Introduction: Release 2.0," Hyperledger Fabric Documentation, Hyperledger, 2017, accessed 20 March 2018. Adapted by Anthony Williams under CC BY 4.0.

PUBLIC VERSUS PRIVATE BLOCKCHAIN CONSENSUS MECHANISMS

On public blockchain, participants submit transactions to the blockchain, but no new data are accepted without consensus. The process by which a network of nodes verifies new transactions is known as a *consensus protocol*. In the public blockchain system, all nodes follow an algorithm that verifies transactions by committing software and hardware resources to solving a problem by brute force (i.e., by solving a cryptographic puzzle). The node that finds the solution first is rewarded, and each new solution, along with the transactions used to verify it, forms the basis for the next puzzle.

TABLE 5-1

POTENTIAL ROLES, RIGHTS, AND RESPONSIBILITIES ASSIGNED TO DIFFERENT GOVERNMENT ACTORS

GOVERNMENT OFFICE	NETWORK ROLE	RIGHTS AND RESPONSIBILITIES
Receiver general	Network proprietor	Proprietors set up and define the purpose of a chain network. After launching a network, they become network owners and can validate transactions and invite other business partners to use or co-own the network.
Central agencies (treasury board, finance)	Network owners	Network owners are stakeholders of a network that can both initiate and validate transactions, invite new members or users to the network, and approve new owners.
Line departments	Network members	Members are participants of a blockchain network that cannot validate transactions but can initiate new transactions on the network.
Government auditors	Network auditors	These individuals or organizations have permission to interrogate transactions.
Citizens, businesses, suppliers, researchers	Network users	End users of a network can read and initiate transactions on a chain network through applications. Unlike network owners and members, users do not own nodes. They transact with the network through a member or owner node.

This process is designed to take time, currently around 10 minutes on the Bitcoin blockchain. Transactions are not considered fully verified for about one to two hours, after which point they are deep enough in the ledger that introducing a competing version of the ledger, known as a *fork*, would be computationally expensive. This delay is a vulnerability of the system, in that a transaction that initially appears verified may lose that status later. It is also a significant obstacle to adoption by financial traders, devices on the Internet of Things, and any participant relying on fast-paced transactions.

The most widely adopted approach to adding a new block to a chain is the *Nakamoto consensus protocol*. In this instance, the rate at which blocks can be created is limited, often by using a proof-of-work mechanism, whereby a processing node can only add a new block by demonstrating that a difficult computational task has been completed. Proof of work is widely used, but the auxiliary effort required to complete the difficult task can be economically inefficient and would not be justified in receiver general context.

Another option is a proof of stake, in which the processing node that can add a new block in the next round is determined by the size of its stakeholding in the global blockchain and/or in that round. Proof of stake can be more computationally efficient, but it has not yet been widely adopted because of concerns that rewarding those who already are most deeply involved in the network inherently creates an increasingly centralized system. Centralization is inimical to a truly robust network, and so a stakeholding approach is not a natural fit for this use case.

Instead of the Nakamoto consensus, private blockchains such as the one proposed here can use conventional replication algorithms. For example, Hyperledger, Stellar, and Ripple use *practical Byzantine fault tolerance*, which provides stronger guarantees about the completion of transactions, is more computationally efficient, and supports fewer processing nodes, all of which must be trusted actors.[344]

HOW PRACTICAL BYZANTINE FAULT TOLERANCE WORKS

When a node in the network receives a message, it runs a computation or operation using that message along with its internal state (i.e., the values of its internal variables at any given time in an object-oriented programming environment).[345] This computation informs how the node interprets that message (e.g., whether to accept a transaction as valid). The node then broadcasts its decision to all other nodes in the network. The blockchain updates according to the consensus decision determined by the total decisions submitted by the nodes—that is, a majority vote of validating nodes on the network.[346]

For the receiver general's single ledger, departments would initiate transactions (e.g., payments to employees or vendors) and the receiver general (and possibly other federal entities) would interrogate the transactions to ensure they are valid. The government could customize its approach to validating transactions. For example, Hyperledger Fabric uses an endorsement policy to define which network members must agree on the results of a transaction before they add it to the ledger.[347] Fabric includes a small domain-specific language for endorsement policies, such as:

- Government of Canada peers A, B, C, and F must all endorse transactions of type P (e.g., payroll transactions)

- A majority (51+%) of peers in the network must endorse transactions of type V (e.g., payments to vendors)

- At least three peers of A, B, C, D, E, F, and G must endorse transactions of type R (e.g., departmental revenues)

Regardless of the protocol used, once network members reach consensus, the transaction data are time-stamped and their corresponding metadata are appended to the ledger and replicated to all other nodes (members) on the network. In this instance, the network would add validated transactions to the Government of Canada's ledger and update the DFMS.

USER EXPERIENCE

A blockchain ledger would introduce several advantageous changes to the user experience for government departments, the receiver general, and government auditors.

Automation of reconciliation and reporting. The ability of departments to enter and verify transactions directly on the blockchain in near real-time would eliminate the need for time-intensive offline or batch reconciliation processes between the RG-GL and the departmental financial management systems. Rather, verified transactions in the blockchain would be used to update the receiver general's ledger and the DFMS simultaneously.

Transparency and granularity. The receiver general and government auditors would gain near real-time visibility into individual transactions (i.e., revenues and payments) conducted across the network of federal departments. Under the current system, the information received on a monthly basis is a summary-level trial balance prepared by all departments by aggregating their detailed financial information to government-wide coding—information the receiver general cannot access otherwise. Since transactions recorded on a blockchain could be coded, a shared blockchain ledger could amalgamate transactions for producing the public accounts of Canada without losing the granularity of transaction data, which would reside in the shared ledger.

Reduced fraud. A blockchain solution would ensure that the government's financial records are tamper-proof and would reduce the scope for entering fraudulent transactions or falsifying information. The use of cryptographically linked blocks would ensure that no one could alter or delete records without detection.

Value-added auditing. A blockchain ledger would allow government auditors to verify a large portion of the most important data behind the financial accounts of individual departments automatically. The cost and time necessary to conduct a financial audit would decline considerably. With blockchain-enabled digitization, auditors could deploy more automation, analytics, and machine-learning capabilities such as automatically alerting relevant parties about unusual transactions on a near real-time basis. Supporting documentation—contracts, purchase orders, and invoices—could be encrypted and securely stored or linked to a blockchain.

These improvements would free auditors to spend time where they could add more value, such as analyzing complex dealings, recommending improvements in public spending process, and ensuring adequate internal controls and processes for departments to measure and report on their performance.

ADAPTATION OF THE RECEIVER GENERAL MANDATE AND WORKFLOW

Introducing a shared blockchain ledger would introduce substantive changes to the receiver general's mandate and workflow. Automating the labor-intensive reconciliation process will free the receiver general to focus more on upgrading the efficacy, timeliness, and transparency of government accounting and reporting functions. Consider the following:

Network governance. As governor of the blockchain network, the receiver general would be responsible for managing participants and their various roles in initiating and validating transactions. The receiver general would also be responsible for any updates to the consensus protocol for verifying transactions.

Blockchain training. Transitioning to blockchain solutions will require education and training for financial executives and departmental leaders. The receiver general could partner with technology leaders in the federal government to educate executives on how blockchain works and how it will transform financial management and accounting.

Data integrity. The success of a blockchain ledger depends on the quality of the data going in. By spending less on manual reconciliations, the receiver general could be more involved in doing quality control of the data management practices at the departmental level.

Data transparency and open government. On a public blockchain, any member of the public could view each record; any person could verify the authenticity of a transaction. This granularity would be overkill for releasing meaningful information about government revenues and spending to Canadians and would compromise the privacy of the individuals and entities that transact with the government. In some instances, it could pose a threat to national security.

However, the receiver general could build external applications that would interface with the blockchain ledger to make information accessible without sacrificing privacy or national security. For example, the receiver general could create smart contracts with rules and algorithms that allowed data in the blockchain ledger to be automatically shared with third parties, once predefined conditions were met. Researchers, journalists, citizens, industry associations, and other interested parties could use such applications.

CHALLENGES AND RISK MANAGEMENT

Blockchain is an emerging technology, and therefore carries some risks for early adopters. On one hand, the flexibility of the blockchain ecosystem offers organizations customized implementation to meet their needs. However, this diversity can impede the development of standards and best practices, creating a burden for training the workforce and building, operating, securing, maintaining, and defending the technology for users in government. What follows are some of the key risks that the receiver general must consider in evaluating the potential for using blockchain to create a single digital ledger for the public accounts of Canada.

Blockchain implementation skills. Blockchain solutions are currently built in modern programming languages. For example, Bitcoin uses C++, Ethereum uses JavaScript and Solidity for smart contracts, and Hyperledger, the Go language and Java. Programmers at established software vendors can shift to blockchain development with minimal requirements, whereas government IT employees may require training in blockchain and underlying programming languages. Sourcing the right talent to manage a government-wide blockchain implementation will be challenging, given the technology industry's current shortage of skilled workers and the government's hiring challenges.

Interoperability with blockchain. Blockchain is not a plug-and-play technology. On the contrary, blockchain solutions need to replace or tightly integrate or interoperate with existing systems. Most federal departments have aging infrastructure or legacy IT systems, which may impede blockchain adoption. With 102 federal departments, each with its own unique financial management system, the transition to a blockchain-enabled ledger will not be smooth. We need to investigate the blockchain compatibility of these systems as part of our feasibility study.

Modernizing policies and procedures. To adopt blockchain across the Government of Canada, each federal department must consider its existing policies, procedures, and financial management practices with an intent to update incompatible elements. According to the blockchain working group of the American Council for Technology–Industry Advisory Council, outdated legacy policies will impede IT operations in transitioning to a distributed model. In particular, legacy data exchange procedures will hinder a blockchain platform's operation and restrict its interaction with other government systems, be they internal or external. A blockchain system will not thrive over time if the participating federal departments cannot evolve with it. "Blockchain is still a very early technology and will require a healthy amount of flexibility and adaptability for any early adopters."[348]

Computational power. Running a government-wide blockchain ledger that records all the transactions of the Government of Canada would require a significant amount of computational power. To reach consensus, each node in a network must solve a cryptographic problem and show a proof of work. The amount of computational power—and electricity consumption—needed in the proof-of-work method increases with the scale of the network.

Security. The security of a blockchain network generally grows with the number of members supporting consensus, as more sharing and agreeing on data means that more nodes would need to collude or be simultaneously manipulated in any attempt to attack the system and alter its individual databases. Theoretically, miners can collude to append false transactions into the blockchain, but the probability of success diminishes with an increasing number of nodes required to verify each transaction.

Nevertheless, the presence of giant mining pools and the other massive bitcoin-mining conglomerates concentrated in countries with low electricity prices is a growing concern within the community, given the risk that such conglomerates could establish the critical mass required to monopolize control over a blockchain effectively.

In the absence of numbers, private blockchains achieve security by giving their operators control over who can read the ledger of verified transactions, who can submit transactions, and who can verify them. In other words, security is based on limiting participation to trusted actors. In the receiver general use case, limiting participation to federal departments should rule out the presence of malicious users.

Implementing blockchain is challenging, but these challenges are not insurmountable. Any new technology always carries risk, but the public sector has a history of successfully, if slowly and cautiously, navigating those risks. The growing adoption of cloud computing is among the most recent examples. Given that the receiver general is preplanning its IT modernization, it has an opportunity to include a blockchain solution in its road maps now and to launch small-scale proofs of concepts and pilot projects in cooperation with willing early adopters. Meanwhile, it can leverage lessons learned and proven best practices from early adopters in other jurisdictions.

IMPLEMENTATION COSTS

Feedback from blockchain vendors suggests that it is too early to offer an accurate estimate of the costs and benefits of designing, building, and implementing a blockchain-enabled ledger for the receiver general. Vendors raised these considerations.

Heterogeneity of financial management systems in the federal government. Each of the 102 departments in the federal government has a unique financial management system. Therefore, we need a more detailed technical assessment of the extent to which existing systems could interoperate with blockchain and whether we would need to upgrade, modify, or replace DFMS wholesale to integrate a blockchain-enabled ledger into the compiling of the public accounts of Canada.

Differing departmental capacities to adjust to blockchain-enabled solutions. We need a similar analysis of capacity building, training, and process redesign needed to support the implementation of blockchain technology. In the launch of the Phoenix pay system, we learned that the ongoing capacity-building and support costs of implementation can easily exceed the cost of the initial technical build and system implementation.

Lack of comparable reference cases. There are no other comparable implementations of blockchain technology in government at this scale. The land and corporate stock registries are significantly less complex than a whole-of-government adoption of a distributed ledger for the public accounts of Canada. Estonia's implementation of blockchain-enabled systems is far-reaching, but Estonia is working with a much smaller bureaucracy and far fewer legacy systems.

Rapidly evolving blockchain ecosystem. Blockchain technologies are still immature and constantly evolving. Interoperability between blockchain and the leading enterprise resource planning and financial management solutions is also advancing; whether and how these advances will roll out to existing users in government is unclear. Thus, the costs of design and implementation will depend on the state of evolution of the component technologies. Given these factors, along with the Government of Canada's experience with the Phoenix pay system, the receiver general should adopt a cautious and incremental approach to blockchain technology.

TRIPLE-ENTRY ACCOUNTING

According to some blockchain enthusiasts, blockchain is disrupting the centuries-old standard of double-entry bookkeeping and giving rise to a new paradigm—triple-entry accounting—that will rock the world of chief financial officers, controllers, corporate auditors, and certified or chartered public accountants. It is hyperbole based on misunderstandings of both double and triple entries.

In the double-entry method, every financial transaction has an equal and opposite effect in at least two different accounts, in the form of debits and credits. It is used to complete this equation:

Assets = Liabilities + Equity

In other words, double-entry bookkeeping allows organizations to maintain records of their assets and liabilities that reflect what they own and owe, and what they have earned and spent over any given period of time.

In 1982, Yuji Ijiri, a professor of accounting and economics at the Graduate School of Industrial Administration at Carnegie Mellon University, added a third component—momentum—after the global standard debit and credit.[349] While he used the phrase, "triple-entry accounting," he did not coin it—Russian scholars did, around 1900—nor did he view his system as paradigm-shifting; he considered double-entry accounting highly extensible.[350]

In 2005, Ian Grigg argued that the cryptographically sealed record of transactions—effectively a shared receipt—was the equivalent of a "third entry" that could extend double-entry systems:

> The digitally signed receipt, with the entire authorization for a transaction, represents a dramatic challenge to double-entry bookkeeping at least at the conceptual level. The cryptographic invention of the digital signature gives powerful evidentiary force to the receipt, and in practice reduces the accounting problem to one of the receipt's presence or its absence. This problem is solved by sharing the records—each of the agents has a good copy. … This leads to the pairs of double entries connected by the central list of receipts; three entries for each transaction.[351]

Ben Taylor, CEO of SoftLedger, a cloud accounting software company, argued that Grigg's use of the phrase is confusing to accounting professionals and misleading to technologists: the presence of a digitally signed receipt is not a fundamental departure from double-entry accounting. He pointed out a common misconception, that "the writing of each piece of information to the blockchain is actually a third entry. It's not."[352]

Numerous blockchain commentators have used "double-entry accounting" to refer to the recording of a single transaction between two parties in the separate accounting records of each party—such as a buyer and a seller recording the sale and the purchase of an asset in their respective books.[353] In this misrepresentation of double-entry accounting, the act of recording a transaction on the blockchain "creates an interlocking system of enduring accounting records" between the two parties, "rather than these entries occurring separately in independent sets of books."[354] Hence, the flawed notion of the third entry.

This misrepresentation is unfortunate, but it should not diminish the value of blockchain in accounting applications. The ability to write transactions to a blockchain in real time and between multiple parties is powerful. A ledger that shows the entire sequence and relationship among transactions provides not simply a credible audit

trail but real-time status—the network state—of all transactions relevant to the parties.

CONCLUSIONS AND RECOMMENDATIONS

In sector after sector, algorithmic techniques have extended well beyond their origins in cryptocurrencies to become tools to record, enable, and secure huge numbers and varieties of transactions, incorporating rules, smart contracts, and digital signatures among many emerging technologies. Jurisdictions ranging from Estonia to the United States are using blockchain to power innovations in business registration, identity management, e-voting, healthcare, and international trade. Based on our research, we recommend the following:

Examine the potential for significant process efficiencies. For the Government of Canada, trial balances, journal entries, sub-ledger extracts, account reconciliations, and supporting spreadsheet files likely exist in various electronic and manual formats. With the proposed blockchain-enabled solution, it could consolidate multiple independent and isolated departmental ledgers into a single shared ledger that would retain a complete, indelible, and authoritative history of all transactions by the government. Entering and verifying transactions directly on the blockchain could eliminate time-intensive offline or batch reconciliation processes between the RG-GL and the departmental financial management systems.

Begin to reimagine the role and responsibilities of government auditors. The receiver general and government auditors would gain near real-time visibility into individual transactions, as opposed to aggregated summaries. With real-time access to unalterable audit evidence (e.g., agreements, purchase orders, and invoices), auditors could improve the pace of financial reporting and auditing. Auditors could spend more time probing complex transactions, recommending how to improve the efficacy and efficiency of public spending, and ensuring that departments have adequate internal controls and processes for measuring and reporting on their performance.

Begin to reimagine the role of the receiver general. Automating the labor-intensive reconciliation process, in particular, will free the receiver general to focus more on upgrading the efficacy, timeliness, and transparency of government accounting and reporting functions. New roles for the receiver general would include managing participants and their various roles in initiating and validating transactions on the ledger as well as building external applications that would boost the transparency of the government's reporting process.

Understand the trade-offs between private and public ledgers. With greater security and access control, a permissioned blockchain solution would allow access to identical copies of a ledger to a limited number of preselected trusted participants, namely each federal department and the receiver general. The benefits of a private or permissioned blockchain include faster transaction verification and network communication and the abilities to fix errors, reverse transactions, restrict access, and reduce the likelihood of outsider attacks. Using a permissioned network, the receiver general could choose to assign differing roles to different departments.

Include a blockchain-enabled ledger in forward-looking IT plans. Blockchain is still an emerging technology and carries some risks for early adopters. Technical staff will require training in blockchain and underlying programming languages. Most federal departments have aging infrastructure and/or legacy IT systems in critical functions, which may impede blockchain adoption. A blockchain system will likely not succeed long term unless the participating federal departments evolve with it. The receiver general has an opportunity to include a blockchain solution in its road map now and to leverage lessons and proven practices of early adopters elsewhere.

Proceed with an incremental approach. In light of the implementation challenges, and the evolving state of blockchain technologies, the receiver general should adopt a cautious and incremental approach to blockchain technology. A proposed first step is an in-depth feasibility study of cost and implementation-related parameters discussed. As a second step, pending the outcome of the feasibility study, the receiver general should work with two or three early adopter departments to design and test a POC and run a multiyear pilot to test assumptions and conclusions of the feasibility study.

QUESTIONS TO ASK IN DEVELOPING PROOF OF CONCEPT

How much does the current system of accounting cost to administer, for a department and for the government as a whole?

How would a blockchain solution affect the mandate and function of those responsible for government accounts?

Will the system align with existing laws and regulations?

Will changes to legal or regulatory frameworks facilitate adoption or effectiveness?

Could the solution leverage existing blockchain-based accounting efforts in either the public or private sectors?

Are there financial or fiduciary risks associated with the solution? If so, could those risks be mitigated?

How would a blockchain ledger change the user experience for government departments and/or affect other stakeholders such as government auditors and the public?

What will such a system cost each department and the government as a whole?

Ultimately, the core question facing the receiver general is: do we go ahead, invest in this emerging technology, and embrace the required changes in technology, processes, and organizational design, or do we focus on improving the existing system and optimizing its processes?

QUESTIONS TO ASK IN AN AFTER-ACTION REVIEW

How much did it cost to build a blockchain POC?

How much did it cost to run a multiyear pilot process, including costs to support the implementation of the blockchain technology, such as investments in process redesign, capacity building, and ongoing technical support?

Were administrative efficiencies realized or demonstrated over the course of the pilot?

Based on these costs and benefits, what are the estimated costs and benefits of scaling the solution across the federal government?

What is the cost-benefit analysis of status quo versus a blockchain-based system?

If departments jointly participate in building and administering a shared blockchain ledger, how will the government account for pro-rata share of costs for each department?

Given the estimated benefits, over what time horizon should the government expect to see a payback on its investment?

Collaborate with stakeholders. The receiver general should work closely with involved departmental financial managers to understand sunk costs, operational costs (i.e., departmental overhead), and costs borne by the receiver general. These will be important data when comparing costs and benefits of the status quo with blockchain-based processes. The receiver general and departmental financial managers should coordinate the tracking and analysis of efficiencies and benefits arising from a blockchain-enabled pilot. Given the learning curve and organizational adjustments in play, participants may not realize efficiencies and benefits until the second year of the pilot, once they better understand its effects on organizational design and financial management processes.

CHAPTER 6

MANAGING BLOCKCHAIN TRANSPARENCY

Strategies for a Private/Open World

Andreas Park

 BLOCKCHAIN TRANSPARENCY IN BRIEF

- The advent of blockchain technology forces us to reconsider the upside and downside of public revelation of transactions and contracts. The implementation, application, and possible regulation of distributed ledgers involve choices that will critically affect information disclosure and economic interactions.

- Blockchain technology can facilitate the monitoring of a firm's investment decisions by storing contracts and transactions in a manner that is comparatively inexpensive and inherently visible to anyone who has access to the Internet.

- It does not matter whether the blockchain is public and permissionless, such as the Bitcoin or Ethereum blockchains, or private and permissioned, such as Ripple or Hyperledger implementations: in principle, transactions are traceable with attribution of actions to identifiers. Therefore, the technology has a native high level of transparency.

- Users can still protect their privacy in both private and public blockchains: some methods are procedural and involve the smart usage of the protocol, whereas others are technological and use mathematics.

INTRODUCTION TO REAL-TIME INFORMATION SYMMETRY

On 19 October 2001, Enron Corp.'s multiyear success story ended without anyone's living happily ever after: the firm announced $638 million in quarterly losses and a $1.2 billion reduction in shareholder equity. Fast forward a few months, following an SEC and US Department of Justice investigation, the world learned that Enron management had fudged the books and hidden massive debt obligations in complex accounting constructs. Enron executives received 24-year prison sentences, which was little consolation to tens of thousands of Enron and Arthur Andersen employees who lost their jobs and pensions and to shareholders who saw $65 billion of equity disappear. Several more accounting scandals later, US Congress passed the Sarbanes-Oxley Act, which tightened disclosure, accounting, and accountability standards.

Taking a step back, let's ask ourselves: what is the root problem that regulators and legislators have been trying to solve? Lenders want to know whether a borrower is likely to pay back a loan, and equity investors want to know whether they are likely to receive a return on their investment, particularly whether the current market price of a public company indeed reflects the intrinsic value of a share. Yet, time and time again, managers of banks, corporations, accounting firms, and government agencies have been caught in lies.

Asymmetric information, when one side of a deal has better information than the other and can use it to the latter's detriment, is toxic for the functioning of markets. For this reason, an elaborate and often burdensome system of regulations exists to reduce this asymmetry by mandating regular and accurate disclosures. Accounting rules give managers leeway to reallocate funds and revenues inside the company. Moreover, accounting reports are published intermittently, and there is ample evidence that managers engage in numerous economically pointless yet costly activities such as earnings "smoothing." Finally, the external certification of the books is expensive.

Supplying intermittent reports was appropriate, time-consuming, and costly in the pre-digital world: management needed to aggregate information from various units and pay a third party to check and verify it before mailing it to shareholders. Today, firms have electronic accounting systems: executives get financial information in real time but have chosen not to share such raw and unaudited data streams with investors.

In principle, blockchain technology allows firms to disclose verified financial transactions publicly, directly, and in real time. It also allows them to disclose an extensive set of contracts. These published deals would be in the form of code that would eliminate ambiguity about a firm's financial condition and commitments. Although fraudulent activities are still possible, many of the deals that led, for instance, to the demise of Enron would no longer be possible.[355] Assets couldn't appear to be owned by two parties at once, hiding liabilities would be impossible, and would-be Enrons couldn't attract such positive media attention and additional funding as Enron did.

THE BENEFITS OF SHARED KNOWLEDGE

A critical component of asset ownership and of a contract is attribution: who holds the asset, and who has established and is party to the contract? A blockchain stores this information by recording asset origination and transactions, and thus changes of ownership within a distributed (as opposed to central) ledger. This complete record of transactions and contracts establishes the current owner of an asset. Ownership is attributed to an address, which is simply a set of letters and numerals and can be thought of as an identifier.

By recording transactions on a blockchain, a network with multiple parties has shared knowledge of past and current ownership of assets. An intrinsic part of the technology is thus that there is some degree of transparency regarding past actions and present ownership. Indeed, by default, the transaction attribution is entirely transparent to anyone with access to the network. In principle, the addresses or IDs are anonymous.

Had Enron's management been required to disclose the firm's addresses publicly, then investors and oversight bodies could have traced the movement of assets and liabilities. The beauty of blockchain-based transactions is that disclosure is inherent. In principle, those with access to the blockchain's information can have the same information about a firm as the firm's managers. This feature may reduce the costs of generating accounting statements and performing audits.[356] There are further cost savings: asymmetric information is a risk, for which financiers require compensation. By reducing information asymmetry, firms reduce risk and lower their cost of capital; they have more money for investment and research, and they can use these funds to build better products and increase employment. Blockchain technology can therefore be a catalyst for incremental economic growth.

HOW MUCH IS *TOO MUCH* TRANSPARENCY?

For all its virtues, transparency affects the economic interactions of market participants, and it can have downsides. For instance, an investment dealer is asked by a client to absorb a large position because the client has a liquidity need. The investment dealer now has a risk on its book that it doesn't want. In a relatively liquid market, this problem may be small because the dealer will likely be able to trade out of the position quickly. But, in a fairly liquid market, the client probably wouldn't have approached the dealer in the first place. In an illiquid market, with few prospective counterparties, the dealer has to worry about a *squeeze*: a well-capitalized bandit trader may be able to move the market against the dealer and force the dealer to liquidate the position at a fire sale price. The dealer does not want the public to see its risky position.

Should we care about the dealer? I believe we must. The risk of a position squeeze is real, dealers want to be compensated, and thus either the cost of trading illiquid assets goes up or markets for illiquid assets collapse altogether.

Put differently, there are legitimate reasons to settle transactions on a highly transparent blockchain and legitimate concerns about such transparency. Indeed, when confronted with the concept of a public blockchain that records all transactions publicly, financial industry executives were put off—not on their watch!

The alternative is a permissioned, private blockchain, organized and controlled by a known and trusted consortium of entities such as banks. The assumption is that the level of visibility of such a private distributed ledger or blockchain is a design choice. But matters are not that simple: even a private blockchain, possibly organized by a consortium of banks still involves the record keeping of everyone's transactions in each node of the distributed network. In other words, even in a private blockchain, our competitors can see our activities.

Is that the end of the discussion? No. If banks have concerns about lack of privacy, then they should not be using the Internet either. Instead, I believe that the discussion around transparency should focus on the desired, socially optimal level of transparency. This level is a critical design choice for firms that wish to establish a private blockchain. Moreover, regulators and lawmakers need to carefully think about what disclosure they require of corporate users of public blockchains.

In this chapter, I outline how the recording of information on a blockchain differs from that in the current world of asset transfers, and who gets to see what information. Changes in transparency have economic consequences and may create winners and loser. I will therefore describe the business cases against and for transparency. Finally, I discuss the technological solutions that exist to reduce the built-in full transparency of blockchains.

NATIVE TRANSPARENCY IN BLOCKCHAIN TECHNOLOGY

OWNERSHIP TRANSFERS: CENTRAL REGISTRIES VERSUS DISTRIBUTED LEDGERS

To illustrate the possible transparency issues, let's look at the workings of blockchain technology and how they relate to the transparency of actions and holdings.

All non-physical, non-registered asset transfers require a mechanism to change the record of ownership. At present, centralized ledgers keep most such records, and only highly trusted parties can access and modify these records. Cash is kept in bank accounts, and a bank account is a central registry. The record of ownership of a house is kept in a property registry. Securities such as stocks, too, are kept in central securities depositories such as the DTCC in the United States or the Canadian Depository for Securities (CDS).[357] Finally, records of most bilateral contracts are commonly kept by the parties involved, and transactions that the terms of the contract trigger thus involve a complicated account-reconciliation process. Consumer loan agreements are usually additionally registered with the credit bureau, such as Equifax or TransUnion.[358]

Blockchain technology is a consensus protocol to change records in distributed ledgers, and its setup defines who can make changes to the ledger and under what circumstances. At its core, a blockchain is an append-only protocol that stores "transactions," where in principle a transaction can be a trade but also text-based information such as a piece of programming code. The key feature of a blockchain is that, by recording transactions, it ensures a consensus on the current owner of an asset. Anyone can explore token transfers on the Ethereum blockchain using the public website *Etherscan.io*, which pulls data from the Ethereum blockchain; or the Bitcoin blockchain using the website *Blockchain.info*.

OWNERSHIP TRANSFERS: PUBLIC VERSUS PRIVATE BLOCKCHAINS

Let's consider the differences in data storage. To date, most firms still store enterprise data in a central database. This setup is simple and easy to understand. Also, since all information is stored and changed at a central location, one party cannot sell the same asset or spend the same dollar twice. Think about a bank account: Bob cannot send the same dollar to both Sue and Alice, and Bob cannot use the same asset as collateral in two transactions. The centralization of data storage prevents this double-spend problem.

There are, however, many concerns with central databases, foremost among them, security: if the database fails because of, say, a major hardware failure, all data might be lost. For that reason, keepers of central databases always make backups—and a backup model is one step closer to a distributed database. Namely, the keepers need to update their backups continuously to avoid data loss and thus need a backup protocol to ensure that data in the backup is accurate.

A distributed database shares features with a central-backup system in that it keeps all information at several locations. The key difference is that in a distributed database, there is no single primary location from which all changes originate. Instead, each site can make changes to the data.

There are numerous advantages to this setting: there is no single point of failure, all data are available locally, and the system can be set up so that the different locations need not trust one another, yet all sites continuously agree on the content of the database. According to Richard Gendal Brown from R3, "[a] system … that [is] operated by multiple parties, none of whom fully trust each other, that nevertheless come[s] into and remain[s] in consensus as to the nature and evolution of a set of shared facts."[359]

However, a side effect of a distributed database is that *all* information is stored at *all* locations. So, for instance, if a set of banks organizes the distributed ledger (wherein each bank is a network node), then every bank holds the information of all other banks' accounts. Such an arrangement raises red flags for executives, and so we need to understand what the information reveals (because storing information is not synonymous with accessing it).

There are two main types of distributed ledgers: *public* and *private*.

A public ledger is permissionless: anyone can become a network node and anyone can, in principle, enter records in the ledger. The most prominent examples are the Bitcoin and Ethereum blockchains. Indeed, the process of becoming a network node is part of using the blockchain: as a first step to use the Ethereum blockchain, one downloads a so-called wallet software; an example is the "Mist wallet." These wallets monitor the Ethereum blockchain to find transactions that have been sent to the wallet. As part of the process, one downloads the information from the Ethereum blockchain and becomes a node.

A private distributed ledger, in contrast, is built by either an individual firm or by a consortium of firms and differs from public distributed ledgers in several key ways. First, a private network can be permissioned and can thus restrict who can use it to record transactions and can view the flow of information and assets across it. For financial institutions, this feature is important as it allows them to comply with KYC legislation, which is a usually a prerequisite for compliance with AML rules. Moreover, in principle, these networks don't need a trustless protocol. A downside is that a consortium solution raises the specter of collusion and rent extraction typical of a trust; for instance, network members may restrict entry, fix prices, and collude on fees. From a competition policy perspective, it may thus be desirable to mandate a trustless protocol to remove a barrier for new entrants wishing to join a consortium network.

Figure 6-1 illustrates the workings of the verification of a blockchain transaction.[360] The key idea is that a user's blockchain address has (implicitly) two components, a public one and a private one.

Everyone can see every transaction linked to the public portion of an address; the private component is used to sign the transaction. Furthermore, the public key is a crucial component in the verification that the user indeed authorized the transaction. The appendix explains how to obtain an address and transfer funds to this address.[361]

FIGURE 6-1

SIGNING AND VERIFYING TRANSACTIONS WITH PUBLIC AND PRIVATE KEYS

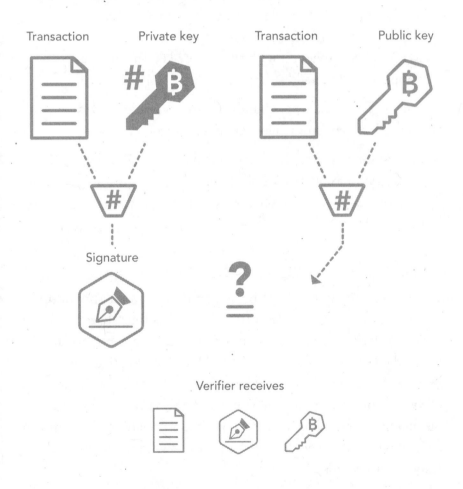

Icons © 2017 Smashicons and Freepick. Used with permission.

IN A NUTSHELL: HOW A BLOCKCHAIN TRANSFER WORKS

Step 0: Two parties agree on a transfer of specific funds or other assets.

Step 1: The buyer (identified by an address) of an item sends a message to the blockchain network asking to initiate the transfer to a seller (an address).

Step 2: The network checks whether the buyer has funds specified and whether the buyer can verify that he or she is authorized to initiate the transfer; this verification requires signing the transaction with the private key/the private component of the address.

Step 3: Transactions are bundled into blocks and added to the chain based on the blockchain's protocol.

Step 4: Once a block has been added to the chain, the transaction has settled. Implicitly, the buyer's account has been decreased and the seller's account increased by the transferred amount.

The takeaway of this discussion is that a blockchain records all transactions with IDs of buyers and sellers, that this information is kept at each node, and that this info is thus shared across a wide network. Critically, one must not mistake a *private* distributed ledger with a blockchain protocol for a solution that guarantees *privacy*. On the contrary, the protocol above and the attribution of ownership to IDs in principle works the same way in a private blockchain. The main difference is that a private blockchain can control whether anyone other than the network members sees the transaction records.

TRANSPARENCY AS A RISK AND AN ASSET

In many situations, transparency is a double-edged sword, and some of the parties that may benefit the most from it are also the most fevered opponents. In the introduction to this chapter, I have already highlighted intermediaries as strong opponents, for instance because absorbing client inventories exposes intermediaries to risk. Transparency of past transactions and holdings may also help them identify possible counterparties.[362]

TRANSPARENCY AS A STRATEGIC RISK

The market for corporate bonds illustrates the complexity of this issue. At the beginning of the last century, corporate bonds were regularly traded on stock exchanges such as the New York Stock Exchange. But over time, this market moved almost entirely to over-the-counter arrangements; even though there have been significant advances in trading technology, this multimillion-dollar market is still surprisingly low-tech, as most trades are arranged in phone conversations or via Bloomberg chat.

The industry also strongly resists attempts to increase transparency, even in terms of post-trade information. For instance, the introduction of the US National Association of Securities Dealers' (NASD) Trade Reporting and Compliance Engine (TRACE) in 2002 and similar efforts by the Investment Industry Regulatory Organization of Canada were met with much resistance. O'Hara, Wang, and Zhou provide one possible explanation: active traders, presumably regular customers, get better prices, and dominant dealers tend to offer worse prices.[363] These findings suggest that dealers have margins to protect. Noncompetitive margins, however, ultimately come at the issuers' expense because investors will price-in liquidity costs.

At the same time, start-up fintech firms such as Algomi, which offer systematic, algorithmic matching of corporate bond trading posi- tions, report that some of their biggest clients are intermediaries. In other words, dealers recognize the usefulness of liquidity-enhancing technology. Similarly, there is ample evidence that market prices after the introduction of TRACE became significantly more precise. More accurate, efficient prices benefit intermediaries as a whole because poor pricing increases a risk.

Sell-side intermediaries are, however, not the only parties that worry about too much transparency. A host of research shows that institutional investors, in particular, are very concerned that competi- tors might imitate their trading strategies. For instance, mutual funds are required to publicly disclose their holdings regularly in 13-F forms; and Christoffersen, Danesh, and Musto document that actively managed mutual funds commonly delay publishing this information for as long as possible.[364] In other words, these funds try to obfuscate their activities for as long as possible, presumably because they worry about losing their competitive advantage. Furthermore, on a more short-term basis, institutional traders spend much effort hiding their trading activities: instead of trading a large quantity in one go, they use complex computer algorithms that "shred" their large orders into tiny pieces. They do this to avoid being detected by the market at large because, as van Kervel and Menkveld report, the longer they spend working their orders over a day, the more likely other smart algorith- mic traders detect these orders and move the price against them.[365]

Over the last 20 years, many firms left the public equity markets: the number of publicly listed firms in the States has dropped by over 40 percent since its height in the late 1990s, and some of the exit- ing firms are household names such as Dell and Safeway. Other highly successful and famous firms such as Uber avoid the public markets deliberately.[366] There are numerous reasons for this trend, but mandated public disclosure for publicly listed firms is an often-cited one.[367] CEOs have to publicly disclose their salaries, and financial disclosure may expose firms to the risk of revealing competitive or strategic business information.

In addition to situations when some parties desire privacy, there are situations where privacy is a necessity. A good example is blockchain-based voting. The underlying idea of using a blockchain for voting is to issue digital, single-use tokens to eligible voters. With a controlled and auditable supply and distribution of tokens, it would be difficult to manipulate a vote. However, at the same time in democratic, political elections, votes must be private, and thus privacy is essential. In other situations, a public vote may be desirable: for instance, in votes during general shareholder assemblies, as recently introduced by the TMX Group, shareholders may want to know if their proxy votes have been used as promised.

Existing blockchain technology can address many of the issues of transparency highlighted here. The arguments presented here are not against the usage of blockchain solutions.

TRANSPARENCY AS A STRATEGIC ASSET

The advent of the Internet and of electronic documents and data vastly increased the information that investors, consumers, trading partners, and regulators can obtain about firms, governments, nongovernmental organizations, and people. Over time, many of these entities have learned to embrace transparency and to use it in their favor. Blockchain technology enables firms to benefit from transparency both directly and indirectly.

Indirect effects: Reputation and perceived integrity

There is a long-standing literature in management science that studies the *indirect* effects of transparency.[368] This literature posits that transparency should be a core principle of responsible management practice, and researchers have found ample evidence that organizations that embrace transparency benefit greatly. These benefits are, in my view, indirect, because many of the reported benefits that derive from a firm's openness improve relationships over time. For instance, in many business dealings, one party gains knowledge about the other, and for a successful relationship, parties need to trust one another that one side of a deal will not exploit this knowledge. A common approach of firms to increase trust is to publish the adopted ethical codes of conduct, which makes it easier for employees to know what is expected and create credibility in business dealings. Furthermore, sharing relevant information with partners and supply-chain members in a timely manner improves trust, and can generally lift a firm's brand.

As Tapscott outlines, there are five elements for firm success with increased transparency and public scrutiny. Firms need to

- Create true value that withstands the scrutiny that transparency brings about.
- Understand customers and build relationship capital.
- Protect customers' privacy.
- Behave with integrity since lapses are caught quickly in a transparent world.
- Be candid as shortcomings can be seen quickly.[369]

Many of these principles apply in a world where financial transactions and contracts are visible on a blockchain. Indeed, Parris et al. define transparency as "[t]he extent to which a stakeholder perceives an organization provides learning opportunities about itself."[370] Transactions and smart contracts (pieces of programming code) visible on a blockchain deliver "hard" information (and thus learning opportunities) in that the information is verifiable and immutable.

An extreme case of transparency is the DAO.[371] Set up as a venture fund, all DAO investments and its entire governance are transparent by design, because the underlying code is open source and visible to all. The basic idea of DAO governance is that owners of DAO tokens would vote on whether or not to fund proposed projects. This autonomous, nonhuman operational model of a DAO is not practical for all firms, but it is a fascinating, stark contrast to "normal" corporate decision-making where executives have great discretion over the usage of funds and where shareholders rarely have a direct say and often have only limited or indirect knowledge about their CEOs' decisions.[372]

As an example for how the "hard" information stored in a blockchain can help an entity, consider a historically corrupt country. How can the government of this country improve its standing? In the end, it is difficult to prove that one is not corrupt. Blockchain technology can be an answer. In the current world, it is often impossible to credibly and efficiently reveal all of a government's relevant transactions and business dealings—but when all transactions and contracts are recorded on a blockchain, nothing remains hidden. And as the money and contract terms can be traced, this government can credibly document that its actions are not furthering corruption.

Direct benefits: Disintermediation, improved governance

There are also direct benefits from transparency: transactions that are recorded on a blockchain are usually of a financial nature, and recording transactions and thus holdings on a blockchain can have *direct* procedural advantages in market interactions. Many financial assets, such as corporate bonds, are very illiquid, meaning that it is difficult for a willing trader to find a counterparty; recent regulatory changes such as the Volcker Rule have exacerbated the situation.[373] One problem is that under the current market structure, where most trades are arranged offline through dealers, it is difficult to know who traded a product in the recent past (and thus might have a continued interest) or who might hold the securities (and might thus be a candidate to trade with). Arguably, greater transparency in this market could increase investor-to-investor interactions (and thus decrease costly intermediation). Malinova and Park show theoretically that a setup with features of a public blockchain (even when market participants take steps to hide their behavior) improves allocative efficiency relative to the traditional, opaque setup where all information about past trading and current holdings remains in silos of information at dealers.[374]

Another example is the market for initial public offerings. During its last boom during the dot-com bubble at the end of the 1990s, this market was fraught with problems. One critical issue was the distribution and access rules to the offerings. Traditionally, the lead underwriting investment bank controls who gets shares in an offering. For popular IPOs, there were numerous conflicts of interest: for instance, a widely reported concern was that underwriting investment banks have an interest to please their best customers by giving them underpriced shares.[375] Another widely reported issue was the process of *laddering*, whereby investors received shares in offers only if they committed to purchase further shares at higher prices.[376] In the current world of investment banking, underwriters cannot easily convince issuers and investors that conflicts of interest play no role in their advice and decision-making. Contrast this with the currently hot (for better or worse) market of ICOs, many of which, for all practical purposes, look like securities offerings.[377] The allocation mechanism in this market is entirely transparent because it is intrinsic to the piece of publicly visible code that determines how tokens are distributed.[378]

In a celebrated paper, David Yermack highlights numerous potential benefits for corporate governance that blockchain technology can bring about.[379] Yermack argued, for instance, that transparent ownership attribution in a blockchain can help address the so-called *empty voting* phenomenon, where an entity gets to vote on economically meaningful decisions without having an economic stake in the firm.[380] The usual assumption is that economic interest in a firm and voting rights are coupled with the ownership of a share. However, derivatives contracts make it possible that a party obtains a large number of voting rights without having an economic stake in the firm.[381] With ownership attribution via a blockchain, it would be transparent at any point in time who owns a stock and who has an economically justified right to vote.

Insider trades, another topic of much contention both in the financial industry and in academia, are a further obvious use case. Insiders are already required to announce their trades and holdings, but there are often significant delays between the transactions and their reporting.[382] Therefore, if all trades were recorded on a blockchain, then—by revealing their public IDs—insiders could credibly and immediately show their trades. All their trades would be visible, which would eliminate costly reporting requirements and could increase public trust.[383] The public would be in the position to understand insider holdings and insider trading better, and firm executives would create trust with their shareholders. This argument applies particularly in jurisdictions where insider trading violations are less strictly enforced than in North America. Finally, transparency of insider trades should reduce the propensity of insiders to engage in illicit trading. As transparency reduces the flexibility of insider traders, it becomes more profitable for outsiders to generate information about firms.

Yermack highlights that the immutability of public blockchains improves (corporate) governance. In the current system, land records can be forged, corporate income statements can be manipulated, and option grants can be backdated. When all these data are recorded on a public blockchain, performing such manipulations becomes prohibitively difficult and expensive.

In finance, transparency of contracts and holdings extends beyond the resolution of adverse selection and moral hazard at the heart of corporate governance and has potentially far-reaching consequences for risk management. One major development in the wake of the 2008 financial crisis was that particular types of derivatives contracts, such as swaps, were forced to be cleared with a newly developed *central counterparty* (CP). The basic idea is that when A wants to sell to B, then A sells to the CP, and the CP sells to B. Why is this necessary?

Imagine that A has also bought from C, but that C goes bust. A would then not be able to deliver to B and may go bust, too. Thus when dealing with A, B faces two counterparty risks: (a) the risk of A's going bust independently and (b) the risk that C goes bust and takes A down with it.

Consider the derivative dealings of AIG prior to the financial crisis in the market for credit default swaps, where it became apparent that AIG had taken large unhedged positions. AIG's default would have triggered defaults of its counterparties, causing a chain reaction all through the financial system. When all trades are cleared by a CP, risk is concentrated at the CP. Although this system can generate a mutually beneficial level of risk sharing, there are problems: because it is a too-big-to-fail entity, the CP needs to be tightly monitored, well-capitalized, and possibly heavily regulated. Moreover, currently, only a small number of contracts qualify for CP clearing. The root cause for the necessity of a CP is that there is insufficient information about the aggregate risk, and that creates moral hazard. As we've known since the path-breaking work of American economist George Akerlof, asymmetric information can lead to the breakdown of a market.

We could argue that the transparency possible with blockchain technology enables a market-based solution: when all financial obligations are visible, we will be able to trace counterparty risk beyond bilateral interactions. Unhedged positions would be visible. Moreover, we would be able to write smart contracts with protective covenants such that counterparties are forced, through the code, to establish hedges in a timely manner, or prevented from engaging in unhedged contracts.

Finally, smart contracts themselves can fundamentally improve economic interactions. As a first step, a smart contract can facilitate the delivery of collateral by automatically transferring the title in the case of a default. Such automation vastly improves the enforcement of collateral, increases its value, reduces risk, and potentially frees up capital.

We use contracts to prove to others (e.g., shareholders) that a transfer of goods will occur (or has been legitimized). We can use smart contracts without blockchains and in non-transparent environments; but in transparent blockchains, parties may be able to sell rights to future payments. In other words, firms may be able to sell cash flows directly from contracts, and they may be able to ensure cash flow risks directly. Furthermore, as Cong, He, and Zheng show, smart contracts can mitigate information asymmetry, leading to enhanced entry and competition and then higher social welfare and consumer surplus.[384]

Altogether, there is a solid business case in favor of the transparency of transactions and contracts that blockchain technology affords, and these advantages go much beyond addressing the concerns that arise from front-page scandals. As it is, the privacy of corporate entities is already limited, especially compared to that of individuals. It is not unreasonable to presume that regulation can simply require blockchain-based disclosure of interactions—and if indeed blockchains become the standard for financial transactions, then this type of disclosure is procedurally inexpensive.

Finally, the validity of the arguments that I present here is confirmed in a recent study by IBM of C-suite executives.[385] The vast majority of executives that have already actively adopted blockchain technology report that the technology will create more trust, for instance, through traceable audit trails of transactions, that reputations can be built by offering transparency about past actions.

SOLVING THE PROBLEM: TECHNOLOGICAL APPROACHES TO PRIVACY IN BLOCKCHAINS

The primary purpose of a blockchain is to ensure the authenticity of the records—by default, distributed ledgers are not set up to guarantee privacy for their users. Indeed, there is ample evidence that transactions in public blockchains are not private, and that individuals' actions can potentially be traced.[386]

As a prerequisite, it is important to separate the concerns that different parties may have. Judging by the tone of the discussions in popular Internet forums, many proponents of cryptocurrencies and particularly bitcoin worry whether their dealings can be traced or detected, for instance, by a government entity. Considering that bitcoin was a popular method of payment for illegal drug purchases on sites such as Silk Road or for ransomware payments, this is not surprising.

In contrast, most enterprise users are used to the government auditing their actions, and they worry less about government knowledge per se. Indeed, they may actually welcome a system that makes traceability easier. Instead, enterprise users are mostly concerned whether their actions are traceable by their competitors, thus diminishing their intellectual property.

PROCEDURAL WORK-AROUNDS: USAGE OF MULTIPLE IDS

So are actions on blockchains always fully traceable and attributable? The answer is no. There are several simple, low-tech, procedural work-arounds that allow users to obfuscate their behavior.

Let me explain the ideas with a concrete example. A mutual fund wants to make a large investment in a recently issued firm whose securities are blockchain-based tokens. The mutual fund would convert fiat currency, such as the Canadian dollar, into a blockchain-based currency such as ether. This transfer would occur at a blockchain-based exchange. The exchange would know who bought the ether (because they have to follow KYC regulations). After the transfer is made, the fund would use the newly purchased ether and buy the crypto security. As I outline in the appendix, usually this transfer is performed in an exchange wallet that combines the actions of numerous market participants. For final settlement, the fund would then transfer the securities to a non-exchange wallet. But the fund does not have to use a known wallet or reveal the wallet ID to the public. Instead, the fund can create a dedicated new wallet. Or the fund can create an arbitrary number of new wallets and split the holding among these. If done carefully, it would be impossible for an outsider to piece together this big purchase. This solution can also be formally programmed using so-called *hierarchical deterministic* (HD) wallets, which algorithmically generate a new public key for every piece of a larger trade.

HD wallets have also been proposed as a solution to privacy in private distributed ledgers. Suppose that a private network is run by a consortium of large banks and brokers. Each of them would create one (or many) HD wallets, and record individual customers' holdings within their own systems. This arrangement is similar to the current settlement of stock trades. Namely, currently, the settlement of stock traders occurs at a central depository, such as the US DTCC or CDS in Canada, and the settlement is at the broker level. The main difference is that HD wallet settlement is on a distributed ledger, and not in a central database. With the distributed ledger there is no informational advantage over the central depository solution, even for someone with access to the ledger (in particular not for Canada where trades usually carry a broker attribution).

Another solution to generate privacy that is related to HD wallets is a merge and re-split operation: under this protocol, several entities anonymously submit new addresses to a smart contract; the contract collects the same number of units of crypto securities from the parties (e.g., 100 bitcoins each), and then the contract redistributes the amounts to the new addresses.[387] From the outside, we could not further follow a trail of money. Needless to say, in a public blockchain without outside control, what I am describing is, for all practical purposes, money laundering. In permissioned blockchains, however, the IDs would be known, and a regulator or tax authority would be able to track individuals. The primary purpose of this endeavor would then be to obfuscate one's behavior to outside observers.

HIGH-TECH SOLUTION: ZERO-KNOWLEDGE PROOFS

In addition to the aforementioned low-tech solutions, modern cryptography offers several high-tech and elegant ways to obtain privacy. The common privacy-related concern regarding a transaction is that the owner of a piece of information wants to provide cryptographic proof that she is a valid owner of that information without having to reveal that information to the validator (i.e., the network).

For example, zero knowledge is critical in blockchain-based voting. For such a vote, one receives a voting token. When casting the vote, the tokenholder needs to verify that she is the legitimate owner of the token; but with secret suffrage, the validator must not see who the owner is because that knowledge might allow the validator to trace the actual vote back to the voter. After all, in public blockchains, each network member keeps a record of all information.

Probably the most sophisticated method yet to solve this problem involves so-called zero-knowledge proofs. Figure 6-2 shows how this verification works.[388]

Here's a standard example of a zero-knowledge proof. Suppose Bob is color-blind but doesn't know it. Alice wants to prove to Bob that there is a difference between green and red. Bob takes two snooker balls, one is red, the other green, but they are otherwise identical. To Bob, they seem completely identical, and he is skeptical that they are actually distinguishable. Alice wants to prove to him that they are in fact differently colored. At the same time, Alice doesn't want Bob to learn which is red and which is green.

Here is the proof system: Bob takes two balls so that he is holding one in each hand. Alice can see the balls but doesn't tell him which is which. Bob then puts both hands behind his back. Next, he either switches the balls between his hands, or leaves them be, with equal chance. He then brings them out from behind his back. Alice now has to "guess" whether or not Bob switched the balls. Of course, Alice can say with certainty whether or not Bob switched them by

FIGURE 6-2

ILLUSTRATION OF ZERO-KNOWLEDGE PROOFS

A prover wants to show that she has the key to a secret door in a cave. Irrespective of whether she goes left or right, she can always use the key and return from either direction. The verifier, not having seen which direction the prover went, demands she returns through the right tunnel. The prover, with the key to the door, opens the door and returns from the right tunnel. Of course, she could have been lucky; someone without the key could have taken the right tunnel in the first place. But they repeat the experiment many times, and the prover's appearing from the correct tunnel by chance diminishes every single time.

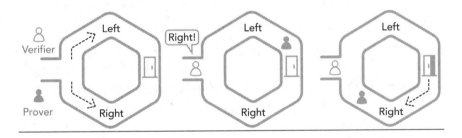

Icons © 2017 Smashicons and Freepick. Used with permission.

simply looking at the colors. If they were the same color and hence indistinguishable, she will guess the correct color with 50 percent probability. Of course, one try is thus not enough, but if Bob and Alice repeat this "proof" many times, the chance vanishes that Alice got it right all the time just by luck. Bob should therefore become convinced that the balls are indeed differently colored. Furthermore, the proof is "zero knowledge" because Bob never learns which ball is green and which one is red; indeed, he gains no knowledge about how to distinguish the balls.[389]

At this writing, the developers of the public blockchain Ethereum are incorporating the option to use a generalized version of zero-knowledge proofs as part of the Ethereum blockchain.

The concept that they employ is zk-SNARK, a protocol whereby someone can reveal only the necessary information to the verifier and no more. Zcash is one example of a cryptocurrency based on zero-knowledge proofs.

When would a company want such an option? Imagine that a firm stores smart contracts on a blockchain. A lender wants to assess the creditworthiness of the firm and asks to reveal what payments the firm can expect based on existing contracts. The firm may not wish to reveal all the details of the contracts (such as counterparties) to the lender. Zero-knowledge proofs are the solution: the firm can prove that it is the recipient of upcoming payments without revealing all the details.

Another blockchain-based cryptocurrency that offers privacy is Monero. It is based on a different concept, the so-called *linkable ring signatures*. The idea is that the system mixes the true ID with a random collection of other IDs for each transaction. In signing a transaction, the user reveals that s/he is the rightful owner without revealing which one. Linkability ensures that double-spending cannot occur. There are several other technological and procedural solutions that can deliver privacy but discussing all of them is beyond the scope of this chapter.

In summary, there are multiple solutions to ensure privacy: some technological (such as zero-knowledge proofs), some procedural (usage of multiple IDs).

IMPLEMENTATION IN PUBLIC VERSUS PRIVATE BLOCKCHAINS

The procedural solutions to obtain privacy that I describe above are intrinsic to public blockchains. The direct downside of the usage of many addresses is that it creates tangible costs: although the creation of IDs is free, each transaction involves a fee, and invoking privacy in this manner comes at a cost. Other than the costs, nothing prevents entities from using an arbitrary number of IDs and from hiding their identity.

While privacy is a right for private citizens, many jurisdictions, such as Canada and the United States, already limit privacy for firms and executives. For instance, firm insiders have to disclose trades in their company's stocks, and mutual funds and some hedge funds are required to disclose their holdings. For firms that use public blockchains, a regulator or lawmaker could impose disclosure requirements. For instance, regulated hedge funds or firms that have issued security-like digital tokens on a blockchain may be required to reveal the addresses that they use from time to time. Doing so is arguably a more elegant solution than the current, administratively burdensome disclosure. Furthermore, as I have argued above, firms and executives may disclose the used addresses proactively to take advantage of the strategic value of transparency.

The usage of high-tech solutions to attain privacy, such as zk-SNARKs, is not contradicting firms using blockchain transparency as a strategic asset. For instance, smart contracts, which are one of the most appealing features of blockchain technology, could involve one party, A, making a delivery to another party, B, while using firm A's IP for tasks that are necessary to make the delivery. Firm A would not want firm B to see its IP, nor does it want the broader public to see the IP. The solution here is to use zk-SNARKs to verify that the tasks have indeed been accomplished. Firms that want to be transparent (e.g., about relevant accounting features) would not have to reveal contract details, but instead they will still be able to announce the final delivery, or they could verifiably display the key parameters of an agreement.

In private or permissioned blockchains, the procedural workarounds from public blockchains apply, too. However, in private blockchains, there are further options. Whether a user can create multiple IDs is a design choice. The economic incentives for the verification and settlement of transactions is also a design choice, as are the costs for using multiple IDs. Private blockchains can also include features that mask user IDs or that limit visibility of subsets of transactions to a selection of parties.

More critical for private blockchains is that users understand the ID setup and that they understand the network governance and the information available to network members. For instance, is the setup identical to that of a public blockchain except that all users have gone through a KYC procedure? Or are there limitations to ID usage? Do all network members use IDs similarly? Do customers of networks have equal access or do some institutions give some customers more information than others?

If indeed leading financial institutions were to introduce private blockchains to facilitate their interactions, then the handling of the information and the identifiers would require much thought (and likely a lengthy legislative and regulatory process). For instance, the main benefit of a blockchain technology is that it enables peer-to-peer interactions, which will lead to further disintermediation. Institutional investors that rely on a bank-consortium-operated private blockchain need to understand what information they or any other party can derive from the blockchain.

A related concern arises for corporate users, that of baseline information. A business partner may make a subset of information visible. For instance, a party may share information to build a reputation as a good business partner. However, if disclosure is selective rather than full, then users cannot construct a baseline for a meaningful comparison.

As this discussion highlights, there are many possible information asymmetries that can arise with private blockchains. Since the existing financial institutions are already heavily regulated, any private blockchain they build would likely also need to be regulated. The regulation would need to ensure the mitigation of information asymmetries between members and nonmembers and the resulting conflicts of interest.

In the history of finance, it has been difficult to change transparency regimes, and such moves have often been met with much resistance.[390] Personally, I believe that the regulation of private or consortium blockchains will quickly become extremely problematic, because it would need to cover multiple strong-willed jurisdictions.

In my view, there are two salient outcomes: the first is that the private, permissioned blockchains are identical to the public ones except that the access to the network is controlled by network members, but all other informational and transparency features are the same as in public blockchains.

The second outcome is that the financial institutions manage to design a distributed ledger that precisely mimics the current world. Indeed, the R3 consortium, formed by most of the world's largest financial institutions, promotes its own version of a distributed ledger, the Corda system. R3 describes this system as an open, distributed ledger that preserves privacy in the sense that a firm that is part of the ledger can see only the information that pertains to it.[391] The best description of Corda, in my view, is that it is a system of bilaterally agreed and verified transactions with conflict resolution provided by (algorithmic) notaries. This system looks like a digitized version of the current world of contracts using some of the features that have been developed and deployed in public blockchains (e.g., smart contracts). Since blockchain technology is often compared to the Internet, the appropriate analogy here is that Corda looks like the AOL of the 21st century.

Finally, public blockchains such as Bitcoin or Ethereum are very secure: the proof-of-work (and possibly proof-of-stake) protocols require an attacker to control more than 51 percent of the respective networks' computing power. At present, obtaining these resources comes at an astronomical cost; therefore, tampering with records is economically infeasible on these blockchains. Private blockchains would become large, lucrative targets for hackers; and depending on the protocol, a single compromised network member could contaminate the entire ledger. The security of private blockchains is a real and significant concern, albeit one beyond the scope of this chapter.[392]

CONCLUSIONS AND RECOMMENDATIONS

When corporate executives first learned about the concept of a blockchain, they quickly realized that the native transparency fundamentally went against the grain of their current procedures—in particular for financial institutions. At first blush, private blockchains then seemed to be the obvious choice—the term "private" suggests that they could maintain the traditional level of total privacy for financial transactions. The truth is more complicated.

Transparency is native to most blockchains, including private ones. We would be wrong to think that a private blockchain is synonymous with privacy or to equate a public blockchain with lack of privacy. Instead, there are technological solutions that allow users to keep their transactions masked. Therefore, transparency and privacy are choices, even in public blockchains.

With that in mind, blockchain users must understand that they send signals when they opt for privacy instead of transparency. Insisting on privacy may come with a reputation loss. As firms consider incorporating blockchain technology into their business operations, they ought to consider the positive potential of high transparency for their business. Transparency increases trust and can help build positive reputations—with business partners, customers, and investors. It can be conceptually complex to add disclosure features to existing systems—but with blockchain technology, being transparent is straightforward, and disclosure can come at no operational cost.

Over the next years, we will likely see implementations of private blockchains that offer *masking* functionality of identifiers. The intrinsic security concerns and the signaling effect notwithstanding, executives who go down this path face important questions regarding the governance of information in private blockchains: Who knows what? Who masks and unmasks identifiers? Who controls and monitors the ensuing protocols? It is crucial not to set up a private blockchain in a manner that creates asymmetric information, adverse selection, and moral hazard, lest we see a whole set of innovation-stymieing regulations.

My hope is that executives embrace the positive network effects of transparency. It is challenging to amend existing disclosure practices, and historically we have seen meaningful changes only in the wake of scandals. The advent of this new technology is a unique opportunity to reconsider and to embrace transparency and to take advantage of the economic benefits of an open world.

APPENDIX TO CHAPTER 6

HOW TO ACCESS THE ETHEREUM BLOCKCHAIN

Items on the Ethereum Blockchain are associated with public addresses, which are combinations of numbers and letters. For instance, my public address is 0xb1f0ab5ba4DBABAACba71baB7d6bF79D64EE397c.

To receive a payment, we need to have such an address. Creating one is straightforward by using, for example, the website *MyEtherWallet.com*. To create an address, we enter an arbitrary string as a password. The website then creates a public ID and a private ID from this information, and it creates a file that contains the relevant information. For the term, "showmethemoney!" I received this information:

Your address:
0x15b71d3db7F17B31e911517252EeE6a7445eA66C

Your private key:
e36979144c398043f8606a349b01acecc1b8a0ffd-
b9a55528710621434fdb538

Note that this information is for illustration only. It is not advice. *No one should use this particular information.* I can now receive payments to this address; by itself, however, the address is not useful. Namely, to make payments, one needs to obtain a wallet. A standard one is Mist, available here: <u>github.com/ethereum/mist/releases</u>.

How can we obtain ether, the native currency of the Ethereum network? There are at least three ways:

1. We become miners, meaning that we use our computer to participate in the verification activities of the Ethereum blockchain. If we succeed in creating blocks of transactions then we obtain newly minted ether as a built-in reward. However, successful mining requires specialized computing equipment—a standard central processing unit is much too slow.

2. A third party sends ether to our address, for instance, in return for a real-world item of value (say, a baby stroller that we sell on Craigslist).

3. We convert fiat currency (e.g., Canadian dollar, US dollar) into ether and send it to this address.

On that last point, as of this writing, converting fiat currency into digital money is a multistep process. First, we need to create an account at a cryptocurrency exchange such as Coinbase, Kraken, Poloniex, or QuadrigaCX. These exchanges perform KYC, meaning that we need to verify our identity by providing a credit card number and a scan of our passport or driver's license. Once the exchange has verified our identity, the exchange creates an account, which we can fund by sending money to the exchange in our name using, say, a credit card or a wire transfer. Needless to say, this process involves non-negligible fees. Once funded, we can then buy ether or other digital assets at these cryptocurrency exchanges. Coinbase, for instance, instantaneously converts fiat currency into ether. However, the conversion transaction has not settled on the blockchain yet—the money is still technically at the exchange. So *if the exchange gets hacked or goes bankrupt, our money is lost*. To be a true owner of ether, we need to transfer funds away from the exchange and send them to an address such as the one listed above.

ACKNOWLEDGMENTS

This book would not have been possible without the contributions of dozens of people. Specifically, we thank the industry experts and entrepreneurs who are shaping this new industry, and who generously agreed to interviews: Joseph Lubin, Collin Myers, and James Beck of ConsenSys; Rune Christensen and Greg Di Prisco of MakerDAO; Tyler and Cameron Winklevoss of Winklevoss Capital Management; Anthony Pompliano of Morgan Creek Digital; Meltem Demirors of CoinShares; Adi Sideman of Props; Bill Barhydt of Abra; Ryan Selkis of Messari; Ethan Buchman of Cosmos and Tendermint; Ron Resnick of the Enterprise Ethereum Alliance; Marley Gray of Microsoft; Emin Gün Sirer of Cornell University; Brendan Eich of Brave Marco; Santori of Blockchain (formerly of Cooley LLP); Lucian Tarnowski of BraveNew, David Treat of Accenture; Damien Vanderveken of SWIFT Lab; Akseli Virtanen of the Economic Space Agency; Jesse Walden of Mediachain; and Starkema Saunders, Jennifer Peve, Michael McClain, Daniel Thieke, and Theresa Paraschac of DTCC.

Thanks go to the outstanding research faculty of the Blockchain Research Institute, including Michael Casey, Primavera De Filippi, Andreas Park, Rachel Robinson, Bob Tapscott, Joel Telpner, Anthony Williams, and others whose work was foundational to this book. Special thanks to Charlie Morris of CM Crypto Capital for his feedback.

Any writer knows the importance of a great editor. We are grateful to have one of the best in the business. The Blockchain Research Institute's Editor-in-Chief Kirsten Sandberg provides structure, clarity, and narrative thrust to every piece of content that the BRI publishes. Our entire editorial team is the engine that drives our content, and we are grateful for all that they do.

We also thank our institute's members for their ongoing participation: Accenture, Aon, Bank of Canada, Bell Canada, BioLife,

BPC Banking Technologies, Brightline (a Project Management Institute initiative), Capgemini, Canadian Imperial Bank of Commerce, Centrica, Cimcorp, Cisco Systems Inc., City of Toronto, the Coca-Cola Company, Deloitte, Delta Air Lines Inc., Depository Trust & Clearing Corporation, ExxonMobil Global Service Company, FedEx Corporate Services, Fujitsu, Government of Ontario, Gowling WLG, Huobi, IBM, ICICI Bank, INSEAD, Institute on Governance, Interac, Intuit, ISED Canada, JumpStart, KPMG, Loblaw Companies, Manulife, Microsoft, MKS (Switzerland) SA, Moog, Nasdaq, Navigator, Ontario Ministry of Health and Long-Term Care, Orange, Philip Morris International Management, Procter & Gamble, PepsiCo, PNC Bank, Raymond Chabot Grant Thornton, Reliance Industries, Revenu Québec, Salesforce, SAP SE, Tata Consultancy Services, Teck Resources, Tencent, Thomson Reuters, TMX Group, University of Arkansas, University Health Network, University of Texas-Dallas, and WISeKey.

We are grateful for our pioneer members: Access Copyright, Aion, Artlery, Attest, Blockchain Guru, Bloq, CarbonX, Cosmos, Decentral Inc., Evrythng, Huobi, Jumpstart, Liechtenstein Cryptoassets Exchange, LongHash, Medicalchain, Navigator Ltd., NEM Foundation, Numeracle, Paycase Financial, PermianChain Technologies Inc., Polymath, SGInnovate, Slant AG, SpaceChain, Sweetbridge, Telos Foundation, Veriphi, and YouBase.

Finally, thanks to our affiliate organizations: Alastria, Blockchain in Transport Alliance, Blockchain Research Institute Nanjing, Chamber of Digital Commerce, Coalition of Automated Legal Applications, Enterprise Ethereum Alliance, Healthcare Information and Management Systems Society, Hyperledger hosted by The Linux Foundation, and the Illinois Chamber of Commerce.

ABOUT THE BLOCKCHAIN RESEARCH INSTITUTE

Co-founded in 2017 by Don and Alex Tapscott, the Blockchain Research Institute is an independent, global think tank established to help realize the new promise of the digital economy. For several years now, we have been investigating the transformative and disruptive potential of blockchain technology on business, government, and society.

Our syndicated research program, which is funded by major corporations and government agencies, aims to fill a large gap in the global understanding of blockchain protocols, applications, and ecosystems and their strategic implications for enterprise leaders, supply chains, and industries. Deliverables include lighthouse cases, big idea white papers, research briefs, roundtable reports, infographics, videos, and webinars.

Our global team of blockchain experts is dedicated to exploring, understanding, documenting, and informing leaders about the market opportunities and implementation challenges of this nascent technology. Research areas include financial services, manufacturing, retail, energy and resources, technology, media, telecommunications, healthcare, and government as well as the management of organizations, the transformation of the corporation, and the regulation of innovation. We also explore blockchain's potential role in the Internet of Things, robotics and autonomous machines, artificial intelligence and machine learning, and other emerging technologies.

Our findings are initially proprietary to our members and are ultimately released under a Creative Commons license to help achieve our mission. To find out more, please visit

blockchainresearchinstitute.org

ABOUT THE CONTRIBUTORS

MICHAEL J. CASEY

Michael Casey is the chief content officer at *CoinDesk*, the leading provider of news, events programming, and research for the blockchain and digital asset community. He is also chairman and co-founder of Streambed Media, an early-stage video production and technology platform that seeks to optimize capital formation and creative output in the digital media industry. Separately, he retains a nonprofit role as senior adviser at the MIT Media Lab's Digital Currency Initiative and is an adjunct professor at Curtin University's Center for Culture and Technology. Until mid-2015, Michael was a senior columnist covering global finance at *The Wall Street Journal*, the culmination of a two-decade career in print journalism. He also hosted online TV shows for WSJ Live and appeared on various networks, including CNBC, CNN, Fox Business, and the BBC. Michael is a frequent speaker on topics of digital innovation, globalization, and the future of media and money. He has been an adviser and consultant to start-ups and large enterprises that are driving, undergoing, or confronting digital transformation. Michael has five acclaimed books to his name, including *The Truth Machine: The Blockchain and the Future of Everything* and *The Age of Cryptocurrency: How Bitcoin and Digital Money Are Challenging the Global Economic Order*, both co-authored with Paul Vigna. A native of Perth, Australia, Michael is a graduate of the University of Western Australia and has higher degrees from Cornell University and Curtin University.

ALEXIS COLLOMB

Alexis Collomb joined the Conservatoire National des Arts et Métiers (CNAM) in 2011 where he has been responsible for its master in finance program, looking after both capital markets and corporate finance tracks. Currently heading the CNAM's economics finance insurance and banking department, he is also scientific co-director of the Blockchain Perspectives Joint Research Initiative within Paris-based ILB think tank. Alexis started his career in investment banking at Donaldson, Lufkin & Jenrette in New York. He later joined Citigroup in London, where he initially worked as equity derivatives strategist, and then as cross-asset strategist. Initially a telecommunications engineer and computer scientist, Alexis also holds a master's degree in engineering-economics systems and a PhD in management science from Stanford University where he was part of the Systems Optimization Laboratory. In addition to innovation financing, his current research focuses on cryptoeconomics, smart contracts, and how distributed ledger technology is affecting the financial world—particularly its post-trade infrastructure—and the insurance industry. A seasoned adviser to start-ups, he currently holds various board positions and is a member of LabEx Refi's scientific committee, a European research group focused on financial regulation.

PRIMAVERA DE FILIPPI

Primavera De Filippi is a researcher at the National Center of Scientific Research in Paris and a faculty associate at the Berkman Klein Center for Internet & Society at Harvard University. She is a member of the Global Future Council on Blockchain Technologies at the World Economic Forum and founder of the Internet Governance Forum's dynamic coalition on blockchain technology COALA. In 2018, Harvard University Press published her book, *Blockchain and the Law*, co-authored with Aaron Wright.

ANDREAS PARK

Andreas Park is an associate professor of finance at the University of Toronto, appointed to the Rotman School of Management, the Institute for Management and Innovation, and the Department of Management at U of T Mississauga. He currently serves as the research director at the FinHub, Rotman's Financial Innovation Lab. He is the co-founder of the LedgerHub, the University of Toronto's blockchain research lab, and a lab economist for blockchain at the Creative Destruction Lab. Andreas teaches courses on blockchain, fintech, and financial market trading, and his current research focuses on the economic impact of technological transformations such as blockchain technology. His work has been published in top journals in economics and finance including *Econometrica*, the *Journal of Finance*, the *Journal of Financial Economics*, and the *Journal of Financial and Quantitative Analysis*.

KLARA SOK

Klara Sok is a research fellow in social sciences at the Conservatoire National des Arts et Métiers at the Lirsa and the Dicen-IdF research centers. She is a founding member of the transdisciplinary Blockchain Perspectives Joint Research Initiative and is preparing her PhD dissertation on blockchain and cryptocurrencies. Klara is interested in the socioeconomic and organizational changes generated by the introduction of bitcoin and other blockchain-based information and communication technologies as alternatives to existing legacy systems, namely for the financial services industry. Her research questions how blockchain might fit into a general-purpose technology category through its ability to automate trusted information flows and publicize value transfer processes in an potentially opposable manner, which could, in turn, smooth financial intermediation processes and incrementally fuel further economic growth. Klara is co-developing OpenResearch, a blockchain-based open peer-review platform. After serving as organizational analyst for the Boston Consulting Group, Klara spent several years as an emerging Asian equity portfolio manager for Edmond de Rothschild Asset Management. She also worked in Cambodia as a consultant for the United Nations (UNCTAD, UNIFEM), the World Bank (International Finance

Corporation), and the World Economic Forum. Klara graduated from Audencia Business School and holds a master's degree in organizational sociology from Sciences Po Paris.

ALEX TAPSCOTT

Alex Tapscott is a globally recognized writer, speaker, investor, and adviser focused on the impact of emerging technologies, such as blockchain and cryptocurrencies, on business, society, and government. He is the co-author (with Don Tapscott) of the critically acclaimed nonfiction best seller, *Blockchain Revolution: How the Technology Behind Bitcoin and Other Cryptocurrencies Is Changing the World*, which has been translated into more than 15 languages. His TEDx San Francisco talk, "Blockchain Is Eating Wall Street," has been viewed over 692,000 times.[393] In 2017, Alex co-founded the Blockchain Research Institute, a multimillion-dollar think tank that is investigating blockchain strategies, opportunities, and use cases. He also received (with Don Tapscott) the Digital Thinking Award, one of Thinkers50's Distinguished Achievement Awards. Previously, Alex was an executive at Canaccord Genuity, Canada's largest independent investment bank. Alex is a graduate of Amherst College (cum laude) and lives in Toronto, Canada. He is an active investor in blockchain projects and some cryptoassets. Mentioned in this book, he owns bitcoin, ether, ATOMs, and Zcash. He also owns stock in Facebook, Amazon, Apple, and Google.

BOB TAPSCOTT

Bob Tapscott is a recognized information technology strategist, author, and speaker, keynoting conferences on the topics of artificial intelligence, fintech, and blockchain. Bob's extensive background in successfully leading large international software projects goes beyond typical technology design and development to include the training, organizational restructuring, and workflow redesign required to deliver, measure, and improve overall corporate performance. As a vice president or a chief information officer, Bob has led the Canadian technology efforts of Citibank, HSBC, and other Schedule II banks in Canada. More recently, Bob has been an author, adviser, and consultant to many organizations, including SAP on master data management, J.P.Morgan on derivatives, and VMware and DIRECTV on strategy. At Jeppesen (now a Boeing company), he designed the system that supplies the directions to the majority of the world's commercial aircraft (both Boeing's and Airbus'). His experience in payments management includes running the clearing and settlement systems for a variety of Canadian banks, and membership on the board to the precursor to Payments Canada, the Canadian Payments Association for both Lloyds Bank and HSBC.

FENNIE WANG

Fennie Wang, a lawyer turned entrepreneur in the blockchain space, leads strategy, legal, and partnerships at the ixo Network, UNICEF's first blockchain investment. The ixo Network is a blockchain-powered platform for collecting, verifying, and tokenizing any project's impact data, which can then be monetized, shared, or traded. Fennie is a US-qualified securities lawyer, who practiced both securities defense (including SEC investigations) and international capital markets in New York and London with leading US law firms WilmerHale and Latham & Watkins. When not working on ixo, she is involved in legal advocacy for the emergent token economy, particularly through her work as a working group coordinator at COALA, a cross-disciplinary policy group in the blockchain and legal space. She started her career as a high yield research analyst at J.P.Morgan. In between Wall Street and law school, she founded a legal services nonprofit in Uganda. She holds a law degree from Columbia, where she was a Harlan Fiske Stone Scholar, and business and legal studies degrees from Berkeley with high honors.

ANTHONY D. WILLIAMS

Anthony Williams is co-founder and president of the DEEP Centre and an internationally recognized authority on the digital revolution, innovation, and creativity in business and society. He is co-author (with Don Tapscott) of the groundbreaking best seller, *Wikinomics: How Mass Collaboration Changes Everything*, and its sequel, *Macrowikinomics: New Solutions for a Connected Planet*. Among other current appointments, Anthony is an expert adviser to the Markle Foundation's *Initiative for America's Economic Future*, a senior fellow with the Lisbon Council in Brussels and the Institute on Governance in Ottawa, and chief adviser to Brazil's Free Education Project, a national strategy to equip two million young Brazilians with the skills required for a 21st-century workforce. His work on technology and innovation has been featured in such publications as the *Huffington Post*, *Harvard Business Review*, and *The Globe and Mail*.

ACRONYMS AND ABBREVIATIONS

ABS, Association of Banks in Singapore

AML, anti-money laundering

API, application programming interface

ASICs, application-specific integrated circuits

ATS, alternative trading system

CDFS, common departmental financial system

CDS, Canadian Depository for Securities

CHAPS, clearing house automated payment system, England's RTGS system

CLS, an acronym originally for continuously linked settlement

COALA, Coalition of Automated Legal Applications

CP, central counterparty

CPM, cost per mille or cost per thousand

CSD, central securities depository

Dapps, Decentralized applications

DeFi, decentralized finance

DFMS, departmental financial management systems

DLT, Distributed ledger technology

DTCC, Depository Trust & Clearing Corporation

ECB, European Central Bank

ECO, ecosystem coin offering

ECSA, Economic Space Agency

EEA, Enterprise Ethereum Alliance

ETF, exchange-traded fund

EVM, Ethereum Virtual Machine

FASt Lane, a mash-up of Federal Acquisition Services (FAS) and Integrated Technology Services (ITS)

FinCEN, Financial Crimes Enforcement Network

FINMA, the Swiss Financial Market Supervisory Authority

FX, foreign exchange

GAAP, generally accepted accounting principles

gpi, SWIFT global payment innovation

GPU, graphics processing unit

GSA, US General Services Administration

HD, hierarchical deterministic

HTTP, hypertext transfer protocol

ICO, initial coin offering

IP, intellectual property

IPFS, InterPlanetary File System

IPO, initial public offering

ISO, International Organization for Standardization

JBA, Japanese Bankers Association

KSI, keyless signature infrastructure

KYC, know your customer

Lantmäteriet, Sweden's land registry authority

LLP, limited liability partnership

LoC, letter of credit

LVTS, larger value transfer system

MAC, message authentication code

MAS, Monetary Authority of Singapore

MSFO, monthly statement of financial operations

MTF, multilateral trading facility

NASD, US National Association of Securities Dealers

NGO, nongovernmental organization

nostro, "ours with you" account

OECD, Organisation for Economic Co-operation and Development

OTC, over the counter

P2P, peer to peer

PDF, portable document format

PKI, public key infrastructure

POC, proof of concept

PoS, proof of stake

PoW, proof of work

PS-GL, payroll systemgeneral ledger

RAIL, real-time asset interchange ledger

RAIN, real-time asset interchange network

RG-GL, receiver general–general ledger

RTGS, real time gross settlement

SAFE, simple agreement for future equity

SAFT, simple agreement for future token

SAFTE, simple agreement for future tokens or equity

SEC, US Securities and Exchange Commission

SegWit, Segregated Witness

SMTP, simple mail transfer protocol

STO, security token offering

SWIFT, Society for Worldwide Interbank Financial Telecommunication

TCP/IP, transmission control and Internet protocols

TGEs token generation events

TRACE, Trade Reporting and Compliance Engine

VC, venture capital or capitalist

vostro, "yours with us" account

XML, extensible markup language

zk-SNARK, zero-knowledge Succinct Non-Interactive ARgument of Knowledge

NOTES

1. Tom Rees, "Carney Defends Facebook's Libra in Call for Digital Payments Revolution," *Telegraph*, Telegraph Media Group Ltd., 15 Oct. 2019. telegraph.co.uk/business/2019/10/15/carney-defends-facebooks-libra-call-digital-payments-revolution, accessed 17 Oct. 2019.

2. Louise Matsakis, "Cryptocurrency Scams Are Just Straight-Up Trolling at This Point," *WIRED*, Condé Nast, 5 Feb. 2018. wired.com/story/cryptocurrency-scams-ico-trolling, accessed 27 Feb. 2018.

3. Anna Irrera, "More than 10 Percent of $3.7 Billion Raised in ICOs Has Been Stolen: Ernst & Young," *Reuters*, Thomson Reuters, 22 Jan. 2018. reuters.com/article/us-ico-ernst-young/more-than-10-percent-of-3-7-billion-raised-in-icos-has-been-stolen-ernst-young-idUSKBN1FB1MZ, accessed 27 Feb. 2018.

4. "Justice Louis D. Brandeis," Louis D. Brandeis Legacy Fund for Social Justice, Brandeis University, 2017. brandeis.edu/legacyfund/bio.html, accessed 4 Nov. 2017.

5. Robert J. Shiller Quotes, *BrainyQuote.com*, BrainyMedia Inc. 2019. brainyquote.com/quotes/robert_j_shiller_824806, accessed 17 Oct. 2019.

6. A paraphrase of Marc Andreessen, "Why Software Is Eating the World," Review, *Wall Street Journal*, Dow Jones & Company, 20 Aug. 2011. wsj.com/articles/SB10001424053111903480904576512250915629460, accessed 8 Sept. 2019.

7. "Motives," *The Quotable Satoshi*, Satoshi Nakamoto Institute, Nov. 2008. satoshi.nakamotoinstitute.org/quotes/motives, accessed 8 Sept. 2019.

8. "Miropayments," *The Quotable Satoshi*, Satoshi Nakamoto Institute, Jan. 2009. satoshi.nakamotoinstitute.org/quotes/micropayments, accessed 8 Sept. 2019.

9. Dan Noyes, "The Top 20 Valuable Facebook Statistics," *Zephoria.com*, Zephoria Inc., last updated July 2019. zephoria.com/top-15-valuable-facebook-statistics, accessed 8 Sept. 2019.

10. Donald J. Trump, Twitter Post, 11 July 2019 (5:15 PM). twitter.com/realdonaldtrump/status/1149472284702208000, accessed 8 Sept. 2019.

11. Jerome Powell, "Fed's Powell: Facebook's Libra Raises 'Serious Concerns' About ..." Video, 00:04:12, *CNBC.com*, CNBC LLC., 11 July 2019. cnbc.com/video/2019/07/11/powell-facebooks-libra-raises-serious-concerns-about-regulation.html, accessed 8 Sept. 2019.

12. Dave Michaels and Paul Vigna, "Facebook Questioned on Cryptocurrency, but Battle Looms with Global Regulators," *Wall Street Journal*, Dow Jones & Company Inc., last updated 16 July 2019. wsj.com/articles/facebook-faces-critics-potential-allies-at-senate-hearing-on-digital-currency-11563289251, accessed 8 Sept. 2019.

13. Dan Noyes, "The Top 20 Valuable Facebook Statistics."

14. Matthew De Silva, "Tencent Created QQ Coin Long before Facebook's Libra," *Quartz*, Quartz Media Inc., 11 July 2019. qz.com/1663249/chinas-tencent-launched-qq-coin-before-long-facebooks-libra-cryptocurrency, accessed 8 Sept. 2019.

15. Bethany McLean, "Nathaniel Popper's 'Digital Gold' Looks at Bitcoin," *New York Times*, New York Times Company, 2 July 2015. nytimes.com/2015/07/05/books/review/nathaniel-poppers-digital-gold-looks-at-bitcoin.html, accessed 8 Sept. 2019.

16. Cameron Winklevoss and Tyler Winklevoss, interviewed by Alex Tapscott, 11 July 2019.

17. Don Tapscott and Alex Tapscott, *Blockchain Revolution: How the Technology Behind Bitcoin and Other Cryptocurrencies Is Changing the World* (New York: Penguin Portfolio, 2018).

18. Blythe Masters, interviewed via telephone by Don and Alex Tapscott, 29 July 2015.

19. 0x, n.d. 0x.org, accessed 8 Sept. 2019.

20. Nikhilesh De, "CFTC: LedgerX 'Not Approved' to Launch 'Physical' Bitcoin Futures," *CoinDesk*, Digital Currency Group, last updated 1 Aug. 2019. coindesk.com/beating-bakkt-ledgerx-is-first-to-launch-physical-bitcoin-futures-in-us, accessed 8 Sept. 2019.

21. Anthony Pompliano, interviewed by Alex Tapscott, 10 July 2019. For more information, see Morgan Creek Digital Assets, digitalassetindexfund.com.

22. Anthony Pompliano, interviewed by Alex Tapscott, 10 July 2019.

23. Marley Gray, interviewed by Alex Tapscott, 17 July 2019.

24. Marley Gray, interviewed by Alex Tapscott, 17 July 2019.

25. "Stablecoin On-chain Transaction Volumes Soar, Outpace Venmo," *TradeBlock Blog*, 12 July 2019. tradeblock.com/blog/stablecoin-on-chain-transaction-volumes-soar-outpace-venmo; PYMNTS, "PayPal Q1 Payments Volume Dips, Venmo User Base Grows," *PYMNTS.com*, What's Next Media and Analytics LLC, 24 April 2019. pymnts.com/earnings/2019/venmo-paypal-q1-payments-volume-user-base, both accessed 8 Sept. 2019.

26. Daniel Palmer, "Walmart Wants to Patent a Stablecoin that Looks a Lot Like Facebook Libra," *CoinDesk*, Digital Currency Group, last updated 2 Aug. 2019. coindesk.com/walmart-wants-to-patent-a-stablecoin-that-looks-a-lot-like-facebook-libra, accessed 8 Sept. 2019.

27. Cameron Winklevoss and Tyler Winklevoss, interviewed by Alex Tapscott, 11 July 2019.

28. Anthony Pompliano, interviewed by Alex Tapscott, 10 July 2019.

29. Ryan Selkis, interviewed by Alex Tapscott, 23 July 2019.

30. Ethan Buchman, interviewed by Alex Tapscott, 10 July 2019.

31. "Top 10 Most Valuable Companies in the World (1997-2019)," Video (4:28), *YouTube.com*, RankingTheWorld, 28 April 2019. youtube.com/watch?v=8WVoJ6JNLO8, accessed 8 Sept. 2019.

32. Michael J. Casey, "The Token Economy: When Money Becomes Programmable," foreword by Don Tapscott, Blockchain Research Institute, 28 Sept. 2017, rev. 28 March 2018.

33. Anthony Williams, "Consolidating Multiple Ledgers with Blockchain: A Single Digital Ledger for the Government of Canada Accounts," foreword by Don Tapscott, Blockchain Research Institute, 16 Nov. 2018.

34. Ethan Buchman, interviewed by Alex Tapscott, 10 July 2019.

35. Anthony Williams, "Consolidating Multiple Ledgers with Blockchain."

36. Anthony Williams, "Consolidating Multiple Ledgers with Blockchain."

37. Steve Lohr, "Calls Mount to Ease Big Tech's Grip on our Data," *New York Times*, New York Times Company, 25 July 2019. nytimes.com/2019/07/25/business/calls-mount-to-ease-big-techs-grip-on-your-data.html, accessed 8 Sept. 2019.

38. Sarah Dai, "China's Central Bank Is Developing Its Own Digital Currency, Even as It Bans Bitcoin and Private Cryptos," *South China Morning Post*, South China Morning Post Publishers Ltd., 5 Nov. 2017. scmp.com/business/companies/article/2118468/chinas-central-bank-studying-its-own-digital-currency-even-it, accessed 8 Sept. 2019.

39. Meltem Demirors, interviewed by Alex Tapscott, 3 July 2019.

40. Greg McMullen, Primavera De Filippi, and Constance Choi, "Blockchain Identity Services: Technical Benchmark of Existing Blockchain-Based Identity Systems," foreword by Don Tapscott, Blockchain Research Institute and Coalition of Automated Legal Applications, 30 July 2019.

41. Greg McMullen, Primavera De Filippi, and Constance Choi, "Blockchain Identity Services."

42. Greg McMullen, Primavera De Filippi, and Constance Choi, "Blockchain Identity Services."

43. Don Tapscott, "A Declaration of Interdependence: Toward a New Social Contract for the Digital Economy," Blockchain Research Institute, rev. 14 Jan. 2019.

44. Ethan Buchman, interviewed by Alex Tapscott, 10 July 2019.

45. James Beck, e-mail message to Alex Tapscott, 7 Aug. 2019.

46. Joseph Lubin, e-mail message to Alex Tapscott, 7 Aug. 2019.

47. Collin Myers, interviewed by Alex Tapscott, 12 July 2019.

48. Collin Myers, interviewed by Alex Tapscott, 12 July 2019.

49. Rune Christensen, interviewed by Alex Tapscott, 24 July 2019.

50. "Total Value Locked (USD) in DeFi," Defi Pulse, n.d. defipulse.com, accessed 8 Sept. 2019.

51. Meltem Demirors, interviewed by Alex Tapscott, 3 July 2019.

52. Greg Di Prisco, interviewed by Alex Tapscott, 17 July 2019.

53. Rune Christensen, interviewed by Alex Tapscott, 24 July 2019.

54. Rune Christensen, interviewed by Alex Tapscott, 24 July 2019.

55. Meltem Demirors, interviewed by Alex Tapscott, 3 July 2019.

56. Bill Barhydt, interviewed by Alex Tapscott, 25 July 2019.

57. Glenn Gruber, "A Tech Reality: If You Don't Like Change, You're Going to Like Irrelevance Even Less," *PhocusWire*, Northstar Travel Group, 20 Dec. 2012. phocuswire.com/A-tech-reality-If-you-don-t-like-change-you-re-going-to-like-irrelevance-even-less, accessed 11 Sept. 2019.

58. Clayton M. Christensen, *The Innovator's Dilemma* (Cambridge, MA: HBS Press, 2013): 98.

59. Donald N. Sull, *Why Good Companies Go Bad, and How Great Managers Remake Them* (Cambridge, MA: HBS Press, 2005).

60. Donald N. Sull, "Why Good Companies Go Bad," *Financial Times*, The Financial Times Ltd., 3 Oct. 2005. donsull.com/wp-content/uploads/2013/07/ft_why_good_go_bad.pdf, accessed 8 Sept. 2019.

61. Steven Zobell, "Why Digital Transformations Fail: Closing the $900 Billion Hole in Enterprise Strategy," *Forbes*, Forbes Media LLC, 13 March 2018. forbes.com/sites/forbestechcouncil/2018/03/13/why-

digital-transformations-fail-closing-the-900-billion-hole-in-enterprise-strategy/#28cfab527b8b, accessed 8 Sept. 2019.

62. Steven Zobell, "Why Digital Transformations Fail."

63. Don Tapscott and Rob Carter, "Blockchain, FedEx, and the Future," *Tech Minutes*, ed. Jason Baker, About FedEx, FedEx Corp., 29 May 2018. about.van.fedex.com/blog/blockchain, accessed 8 Sept. 2019.

64. "Largest Number of Banks to Join Live Application of Blockchain Technology," J.P.Morgan, JPMorgan Chase & Co., n.d. jpmorgan.com/global/treasury-services/IIN, accessed 8 Sept. 2019.

65. "J.P.Morgan Demonstrates the Potential of Blockchain-Based Prototype," J.P.Morgan, JPMorgan Chase & Co., 16 May 2018. jpmorgan.com/country/US/en/detail/1320567520828, accessed 8 Sept. 2019.

66. "J.P.Morgan Creates Digital Coin for Payments," J.P.Morgan, JPMorgan Chase & Co., 14 Feb. 2019. jpmorgan.com/global/news/digital-coin-payments, accessed 8 Sept. 2019.

67. Marie Huillet, "Jamie Dimon Comments on Bitcoin Yet Again, Says He Doesn't Give a Sh*t about It," *Cointelegraph*, Tabula Publishing Ltd., 1 Nov. 2018. cointelegraph.com/news/jamie-dimon-comments-on-bitcoin-yet-again-says-he-doesnt-give-a-sht-about-it, accessed 8 Sept. 2019.

68. Max Raskin and David Yermack, "Digital Currencies, Decentralized Ledgers, and the Future of Central Banking," eds. Peter Conti-Brown and Rosa Lastra, *SSRN.com*, 1 May 2016. Elsevier, papers.ssrn.com/sol3/papers.cfm?abstract_id=2773973, accessed 8 Sept. 2019.

69. Elizabeth Schulze, "Cryptocurrencies Are 'Clearly Shaking the System,' IMF's Lagarde Says," *CNBC.com*, CNBC LLC, 10 April 2019. cnbc.com/2019/04/11/cryptocurrencies-fintech-clearly-shaking-the-system-imfs-lagarde.html, accessed 11 Sept. 2019.

70. Donald J. Trump, Twitter post, 11 July 2019 (5:25 PM). twitter.com/realdonaldtrump/status/1149472282584072192, accessed 8 Sept. 2019.

71. Barry Eichengreen, "As Monetary Policy Reaches Its Limits, It's Time for Governments to Spend," *The Guardian*, Guardian News & Media Ltd., 11 March 2016. theguardian.com/business/2016/mar/11/as-monetary-policy-reaches-its-limits-its-time-for-governments-to-start-spending, accessed 8 Sept. 2019.

72. Adam Hayes, "Decentralized Banking: Monetary Technocracy in the Digital Age," *SSRN.com*, last revised 21 July 2016. Elsevier, papers.ssrn.com/sol3/papers.cfm?abstract_id=2807476, accessed 8 Sept. 2019.

73. Adam Hayes, "Decentralized Banking: Monetary Technocracy in the Digital Age."

74. Kimberly Amadeo, "What Too Big to Fail Means," *The Balance*, Dotdash, last updated 30 May 2019. thebalance.com/too-big-to-fail-3305617, accessed 8 Sept. 2019.

75. Matt Stoller, "Launching a Global Currency Is a Bold, Bad Move for Facebook," *New York Times*, New York Times Company, 19 June 2019. nytimes.com/2019/06/19/opinion/facebook-currency-libra.html, accessed 8 Sept. 2019.

76. David Z. Morris, "Facebook's Libra Currency Could Threaten the Global Financial System. Here's How," *Fortune*, Fortune Media IP Ltd., 18 July 2019. fortune.com/2019/07/18/facebook-libra-cryptocurrency-washington-hearings-financial-system, accessed 8 Sept. 2019.

77. David Z. Morris, "Facebook's Libra Currency Could Threaten the Global Financial System. Here's How."

78. John Biggs, "Indian Panel Proposes Fines and Jail Time for Cryptocurrency Use," *CoinDesk*, Digital Currency Group, 23 July 2019. coindesk.com/indian-panel-proposes-ban-and-jail-time-for-cryptocurrency-use, accessed 8 Sept. 2019.

79. Bill Barhydt, interviewed by Alex Tapscott, 25 July 2019.

80. Max Raskin and David Yermack, "Digital Currencies, Decentralized Ledgers, and the Future of Central Banking," eds. Peter Conti-Brown and Rosa Lastra, *SSRN.com*, 1 May 2016, p. 15.

81. Donald J. Trump, Twitter Post, 23 Aug. 2019 (7:59 AM). twitter.com/realdonaldtrump/status/1164914959131848705; Mark Carney, "The Growing Challenges for Monetary Policy in the Current International Monetary and Financial System," Speech, Bank of England, Jackson Hole Symposium, Kansas City, MO, 23 Aug. 2019. bankofengland.co.uk/-/media/boe/files/speech/2019/the-growing-challenges-for-monetary-policy-speech-by-mark-carney.pdf, both accessed 8 Sept. 2019.

82. Mark Carney, "Enabling the Fintech Transformation–Revolution, Restoration, or Reformation?" Speech, Lord Mayor's Banquet for Bankers and Merchants, London, England, 16 June 2016. bis.org/review/r160621e.pdf, accessed 8 Sept. 2019.

83. John Barrdear and Michael Kumhof, "The Macroeconomics of Central Bank Issued Digital Currencies," Staff Working Paper No. 605, Bank of England, July 2016. bankofengland.co.uk/-/media/boe/files/working-paper/2016/the-macroeconomics-of-central-bank-issued-digital-currencies.pdf, accessed 8 Sept. 2019.

84. Michael Kumhof and Clare Noone, "Central Bank Digital Currencies—Design Principles and Balance Sheet Implications," Staff Working Paper No. 725, Bank of England, May 2018. bankofengland.co.uk/-/media/boe/files/working-paper/2018/central-bank-digital-currencies-design-principles-and-balance-sheet-implications.pdf, accessed 8 Sept. 2019.

85. Mark Carney, "The Growing Challenges for Monetary Policy in the Current International Monetary and Financial System," Speech.

86. Meltem Demirors, interviewed by Alex Tapscott, 3 July 2019.

87. Fon Mathuros, "World Economic Forum 2018 to Call for Strengthening Cooperation in a Fractured World," WEForum.org, World Economic Forum, 20 Sept. 2017. weforum.org/press/2017/09/world-economic-forum-2018-to-call-for-strengthening-cooperation-in-a-fractured-world, accessed 8 Sept. 2019.

88. Rachel W. Robinson, "Distributed and Collaborative Marketplaces: Blockchain Serving the Unbanked," foreword by Alex Tapscott, Blockchain Research Institute, 22 Jan. 2018.

89. Rachel W. Robinson, "Distributed and Collaborative Marketplaces: Blockchain Serving the Unbanked."

90. Marc Goodman, *Future Crimes: Inside the Digital Underground and the Battle for Our Connected World*, reprint edition (New York: Doubleday, Penguin Random House, 2016).

91. Bruce Sterling, "Reading about Facebook Libra," *WIRED*, Condé Nast, 31 July 2019. wired.com/beyond-the-beyond/2019/07/reading-facebook-libra, accessed 8 Sept. 2019.

92. "Report of Investigation Pursuant to Section 21(a) of the Securities Exchange Act of 1934: The DAO," Release No. 81207, US Securities and Exchange Commission, 25 July 2017. sec.gov/litigation/investreport/34-81207.pdf; Dave Michaels and Paul Vigna, "SEC Chief Fires Warning Shot against Coin Offerings," *Wall Street Journal*, Dow Jones & Company Inc., last updated 9 Nov. 2017. wsj.com/articles/sec-chief-fires-warning-shot-against-coin-offerings-1510247148; and "SEC Qualifies First Token Offerings under Regulation A," *Cooley.com*, Cooley LLP, 18 July 2019. cooley.com/news/insight/2019/2019-07-18-sec-qualifies-first-token-offerings-under-regulation-a, all accessed 8 Sept. 2019.

93. Cooley, "SEC Qualifies First Token Offerings under Regulation A."

94. Quoted in "Circle Reveals Why Most Start-ups Are Wary of the US Market," *TOPNEWS*, 5 Aug. 2019. topnews.one/33040-circle-reveals-why-most-startups-are-wary-of-the-us-market.html, accessed 11 Sept. 2019.

95. "Section 230 of the Communications Decency Act," *EFF.org*, Electronic Frontier Foundation, n.d. eff.org/issues/cda230, accessed 8 Sept. 2019.

96. Joel S. Telpner, "The Lion, the Unicorn, and the Crown: Striking a Balance between Regulation and Blockchain Innovation," foreword by Don Tapscott, Blockchain Research Institute, 10 May 2018.

97. Ryan Selkis, interviewed by Alex Tapscott, 23 July 2019.

98. William Hinman, "Digital Asset Transactions: When *Howey* Met Gary (Plastic)," Speech, *SEC.gov*, Yahoo Finance All Markets Summit: Crypto, San Francisco, CA, 14 June 2018. sec.gov/news/speech/speech-hinman-061418, accessed 7 Oct. 2019.

99. "*CoinDesk* ICO Tracker: All-Time Cumulative ICO Funding," *CoinDesk*, Digital Currency Group, as of 18 Aug. 2017. coindesk.com/ico-tracker.

100. Garrett Hardin, "The Tragedy of the Commons," *Science* 162, No. 3859 (13 Dec. 1968): 1243–1248. American Association for the Advancement of Science, science.sciencemag.org/content/162/3859/1243, accessed 18 Sept. 2017.

101. Edella Schlager and Elinor Ostrom, "Property-Rights Regimes and Natural Resources: A Conceptual Analysis," *Land Economics* 68, No. 3 (University of Wisconsin Press: Aug. 1992): 249-262. JSTOR, jstor.org/stable/3146375, accessed 22 April 2010.

102. "Total Market Capitalization," *CoinMarketCap.com*. coinmarketcap.com/charts, accessed 22 Aug. 2017.

103. Oscar Williams-Grut, "Goldman: 'It's Getting Harder for Institutional Investors to Ignore Cryptocurrencies,'" *Business Insider*, Insider Inc., 10 Aug. 2017. businessinsider.com/goldman-sachs-cryptocurrencies-bitcoin-ethereum-icos-2017-8, accessed 22 Aug. 2017.

104. Gertrude Chavez-Dreyfuss, "Interview: Blockchain Start-up Gnosis to Freeze Tokens after Strong Sale," Reuters, *CNBC.com*, 25 April 2017. cnbc.com/2017/04/25/reuters-america-interview-blockchain-start-up-gnosis-to-freeze-tokens-after-strong-sale.html, accessed 18 Sept. 2017.

105. Mr. Justice Murphy, Opinion, *Securities and Exchange Commission v. W. J. Howey Co. et al.*, 328 US 293 (66 S.Ct. 1100, 90 L.Ed. 1244), No. 843, 27 May 1946. Legal Information Institute, Cornell Law School, law.cornell.edu/supremecourt/text/328/293, accessed 15 Sept. 2017.

106. Benjamin Roberts, interviewed by Don Tapscott, 20 June 2017. (Transcript shared with Michael Casey.)

107. "SEC Issues Investigative Report Concluding DAO Tokens, a Digital Asset, Were Securities," *SEC.gov*, US Securities and Exchange

Commission, 25 July 2017. sec.gov/news/press-release/2017-131, accessed 15 Sept. 2017.

108. John Ruwitch and Jemima Kelly, "China Hits Booming Cryptocurrency Market with Coin Fundraising Ban," *Reuters.com*, Thomson Reuters, 4 Sept. 2017. reuters.com/article/us-china-finance-digital/china-hits-booming-cryptocurrency-market-with-coin-fundraising-ban-idUSKCN1BF0R7, accessed 15 Sept. 2017.

109. Emin Gün Sirer, interviewed by Michael Casey, 22 June 2017.

110. Balaji S. Srinivasan, "Thoughts on Tokens," *Medium*, 21.co, 27 May 2017. news.21.co/thoughts-on-tokens-436109aabcbe, accessed 15 Sept. 2017.

111. Fred Wilson, "The Golden Age of Open Protocols," AVC [a venture capitalist], 31 July 2016. avc.com/2016/07/the-golden-age-of-open-protocols, accessed 15 Sept. 2017.

112. Lucian Tarnowski, interviewed by Michael Casey, 5 July 2017.

113. Harlan T. Wood, James E. Foley, and Alex Alekseyenko, "Gravity, a Distributed Smart Contracts Protocol," Economic Space Agency, n.d. economicspace.agency/gravity, accessed 18 Sept. 2017.

114. Akseli Virtanen, interviewed by Michael Casey, 4 July 2017.

115. Gregor Aisch, Wilson Andrews, and Josh Keller, "The Cost of Mobile Ads on 50 News Websites," *New York Times*, New York Times Company, 1 Oct. 2015. nytimes.com/interactive/2015/10/01/business/cost-of-mobile-ads.html, accessed 18 Sept. 2017.

116. ANA and White Ops, "Bot Baseline 2016-2017: Fraud in Digital Advertising," *ANA.net*, Association of National Advertisers and White Ops, May 2017. ana.net/content/show/id/botfraud-2017, accessed 18 Sept. 2017.

117. "US Ad Blocking to Jump by Double Digits This Year: More than 25% of Internet Users Will Block Ads This Year," *eMarketer.com*, eMarketer Inc., 21 June 2016. emarketer.com/Article/US-Ad-Blocking-Jump-by-Double-Digits-This-Year/1014111, accessed 18 Sept. 2017.

118. "The World's Most Valuable Resource Is No Longer Oil, but Data," *The Economist*, Economist Newspaper Ltd., 6 May 2017. economist.com/news/leaders/21721656-data-economy-demands-new-approach-antitrust-rules-worlds-most-valuable-resource, accessed 15 Sept. 2017.

119. Jonathan Keane, "$35 Million in 30 Seconds: Token Sale for Internet Browser Brave Sells Out," *CoinDesk*, Digital Currency Group, 31 May 2017. coindesk.com/35-million-30-seconds-token-sale-internet-browser-brave-sells, accessed 15 Sept. 2017.

120. "BAT Top 100 Token Holders," *Etherscan.io*, EtherScan, 15 Sept. 2017. etherscan.io/token/tokenholderchart/0x0d8775f648430679a709e 98d2b0cb6250d2887ef, accessed 15 Sept. 2017.

121. Brendan Eich, interviewed by Michael Casey, 29 June 2017.

122. Vitalik Buterin (@VitalikButerin), Twitter post, 31 May 2017 (10:44 AM) twitter.com/VitalikButerin/status/869972830191984641; and 31 May 2017 (10:45 AM). twitter.com/VitalikButerin/status/869973222330032129, both accessed 18 Sept. 2017.

123. Mo Marshall, "Three Lessons from Tezos' Record-Setting Blockchain Fundraise," *VentureBeat*, 21 July 2017. venturebeat.com/2017/07/21/3-lessons-from-tezos-record-setting-blockchain-fundraise, accessed 18 Sept. 2017.

124. Chris Burniske and Jack Tatar, *Cryptoassets: The Innovative Investors Guide to Bitcoin and Beyond* (New York: McGraw-Hill Education, 2017): 55.

125. Chris Burniske and Jack Tatar, *Cryptoassets: The Innovative Investors Guide to Bitcoin and Beyond* (New York: McGraw-Hill Education, 2017): 127.

126. Joichi Ito, "My View on the Current Situation of Bitcoin and the Blockchain," *Joi Ito Blog*, 22 Feb. 2016. joi.ito.com/weblog/2016/02/22/my-view-on-the-.html, accessed 18 Sept. 2017.

127. "Bitcoin Energy Consumption Index," *Digiconomist*, as of 15 Sept. 2017. digiconomist.net/bitcoin-energy-consumption.

128. Molly Webster, "The Ceremony," *RadioLab.org*, WNYC Studios, 14 July 2017. radiolab.org/story/ceremony, accessed 15 Sept. 2017.

129. Zooko Wilcox and Jack Grigg, "Why Equihash?" *Zcash Blog*, 15 April 2016. z.cash/blog/why-equihash.html, accessed 22 Aug. 2017.

130. Rhett Creighton, "Zcash Miners: Stop Paying 20% Genius Tax," *DecentralizeToday*, 30 Oct. 2016. decentralize.today/zcash-miners-stop-paying-20-genius-tax-486d9f40884f, accessed 15 Sept. 2017.

131. Molly Webster, "The Ceremony," prods. Matt Kielty and Molly Webster, *RadioLab.org*, WNYC Studios, New York Public Radio and Alfred P. Sloan Foundation, 14 July 2017. radiolab.org/story/ceremony, accessed 15 Sept. 2017.

132. Comment made on stage at Consensus Conference, 22 May 2017.

133. "[1025] Projects Built on Ethereum," *State of the Ðapps*, n.d. stateofthedapps.com, as of 7 Feb. 2018. See also github.com/state-of-the-dapps.

134. Kathleen (McCaffrey) Breitman, "Dear Legal Insurrection Readers, Remember Me?" *Legal Insurrection*, 17 July 2017. legalinsurrection.com/2017/07/dear-legal-insurrection-readers-remember-me, accessed 15 Sept. 2017.

135. Dom Galeon, "Ethereum Co-Founder Takes to Twitter to Disagree with Tezos Blockchain Plan," *Futurism.com*, 11 July 2017. futurism. com/ethereum-co-founder-takes-to-twitter-to-disagree-with-tezos-blockchain-plan, accessed 15 Sept. 2017.

136. Arthur Breitman, "Why Governance Matters," *Medium*, A Medium Corp., 28 Aug. 2016. medium.com/tezos/why-governance-matters-9c6458044037, accessed 15 Sept. 2017.

137. Robin Hanson, "Futarchy: Vote Values, but Bet Beliefs," George Mason University, n.d. mason.gmu.edu/~rhanson/futarchy.html, accessed 15 Sept. 2017.

138. L.M. Goodman, "Tezos: A Self-Amending Crypto-Ledger," Tezos, 3 Aug. 2014. tezos.com/static/papers/position_paper.pdf, accessed 15 Sept. 2017.

139. Kathleen Breitman interviewed by Paul Vigna, as part of research for a book, co-authored with Michael J. Casey, *The Truth Machine: The Blockchain and the Future of Everything* (New York: St. Martin's Press, 2018).

140. "Diversifying the Portfolio of the Tezos Foundation," Tezos Stiftung, 18 July 2017. steemit.com/tezos/@melea/tezos-news-tezos-foundation-diversifying-the-portfolio, accessed 11 Nov. 2019.

141. JD Alois, "After Raising a $232 Million ICO, Tezos Gives Back with $50 Million Commitment to Companies Using Their Platform," *Crowdfund Insider,* 10 Aug. 2017. crowdfundinsider.com/2017/08 /120569-raising-232-million-ico-tezos-gives-back-50-million-commitment-companies-looking-use-tezos-platform, accessed 15 Sept. 2017.

142. Avi Mizrahi, "ICONOMI to Buy Back and Burn Its Tokens to Increase Value," *Finance Magnates*, 29 March 2017. financemagnates.com/ cryptocurrency/trading/iconomi-buy-back-burn-tokens-increase-value, accessed 15 Sept. 2017.

143. Penguinpablo71, "Steem Stats: Active Users," *Steemit.com*, Steemit Inc., 13 July 2017. steemit.com/steemit/@penguinpablo/steem-stats-active-users, accessed 15 Sept. 2017.

144. Daniel Larimer (bytemaster), Josh Lavin (hkshwa), et al., "EOS.IO Technical White Paper," *GitHub*, GitHub Inc. and Block.one, 26 June 2017, updated 24 Nov. 2017. github.com/EOSIO/Documentation/blob/ master/TechnicalWhitePaper.md, accessed 1 Dec. 2017.

145. "Frequently Asked Questions," EOS, n.d. eos.io/faq.html, accessed 22 Aug. 2017.

146. Will Stephens, "It's Official! EOS CrowdSale LARGEST ICO Ever—Now Raised over $150M," *Steemit.com*, Steemit Inc., 1 July 2017. steemit.com/cryptocurrency/@willstephens/it-s-official-eos-crowdsale-largest-ico-ever-now-raised-over-usd150m, accessed 15 Sept. 2017.

147. ICO Alert. icoalert.com, accessed 17 Aug. 2017.

148. Ryan Merkley, "State of the Commons," Creative Commons, 28 April 2017. stateof.creativecommons.org, accessed 18 Sept. 2017.

149. "MetaX Completes $10 Million adToken (ADT) Sale," *Cision PRWeb*, Vocus PRW Holdings LLC, 28 June 2017. prweb.com/releases/2017/06/prweb14467717.htm, accessed 15 Sept. 2017.

150. AdChain, "What's the difference between adToken and BAT?" *Medium*, A Medium Corp., 2 June 2017. medium.com/@AdChain/whats-the-difference-between-adtoken-and-bat-a783a9ea106a, accessed 15 Sept. 2017.

151. Maciej Olpinski, "Userfeeds Got Funded! Here's How We Plan to Bring 'Skin in the Game' Back to Discovery Algorithms," *Userfeeds Blog*, A Medium Corp., 3 May 2017. blog.userfeeds.io/userfeeds-got-funded-heres-how-we-plan-to-bring-skin-in-the-game-back-to-discovery-algorithms-71f7afcb886d, accessed 15 Sept. 2017.

152. Jesse Walden, interviewed by Michael Casey, 25 March 2017.

153. Julien Rath, "Spotify Acquired Blockchain Start-up Mediachain," *Business Insider*, Insider Inc., 26 April 2017. businessinsider.com/spotify-acquired-blockchain-startup-mediachain-2017-4, accessed 1 Dec. 2017.

154. Vinny Lingham, "Why Tokens Are Eating the World," *Vinny Lingham Blog*, 17 July 2017. vinnylingham.com/why-tokens-are-eating-the-world-b4174235c87b, accessed 15 Sept. 2017.

155. Cade Metz, "Forget Bitcoin. The Blockchain Could Reveal What's True Today and Tomorrow," *WIRED*, Condé Nast, March 2017. wired.com/2017/03/forget-bitcoin-blockchain-reveal-whats-true-today-tomorrow, accessed 7 Sept. 2017.

156. Exergy, *Thermopedia*, 11 Feb. 2011. thermopedia.com/content/745, accessed 13 Sept. 2017.

157. For a good summary of how the *Howey* test pertains to ICOs, see Gregory J. Nowak and Joseph C. Guagliardo, "Blockchain and Initial Coin Offerings: SEC Provides First US Securities Law Guidance," Harvard Law School Forum on Corporate Governance and Financial Regulation, 9 Aug. 2017. corpgov.law.harvard.edu/2017/08/09/blockchain-and-initial-coin-offerings-sec-provides-first-u-s-securities-law-guidance, accessed 7 Sept. 2017.

158. Marco Santori, interviewed by Michael Casey, 26 June 2017.

159. As per the Crypto Company's website, see thecryptocompany.com.

160. Don Tapscott and Alex Tapscott, "Realizing the Potential of Blockchain: A Multistakeholder Approach to the Stewardship of Blockchain and Cryptocurrencies," White Paper, World Economic Forum, June 2017. www3.weforum.org/docs/WEF_Realizing_Potential_Blockchain.pdf, accessed 22 Aug. 2017.

161. Neha Narula, "Cryptographic Vulnerabilities in IOTA," *Medium*, A Medium Corp., 7 Sept. 2017. medium.com/@neha/cryptographic-vulnerabilities-in-iota-9a6a9ddc4367, accessed 7 Sept. 2017.

162. Laura Shin, "Want to Hold an ICO? CoinList Makes It Easy—and Legal," *Forbes*, Forbes Media LLC, 19 July 2017. forbes.com/sites/laurashin/2017/05/18/want-to-hold-an-ico-coinlist-makes-it-easy-and-legal/#ab2fbc97ce5e, accessed 15 Sept. 2017.

163. Laura Shin, "Crypto Boom: 15 New Hedge Funds Want in on 84,000% Returns," *Forbes*, Forbes Media LLC, 12 July 2017. forbes.com/sites/laurashin/2017/07/12/crypto-boom-15-new-hedge-funds-want-in-on-84000-returns/#549c2824416a, accessed 15 Sept. 2017.

164. Laura Shin, "Crypto Boom: 15 New Hedge Funds Want in on 84,000% Returns."

165. William Mougayar, *The Business Blockchain: Promise, Practice, and Application of the Next Internet Technology* (Hoboken: John D. Wiley & Sons, 2016): 68-69.

166. John Markoff, "Entrepreneurs See a Web Guided by Common Sense," *New York Times*, New York Times Company, 11 Nov. 2006. nytimes.com/2006/11/12/business/12web.html, accessed 3 Feb. 2018.

167. Joseph Lubin, "Announcing 'The Brooklyn Project' for Token Launches," *ConsenSys.net*, ConsenSys Media, 30 Nov. 2017. media.consensys.net/announcing-the-brooklyn-project-for-token-launches-22ba89279f5f, accessed 3 Feb. 2018.

168. Sources of Figure 3-1 data: Oscar Williams-Grut, "The 11 Biggest ICO Fundraises of 2017," *Business Insider*, Insider Inc., 1 Jan. 2018. businessinsider.com/the-10-biggest-ico-fundraises-of-2017-2017-12; and "CoinDesk ICO Tracker," *CoinDesk*, Digital Currency Group, 1 Jan. 2018. coindesk.com/ico-tracker, both accessed 26 Feb. 2018.

169. Elinor Ostrom, "Tragedy of the Commons," eds. Steven N. Durlauf and Lawrence E. Blume, *The New Palgrave Dictionary of Economics*, 2nd ed., Palgrave Macmillan, Macmillan Publishers Ltd., 2008. dictionaryofeconomics.com/article?id=pde2008_T000193, accessed 3 Feb. 2018.

170. Garrett Hardin, "The Tragedy of the Commons," *Journal of Natural Resources Policy Research* 1, No. 3, 2009: 243-253. Taylor and Francis, <u>doi. org/10.1080/19390450903037302</u>, accessed 3 Feb. 2018.

171. In the context of a blockchain-based system, *overexploitation* refers to the risk of network overload, deriving from too many transactions sent to the networks, without enough computational resources to process these transactions. This problem has been solved through the introduction of dynamically adjusted transaction fees (paid in tokens), which allow the system to self-manage these transactions without third-party intervention. *Under-allocation* refers instead to the risk of there not being a sufficient amount of computational resources contributed to the network, thereby hindering the security thereof. Most blockchain-based networks have solved this problem through the probabilistic allocation of a "block reward" to all those who contribute resources to the network.

172. SEC Chair Jay Clayton, "Statement on Cryptocurrencies and Initial Coin Offerings," *SEC.gov*, US Securities and Exchange Commission, 11 Dec. 2017. <u>sec.gov/news/public-statement/statement-clayton-2017-12-11</u>, accessed 1 Feb. 2018.

173. The seminal white paper describing the Bitcoin protocol was circulated on a cryptographic mailing list by a certain Satoshi Nakamoto in 2008. See Satoshi Nakamoto, "Bitcoin: A Peer-to-Peer Electronic Cash System," White Paper, *Bitcoin.org*, 1 Nov. 2008. <u>bitcoin.org/bitcoin.pdf</u>, accessed 5 Feb. 2018.

174. From an economic standpoint, public goods are resources that are both non-excludable and non-rivalrous in consumption. More specifically, according to Gravelle and Rees, "The defining characteristic of a public good is that it is *non-rival*: consumption of it by one individual does not actually or potentially reduce the amount available to be consumed by another individual." See Hugh Gravelle and Ray Rees, Ch. 14, "Market Failure and Government Failure," *Microeconomics*, 3rd ed. (Harlow, Essex: Pearson Education Ltd., 2004): 326. A quasi-public good is a resource that presents the characteristics of a public good, but that might be subject to partial excludability, partial rivalry, or partial diminishability. Bitcoin is only partially non-rival because, although one person using the Bitcoin network will generally have no impact on the usability of the system for others, if too many people are using the network at the same time, it might actually lead to a potential congestion of the system. It is partially excludable, because, to execute a transaction on the Bitcoin network, one needs to spend (and therefore first to acquire) some fraction of bitcoin.

175. In principle, the incentives of individual miners are aligned with the public good. Indeed, we consider here that any "selfish mining" strategy

should yield a negative expected profit for its operator. For more details on the notion of selfish mining, see Ittay Eyal and Emin Gün Sirer, "Majority Is not Enough: Bitcoin Mining Is Vulnerable," *ArXiv.org*, Cornell University Library, NSF Trust STC, and DARPA, 15 Nov. 2013. arxiv.org/abs/1311.0243, accessed 5 Feb. 2018.

176. "Vitalik Buterin," *Bitcoin Magazine*, BTC Media LLC, n.d. bitcoinmagazine.com/authors/vitalik-buterin, accessed 31 Jan. 2018.

177. See Vitalik Buterin, "A Next-Generation Smart Contract and Decentralized Application Platform," *Ethereum/Wiki*, GitHub Inc., Nov. 2013, first edited on GitHub by HeikoHeiko 1 Sept. 2014, and last updated by James Ray, 3 Feb. 2018. github.com/ethereum/wiki/wiki/White-Paper, accessed 6 Feb. 2018. From its introduction: "A blockchain with a built-in fully fledged Turing-complete programming language that can be used to create 'contracts' that can be used to encode arbitrary state transition functions, allowing users to create [any application] simply by writing up the logic in a few lines of [smart contract] code."

178. VitalikButerin, Administrator, "So Where Did the Name Ethereum Come from?" *Ethereum Community Forum*, Ethereum Foundation, March 2014. forum.ethereum.org/discussion/655/so-where-did-the-name-ethereum-come-from, accessed 1 Feb. 2018.

179. The token sale went live on 30 July 2014, before the Ethereum platform had been built. Promises for 11.9 million tokens were sold to the public, with an expectation that these promises would be converted into ether as soon as the platform launched.

180. However, about a month later, a code weakness was detected and exploited by an attacker leading to its demise, and triggering a governance crisis that resulted in a hard fork of the Ethereum blockchain supported by the majority of Ethereum developers, while the remaining part of the community decided to maintain the original blockchain—which became Ethereum Classic.

181. See Slock.it GmbH, slock.it. For a technical analysis of the DAO, see Christoph Jentzsch, "The History of the DAO and Lessons Learned," *Slock.it Blog*, A Medium Corp., 24 Aug. 2016. blog.slock.it/the-history-of-the-dao-and-lessons-learned-d06740f8cfa5, accessed 1 Feb. 2018.

182. Curators acted as a "failsafe mechanism" whose mission was to ensure a network distribution preventing project submitters from colluding into a 51 percent attack, meaning checking on their identity (the "Who's Who of crypto") to ensure the network decision process might not be subject to alliances. For a short explanation on the curator role, see Stephan Tual, "Vitalik Buterin, Gavin Wood, Alex Van De Sande, Vlad

Zamfir Announced amongst Exceptional DAO Curators," *Slock.it Blog*, A Medium Corp., 25 April 2016. blog.slock.it/vitalik-buterin-gavin-wood-alex-van-de-sande-vlad-zamfir-announced-amongst-stellar-dao-curators-44be4d12dd6e, accessed 3 Feb. 2018. For more details, see Stephan Tual, "On DAO Contractors and Curators," *Slock.it Blog*, A Medium Corp., 9 April 2016. blog.slock.it/on-contractors-and-curators-2fb9238b2553, accessed 3 Feb. 2018.

183. This is the standard principal/agent model in economics, whereby the owner (acting as principal) hires a manager (the agent) to run and manage the day-to-day operations of the firm. The agent's incentives need to be properly configured so that the agent's behavior will conform to the principal's set objective.

184. Sources of data in this paragraph and Figure 3-2: Oscar Williams-Grut, "The 11 Biggest ICO Fundraises of 2017," *Business Insider*, Insider Inc., 1 Jan. 2018. businessinsider.com/the-10-biggest-ico-fundraises-of-2017-2017-12; "Cryptocurrency ICO Stats 2017," *CoinSchedule*, CoinSchedule.com, 26 Feb. 2018. coinschedule.com/stats. html?year=2017; "IOTA: ICO Overview with Rating and Review," *TokenTops.com*, 21 Dec. 2015. tokentops.com/ico/iota, all accessed 26 Feb. 2018.

185. Sanjeev Verma, Nghi Bui, and Chelsea Lam, "Munchee Token: A Decentralized Blockchain Based Food Review/Rating Social Media Platform," White Paper, Munchee Inc., 16 Oct. 2017, p. 11. theventurealley.com/wp-content/uploads/sites/5/2017/12/Munchee-White-Paper.pdf, accessed 3 Feb. 2018. For instance, page 11 of MUN's white paper refers to the "Munchee token (MUN) [as] a method of exchange inside of the Munchee ecosystem."

186. SEC, "Report of Investigation Pursuant to Section 21(a) of the Securities Exchange Act of 1934: The DAO," Release No. 81207, *SEC. gov*, US Securities and Exchange Commission, 25 July 2017. sec.gov/litigation/investreport/34-81207.pdf; and "SEC Issues Investigative Report Concluding DAO Tokens, a Digital Asset, Were Securities," Press Release 2017-131, *SEC.gov*, US Securities and Exchange Commission, 25 July 2017. sec.gov/news/press-release/2017-131, both accessed 1 Feb. 2018.

187. SEC, "Report of Investigation Pursuant to Section 21(a) of the Securities Exchange Act of 1934: The DAO."

188. SEC, "Report of Investigation Pursuant to Section 21(a) of the Securities Exchange Act of 1934: The DAO."

189. SEC Chair Jay Clayton, "Statement on Cryptocurrencies and Initial Coin Offerings," *SEC.gov*, US Securities and Exchange Commission,

11 Dec. 2017. sec.gov/news/public-statement/statement-clayton-2017-12-11, accessed 1 Feb. 2018.

190. SEC Chair Jay Clayton, "Statement on Cryptocurrencies and Initial Coin Offerings," *SEC.gov*, US Securities and Exchange Commission, 11 Dec. 2017.

191. SEC, "In the Matter of MUNCHEE INC., Respondent; Order Instituting Cease-and-Desist Proceedings Pursuant to Section 8A of the Securities Act of 1933, Making Findings, and Imposing a Cease-and-Desist Order," Securities Act of 1933 Release No. 10445, Administrative Proceeding File No. 3-18304, *SEC.gov*, US Securities and Exchange Commission, 11 Dec. 2017: p. 6, pt. 18. sec.gov/litigation/admin/2017/33-10445.pdf, accessed 2 Feb. 2018.

192. SEC, "In the Matter of MUNCHEE INC., Respondent": p. 9, para. 35. sec.gov/litigation/admin/2017/33-10445.pdf, accessed 2 Feb. 2018.

193. SEC Chair Jay Clayton, "Statement on Cryptocurrencies and Initial Coin Offerings," *SEC.gov*, US Securities and Exchange Commission, 11 Dec. 2017.

194. SEC, "In the Matter of MUNCHEE INC., Respondent": p. 5, para. 16. sec.gov/litigation/admin/2017/33-10445.pdf, accessed 2 Feb. 2018.

195. SEC, "In the Matter of MUNCHEE INC., Respondent": p. 6, para. 17. sec.gov/litigation/admin/2017/33-10445.pdf, accessed 2 Feb. 2018.

196. "Nick Morgan: The DAO, the SEC, and the ICO Boom," *Epicenter*, hosted by Brian Fabian Crain, Sebastien Couture, and Meher Roy, episode 198, Epicenter Media Ltd., 29 Aug. 2017. epicenter.tv/episode/198, accessed 2 Feb. 2018.

197. SEC, "In the Matter of MUNCHEE INC., Respondent": pp. 6-7, points 21-24; p. 9, point 33. sec.gov/litigation/admin/2017/33-10445.pdf, accessed 2 Feb. 2018.

198. Automation also brings about an interesting gray area concerning the very nature of "managerial efforts." What happens if tokens are sold for a DAO once (and only once) it is up and running, and operated by algorithmic governance? And suppose the objective of this DAO were solely to generate profits through automated trading rules for its token-holders. A judge may find herself in a gray area where it is not clear that the fourth prong of the *Howey* test is met, while it is clear that in this profit-only oriented case, the token should be treated as an investment security. There again, a clear determination of substance over form will undoubtedly be needed.

199. "Why Switzerland?" *CryptoValley.Swiss*, Crypto Valley Association, n.d. cryptovalley.swiss/why-switzerland, accessed 3 Feb. 2018.

200. See ProPublica's records for the Linux Foundation here, projects. propublica.org/nonprofits/organizations/460503801, and the Mozilla Foundation here projects.propublica.org/nonprofits/ organizations/200097189, both accessed 3 Feb. 2018.

201. Swiss Civil Code of 10 Dec. 1907 (status as of 1 Sept. 2017), articles 80-89. admin.ch/opc/en/classified-compilation/19070042/index.html, accessed 7 Feb. 2018.

202. "About the Ethereum Foundation: Mission and Vision Statement," *Ethereum Project*, Ethereum Foundation (Stiftung Ethereum), 14 July 2014. ethereum.org/foundation, accessed 3 Feb. 2018.

203. "AML News and Trends Cryptocurrencies ICOs Latest FINMA Guidelines on ICOs; How to Do KYC for Your Token Holders," *Competitive Compliance*, Competitive Compliance GmbH, 3 Oct. 2017. competitivecompliance.com/single-post/2017/10/04/Latest-FINMA-Guidelines-on-ICOs-How-to-do-KYC-for-your-token-holders, accessed 3 Feb. 2018.

204. Juan Batiz-Benet, Jesse Clayburgh, and Marco Santori, "The SAFT Project: Toward a Compliant Token Sale Framework," *SaftProject.com*, Protocol Labs Inc. and Cooley LLP, 2 Oct. 2017. saftproject.com/static/ SAFT-Project-Whitepaper.pdf, accessed 7 Feb. 2018. For more detail, see the final three paragraphs of p. 1.

205. Juan Batiz-Benet, Jesse Clayburgh, and Marco Santori, "The SAFT Project: Toward a Compliant Token Sale Framework."

206. Cardozo Blockchain Project, "Not so Fast, Risks Related to the Use of 'SAFT' for Token Sales," Research Report 1, co-directed by Aaron Wright and Jeanne Schroeder, Benjamin N. Cardozo School of Law, Yeshiva University, 21 Nov. 2017. cardozo.yu.edu/sites/default/files/ Cardozo%20Blockchain%20Project%20-%20Not%20So%20Fast%20 -%20SAFT%20Response_final.pdf, accessed 3 Feb. 2018.

207. Jack du Rose, "SAFTE: A Simple Agreement for Future Tokens (or Equity)," *Colony*, Collectively Intelligent Ltd., 18 April 2017. blog.colony. io/a-simple-agreement-for-future-tokens-or-equity-b8ef08608347, accessed 1 Feb. 2018.

208. Carolynn Levy and Cadràn Cowansage, "SAFE Primer," *YCombinator. com*, Y Combinator LLC, 28 June 2017. ycombinator.com/docs/SAFE_ Primer.rtf, accessed 3 Feb. 2018.

209. In this case, the convertible loan holder would—because of an immediate need for cash or other reasons—decide neither to participate in the token issuance nor to convert his/her loan into equity.

210. Office of Investor Education and Advocacy, "Rule 506 of Regulation D," *SEC.gov*, US Securities and Exchange Commission, 16 Jan. 2013,

updated 27 Nov. 2017. sec.gov/fast-answers/answers-rule506htm.html, accessed 1 Feb. 2018.

211. "Eliminating the Prohibition against General Solicitation and General Advertising in Rule 506 and Rule 144A Offerings: A Small Entity Compliance Guide," *SEC.gov*, US Securities and Exchange Commission, 20 Sept. 2013. sec.gov/info/smallbus/secg/general-solicitation-small-entity-compliance-guide.htm, accessed 1 Feb. 2018.

212. "Rule 144: Selling Restricted and Control Securities," Investor Publications, *SEC.gov*, US Securities and Exchange Commission, 16 Jan. 2013. sec.gov/reportspubs/investor-publications/investorpubsrule144htm.html, accessed 1 Feb. 2018.

213. SEC, "Final Rules: Release No. 33-9741: Amendments for Small and Additional Issues Exemptions under the Securities Act (Regulation A)," *SEC.gov*, Division of Corporation Finance, US Securities and Exchange Commission, June 2015. sec.gov/rules/final/2015/33-9741.pdf, accessed 3 Feb. 2018.

214. Anzhela Knyazeva, "Regulation A+: What Do We Know So Far?" *SEC.gov*, Division of Economic and Risk Analysis, US Securities and Exchange Commission, Nov. 2016. sec.gov/files/Knyazeva_RegulationA%20.pdf, accessed 3 Feb. 2018.

215. SEC Chair Jay Clayton, "Statement on Cryptocurrencies and Initial Coin Offerings," *SEC.gov*, US Securities and Exchange Commission, 11 Dec. 2017. sec.gov/news/public-statement/statement-clayton-2017-12-11, accessed 1 Feb. 2018.

216. Article 4(1), point (44)(c) of Markets in Financial Instruments Directive (MiFID) II includes in its scope "any other securities giving the right to acquire or sell any such transferable securities or giving rise to a cash settlement determined by reference to transferable securities, currencies, interest rates or yields, commodities or other indices or measures." See "Directive 2014/65/EU of the European Parliament and of the Council of 15 May 2014 on markets in financial instruments and amending Directive 2002/92/EC and Directive 2011/61/EU," eur-lex.europa.eu/legal-content/EN/TXT/HTML/?uri=CELEX:32014L0065&from=EN, accessed 5 Feb. 2018.

217. "FinCEN's Mandate from Congress," *Financial Crimes Enforcement Network*, US Department of Treasury, n.d. fincen.gov/resources/fincens-mandate-congress, accessed 3 Feb. 2018.

218. Vlad Zamfir, "A Safe Token Sale Mechanism," *Medium*, A Medium Corp., 13 March 2017. medium.com/@Vlad_Zamfir/a-safe-token-sale-mechanism-8d73c430ddd1, accessed 1 Feb. 2018.

219. Vlad Zamfir, "A Safe Token Sale Mechanism," *Medium*, A Medium Corp., 13 March 2017.

220. Sanjeev Verma, Nghi Bui, and Chelsea Lam, "Munchee Token: A Decentralized Blockchain Based Food Review/Rating Social Media Platform," White Paper, Munchee Inc., 16 Oct. 2017, updated 14 Nov. 2017, p. 22. s3.amazonaws.com/munchee-docs/Munchee+White+Paper+-+EN.pdf, accessed 3 Feb. 2018.

221. "Questions of Cash: 'Foreign Currency Cheques Are a Nightmare,'" *The Independent*, Independent Print Ltd., 13 May 2011. independent.co.uk/money/spend-save/questions-of-cash-foreign-currency-cheques-are-a-nightmare-2283754.html, accessed 8 Jan. 2018.

222. Grovetta N. Gardineer, "Dodd–Frank Wall Street Reform and Consumer Protection Act–Regulations CC and Q," *OCC Bulletin 2011-25*, Office of the Comptroller of the Currency, US Department of Treasury, 24 June 2011. occ.treas.gov/news-issuances/bulletins/2011/bulletin-2011-25.html, accessed 8 Jan. 2018.

223. Ted Cordero, "One-day Clearing of Checks to Start in January 2017: BSP Enjoins Banks to Participate," *GMANetwork*, GMA Network Inc., 14 Sept. 2016. gmanetwork.com/news/money/economy/581315/1-day-clearing-of-checks-to-start-in-january-2017/story, accessed 31 Oct. 2017.

224. Neville Arjani and Darcey McVanel, "A Primer on Canada's Large Value Transfer System," *BankofCanada.ca*, Bank of Canada, 1 March 2006. bankofcanada.ca/wp-content/uploads/2010/05/lvts_neville.pdf, accessed 8 Jan. 2018.

225. "Canada's Major Payments Systems," *Bank of Canada.ca*, Bank of Canada, n.d. bankofcanada.ca/core-functions/financial-system/canadas-major-payments-systems, accessed 8 Jan. 2018.

226. "Bank of England to Take Over Running of Chaps as RTGS Make-over Comes Onstream," *Finextra Research*, Finextra Research, 9 May 2017. finextra.com/newsarticle/30535/bank-of-england-to-take-over-running-of-chaps-as-rtgs-make-over-comes-onstream, accessed 31 Oct. 2017.

227. Mike Derins, "How Banks Are Keeping Up with Venmo in Attracting Millennials," *Mobile Payments Today*, Networld Media Group LLC, 22 Sept. 2017. mobilepaymentstoday.com/articles/how-banks-are-keeping-up-with-venmo-in-attracting-millennials, accessed 8 Jan. 2018.

228. Jason Del Rey, "America's Biggest Banks Have Announced Their Venmo Competitor, Zelle," *CNBC*, CNBC, 24 Oct. 2016. cnbc.com/2016/10/24/americas-biggest-banks-have-announced-their-venmo-competitor-zelle.html, accessed 8 Jan. 2018.

229. Tyler Durden, "Apple's $700 Billion Market Cap Is Nothing Compared to Dutch East India Company at Its Peak," *Business Insider*, Insider Inc.,

11 Feb. 2015. businessinsider.com/apples-market-cap-in-fx-inflation-adjusted-context-2015-2, accessed 31 Oct. 2017.

230. William Dalrymple, "The East India Company: The Original Corporate Raiders," *The Guardian*, Guardian News and Media, 4 March 2015. theguardian.com/world/2015/mar/04/east-india-company-original-corporate-raiders, accessed 8 Jan. 2018.

231. T.G. Percival Spear, "Robert Clive," *Encyclopædia Britannica*, Encyclopædia Britannica Inc., 15 Dec. 2016. britannica.com/biography/Robert-Clive, accessed 31 Oct. 2017.

232. Paritosh Bansal, "Goldman's Share of AIG Bailout Money Draws Fire," with Lilla Zuill and Kevin Drawbaugh, *Reuters*, Thomson Reuters, 18 March 2009. reuters.com/article/us-aig-goldmansachs-sb/goldmans-share-of-aig-bailout-money-draws-fire-idUSTRE52H0B520090318, accessed 31 Oct. 2017.

233. ISO 20022 Registration Authority, "ISO 20022: Universal Financial Industry Message Scheme," *ISO 20022*, International Organization for Standardization, 29 Dec. 2017. iso20022.org, accessed 31 Oct. 2017.

234. SWIFT, "Data Standards: BIC (Business Identifier Code)," *SWIFT*, Society for Worldwide Interbank Financial Telecommunication, n.d. swift.com/standards/data-standards/bic, accessed 8 Jan. 2018.

235. SWIFT, "SWIFT FIN Traffic and Figures," *SWIFT*, Society for Worldwide Interbank Financial Telecommunication, n.d. swift.com/about-us/swift-fin-traffic-figures, accessed 8 Jan. 2018.

236. Adrienne Fuller, "How Much Do Banks Really Charge for Wire Transfers?" *Finder.com*, Finder US, 26 Oct. 2017. finder.com/bank-fees-wire-transfers; Spencer Tierney, "Wire Transfers: What Banks Charge," *NerdWallet*, NerdWallet, Inc., 15 Nov. 2017. nerdwallet.com/blog/banking/wire-transfers-what-banks-charge, both accessed 8 Jan. 2018.

237. Foreign exchange rates calculator, TD Bank Group, as of 18 Aug. 2017. tdcanadatrust.com/products-services/banking/foreign-currency-services/rates.jsp, accessed 18 Aug. 2017.

238. Citibank, "Important Notice Regarding Agreement for Online Funds Transfers," *Citibank Online: Agreement for Online Funds Transfers*, Citibank, 18 Oct. 2014. online.citi.com/JRS/forms/wire_xfrs_tsandcs.html, accessed 8 Jan. 2018.

239. Damien Vanderveken, interviewed via telephone by Bob Tapscott, 19 Sept. 2017; e-mail to Bob, 7 Dec. 2017.

240. Damien Vanderveken, interviewed via telephone by Bob Tapscott, 19 Sept. 2017; e-mail to Bob, 7 Dec. 2017.

241. CLS, "Currencies," *CLS: Trusted Market Solutions*, Continuous Linked Settlement, n.d. cls-group.com/About/Pages/Currencies.aspx, accessed 8 Jan. 2018.

242. CLS, "CLS Empowers Clients," *CLS: Trusted Market Solutions*, Continuous Linked Settlement, n.d. cls-group.com/About/Pages/default. aspx, accessed 8 Jan. 2018.

243. CLS, "How It Works," *CLS: Trusted Market Solutions*, Continuous Linked Settlement, n.d. cls-group.com/ProdServ/Settlement/Pages/How. aspx, accessed 8 Jan. 2018.

244. Lee Oliver, "Trading Technology: CLS Blocks FXMarketSpace's Plan to Pre-Net Cash Trades," *Euromoney*, Euromoney Institutional Investor PLC, 27 Nov. 2006. euromoney.com/article/b1321tw6ss6432/trading-technology-cls-blocks-fxmarketspaces-plan-to-pre-net-cash-trades, accessed 8 Jan. 2018.

245. "Special FX: CLS Keeps the Market Safe from Settlement Risk but Needs to Add More Currencies," *The Economist*, The Economist Newspaper Ltd., 21 Sept. 2013. economist.com/news/finance-and-economics/21586540-cls-keeps-market-safe-settlement-risk-needs-add-more; Richard Levich, "Why Foreign Exchange Transactions Did Not Freeze Up during the Global Financial Crisis: The Role of the CLS Bank," *VOX*, Centre for Economic Policy Research, 10 July 2009. voxeu. org/article/clearinghouse-saved-foreign-exchange-trading-crisis, both accessed 8 Jan. 2018.

246. See Basel Committee on Banking Supervision, "Basel III: International Regulatory Framework for Banks," *BIS.org*, Bank for International Settlements, 7 Dec. 2017. bis.org/bcbs/basel3.htm; FASB. "Financial Accounting Standards," Financial Accounting Standards Board, n.d. fasb.org, both accessed 9 Jan. 2018.

247. Eyder Peralta, "Report: Fed Committed $7.77 Trillion to Rescue Banks," *NPR.org*, National Public Radio, 28 Nov. 2011. npr.org/sections/thetwo-way/2011/11/28/142854391/report-fed-committed-7-77-trillion-to-rescue-banks, accessed 8 Jan. 2018.

248. Aruna Viswanatha, "Banks to Pay $5.6 Billion in Probes," *Wall Street Journal*, Dow Jones & Company, 20 May 2015. wsj.com/articles/global-banks-to-pay-5-6-billion-in-penalties-in-fx-libor-probe-1432130400, accessed 8 Jan. 2018.

249. Erik Larson, Tom Schoenberg, and Chris Dolmetsch, "As Big Banks' FX Case Ends, Judge Urges Probe of Traders," *Bloomberg Markets*, Bloomberg LP, 5 Jan. 2017. bloomberg.com/news/articles/2017-01-05/rbs-jpm-citi-barclays-fined-2-5-billion-in-fx-rigging-case, accessed 8 Jan. 2018.

250. Ken Sweet, Associated Press, "Equifax Says 2.5 Million More Americans May Be Affected by Hack," *Bloomberg.com*, Bloomberg LP, 2 Oct. 2017. bloomberg.com/news/articles/2017-10-02/urgent-equifax-2-5-million-more-americans-may-be-affected-by-hack, accessed 8 Jan. 2018.

251. Patrick Rucker, "US Fines HSBC $175 Million for Lax Forex Trading Oversight," with Lawrence White, *Reuters*, Thomson Reuters, 29 Sept. 2017. reuters.com/article/us-hsbc-fed-fine/u-s-fines-hsbc-175-million-for-lax-forex-trading-oversight-idUSKCN1C4283; David McLaughlin, Chris Dolmetsch, and David Voreacos, "Western Union to Pay $586 Million Over Failure to Stop Fraud," *Bloomberg.com*, Bloomberg LP, 19 Jan. 2017. bloomberg.com/news/articles/2017-01-19/western-union-admits-to-aiding-wire-fraud-to-pay-586-million, both accessed 9 Jan. 2018.

252. Jesse Hamilton, "Wells Fargo Is Fined $185 Million Over Unapproved Accounts," *Bloomberg.com*, Bloomberg LP, 8 Sept. 2016. bloomberg.com/news/articles/2016-09-08/wells-fargo-fined-185-million-over-unwanted-customer-accounts, accessed 9 Jan. 2018.

253. William K. Black, *The Best Way to Rob a Bank Is to Own One: How Corporate Executives and Politicians Looted the S&L Industry*, 2nd ed. (Austin: University of Texas Press, 2014).

254. Elizabeth Dexheimer, "The Senate Voted to Make It Harder to Sue Banks," *Bloomberg Politics*, Bloomberg LP, 24 Oct. 2017. bloomberg.com/news/articles/2017-10-25/consumer-bureau-s-arbitration-rule-overturned-by-vote-in-senate, accessed 8 Jan. 2018.

255. Donna Borak and Ted Barrett, "Senate Kills Rule that Made It Easier to Sue Banks," *CNN*, Cable News Network, 25 Oct. 2017. cnn.com/2017/10/24/politics/senate-cfpb-arbitration-repeal/index.html, accessed 9 Jan. 2018.

256. Jeff Stein, "37 of 38 Economists Said the GOP Tax Plans Would Grow the Debt. The 38th Misread the Question," *The Washington Post*, WP Company, 22 Nov. 2017. washingtonpost.com/news/wonk/wp/2017/11/22/37-of-38-economists-said-the-gop-tax-plans-would-grow-the-debt-the-38th-misread-the-question, accessed 9 Jan. 2018.

257. Elizabeth Dexheimer, "Bipartisan Bank-Relief Bill Wins Approval from Senate Panel," *Bloomberg.com*, Bloomberg LP, 5 Dec. 2017. bloomberg.com/news/articles/2017-12-05/bipartisan-bank-relief-bill-wins-approval-from-key-senate-panel, accessed 9 Jan. 2018.

258. "TransferWise Borderless Account," *TransferWise*, TransferWise Ltd., n.d. transferwise.com/ca/borderless, accessed 9 Jan. 2018.

259. "TransferWise Was Born of Frustration," *TransferWise*, TransferWise Ltd., n.d. transferwise.com/de/about, accessed 9 Jan. 2018.

260. "Sir Richard Branson Joins Our Mission to Stamp out Hidden Charges," *TransferWise*, TransferWise Ltd., 28 June 2016. transferwise.com/us/blog/sir-richard-branson-joins-our-mission-to-stamp-out-hidden-fees, accessed 9 Jan. 2018.

261. TD Helps, "How Do I Send a Wire Transfer?" *TD Bank Group*, Toronto-Dominion Bank, 31 Oct. 2017. td.intelliresponse.com/mortgages/index.jsp, accessed 31 Oct. 2017. A wire transfer takes approximately three to five business days to be processed. Transfer costs are $30–$80.

262. "Transforming the Way the World Moves Money," *nanopay*, nanopay Corporation, n.d. nanopay.net, accessed 9 Jan. 2018.

263. "Apple Pay: Cashless Made Effortless," *Apple.com*, Apple Inc., n.d. apple.com/apple-pay, accessed 9 Jan. 2018.

264. Facebook Help Center, "Payments in Messenger," *Facebook.com*, Facebook Inc., n.d. facebook.com/help/messenger-app/750020781733477, accessed 9 Jan. 2018.

265. Faster Payments Task Force, "The US Path to Faster Payments," Fasterpaymentstaskforce.org, Federal Reserve Banks, n.d. fasterpaymentstaskforce.org, accessed 9 Jan. 2018.

266. Faster Payments Task Force, "The US Path to Faster Payments: Faster Payments Final Report, Part One: The Faster Payments Task Force Approach," Federal Reserve Banks, Jan. 2017. fedpaymentsimprovement.org/wp-content/uploads/path-to-faster-payments.pdf, accessed 9 Jan. 2018. See also Faster Payments Task Force, "The US Path to Faster Payments: Faster Payments Final Report, Part Two: A Call to Action," Federal Reserve Banks, July 2017. fasterpaymentstaskforce.org/wp-content/uploads/faster-payments-task-force-final-report-part-two.pdf.

267. Faster Payments Task Force, "The US Path to Faster Payments: Faster Payments Final Report, Part One: The Faster Payments Task Force Approach," Federal Reserve Banks, Jan. 2017. fedpaymentsimprovement.org/wp-content/uploads/path-to-faster-payments.pdf, accessed 9 Jan. 2018.

268. Angela Scott-Briggs, "Fintech Companies Urge the Federal Reserve to Use Cryptocurrency," *TechBullion*, TechBullion, 30 July 2017. techbullion.com/fintech-companies-urge-federal-reserve-use-cryptocurrency, accessed 9 Jan. 2018.

269. Wolfie Zhao, "Faster Payments? Start-up Pitches Federal Reserve Group on Cryptocurrency," *CoinDesk*, Digital Currency Group, Inc., 21 July 2017. coindesk.com/faster-payments-startup-pitches-federal-reserve-group-cryptocurrency, accessed 9 Jan. 2018.

270. John Ginovsky, "Faster US Payments by 2020?" *Banking Exchange*, Simmons-Boardman Publishing Corp., 21 July 2017. bankingexchange. com/news-feed/item/6963-faster-u-s-payments-by-2020, accessed 9 Jan. 2018.

271. Leigh Angres and Jorge Salazar, "The Federal Budget in 2017: An Infographic," Congressional Budget Office, US Congress, 5 March 2018. cbo.gov/publication/53624, accessed 7 Oct. 2019. *CoinMarketCap.com*, coinmarketcap.com/charts, accessed 10 Jan. 2018.

272. "Distributed Ledger Technology: Hype or History in the Making?" *News and Reports*, European Central Bank, n.d. ecb.europa.eu/paym/intro/ news/articles 2016/html/mip qr 1 article 3 distributed ledger tech. en.html, accessed 9 Jan. 2018.

273. David Treat, interviewed via telephone by Bob Tapscott, 24 Oct. 2017; e-mail to Bob, 6 Dec. 2017.

274. David Treat, interviewed via telephone by Bob Tapscott, 24 Oct. 2017; e-mail to Bob, 6 Dec. 2017. See also Nick Saint, "If You're Not Embarrassed by the First Version of Your Product, You've Launched Too Late," *Business Insider*, Insider Inc., 13 Nov. 2009. businessinsider.com/the-iterate-fast-and-release-often-philosophy-of-entrepreneurship-2009-11, accessed 8 Jan. 2018.

275. Damien Vanderveken, interviewed via telephone by Bob Tapscott, 19 Sept. 2017; e-mail to Bob, 7 Dec. 2017.

276. "SWIFT gpi: Delivering the Future of Cross-Border Payments, Today," *SWIFT*, Society for Worldwide Interbank Financial Telecommunication, Jan. 2017. swift.com/file/31751/download?token=BK pC-m9, accessed 9 Jan. 2018.

277. "The Technological Transformation of Cross-Border Payments," *SWIFT*, Society for Worldwide Interbank Financial Telecommunication, n.d. swift.com/our-solutions/global-financial-messaging/payments-cash-management/swift-gpi/the-technological-transformation-of-cross-border-payments, accessed 9 Jan. 2018.

278. Damien Vanderveken, interviewed via telephone by Bob Tapscott, 19 Sept. 2017; e-mail to Bob, 7 Dec. 2017.

279. SWIFT, "Distributed Ledgers, Smart Contracts, Business Standards and ISO 20022," Information Paper, Society for Worldwide Interbank Financial Telecommunication, 7 Sept. 2016, modified 6 Nov. 2017. swift. com/news-events/events/iso-20022-information-session/document-centre, accessed 8 Jan. 2018.

280. SWIFT, "Distributed Ledgers, Smart Contracts, Business Standards and ISO 20022."

281. SWIFT, "Distributed Ledgers, Smart Contracts, Business Standards and ISO 20022."

282. Marc Hochstein, "IBM, Hyperledger Join Blockchain Identity Consortium," *CoinDesk*, Digital Currency Group, 11 Oct. 2017. coindesk.com/ibm-hyperledger-join-blockchain-identity-consortium, accessed 9 Jan. 2018.

283. "Rippled: The Core Peer-to-Peer Server that Manages the XRP Ledger," *Ripple*, Ripple, n.d. ripple.com/build/rippled-apis; Warren Anderson, "Ripple Consensus Ledger Can Sustain 1000 Transactions per Second," *Ripple*, Ripple, 28 Feb. 2017. ripple.com/dev-blog/ripple-consensus-ledger-can-sustain-1000-transactions-per-second, both accessed 9 Jan. 2018.

284. Michael del Castillo, "American Express Opens First Blockchain Corridor With Ripple Tech," *CoinDesk*, Digital Currency Group, 16 Nov. 2017. coindesk.com/american-express-opens-first-blockchain-corridor-ripple-tech, accessed 9 Jan. 2018.

285. Theresa Paraschac, e-mail to Bob Tapscott, 12 Dec. 2017.

286. Theresa Paraschac, e-mail to Bob Tapscott, 12 Dec. 2017.

287. Starkema Saunders, Jennifer Peve, Michael McClain, and Daniel Thieke, interviewed via telephone by Bob Tapscott, 31 Oct. 2017. Theresa Paraschac, e-mail to Bob Tapscott, 12 Dec. 2017.

288. Starkema Saunders, Jennifer Peve, Michael McClain, and Daniel Thieke, interviewed via telephone by Bob Tapscott, 31 Oct. 2017.

289. Theresa Paraschac, e-mail to Bob Tapscott, 12 Dec. 2017.

290. Theresa Paraschac, e-mail to Bob Tapscott, 12 Dec. 2017.

291. Theresa Paraschac, e-mail to Bob Tapscott, 12 Dec. 2017.

292. Starkema Saunders et al., interviewed via telephone by Bob Tapscott, 31 Oct. 2017.

293. Committee on Payment and Settlement Systems, "International Payment Arrangements," *Red Book 2003*, Bank for International Settlements, n.d. bis.org/cpmi/publ/d53p16.pdf, accessed 9 Jan. 2018.

294. "Ingenico Group: More than 35 Years of Innovation," *Ingenico Group*, Ingenico Group, 2018. ingenico.com/about-ingenico-group/about-us/our-history, accessed 9 Jan. 2018.

295. Joe Weisenthal, "The Bill Gross Blunder That Led To His Demise," *Business Insider*, Insider Inc., 2 Oct. 2014. businessinsider.com/this-was-the-bill-gross-blunder-that-led-to-his-downfall-2014-10, accessed 9 Jan. 2018.

296. Brian Chappatta, "The US Yield Curve Is Flattening and Here's Why It Matters," *Bloomberg.com*, Bloomberg LP, 13 Nov. 2017. bloomberg.com/news/articles/2017-11-13/the-u-s-yield-curve-is-flattening-and-here-s-why-it-matters, accessed 9 Jan. 2018.

297. Jason M. Tyra, "Triple Entry Bookkeeping with Bitcoin," *Bitcoin Magazine*, BTC Inc., 10 Feb. 2014. bitcoinmagazine.com/articles/triple-entry-bookkeeping-bitcoin-1392069656, accessed 9 Jan. 2018.

298. "Cryptocurrency," *Oxford Dictionaries: US English*, Oxford University Press, n.d. lexico.com/en/definition/cryptocurrency, accessed 9 Jan. 2018.

299. Leo Melamed, "Revisiting Bretton Woods," *Futures Magazine*, The Alpha Pages, 27 June 2017. futuresmag.com/2017/06/27/revisiting-bretton-woods, accessed 9 Jan. 2018.

300. Alexandra Ulmer and Deisy Buitrago, "Venezuela Wants to Launch a Cryptocurrency Backed by Oil Reserves Called the 'Petro,'" *Business Insider*, Insider, Inc., 3 Dec. 2017. businessinsider.com/venezuela-launch-cryptocurrency-called-petro-2017-12, accessed 9 Jan. 2018.

301. Christine Lagarde, "Central Banking and Fintech—A Brave New World?" Speech, Bank of England, London, 29 Sept. 2017. International Monetary Fund, imf.org/en/News/Articles/2017/09/28/sp092917-central-banking-and-fintech-a-brave-new-world, accessed 9 Jan. 2018.

302. Jeffrey A. Tucker, "IMF Head Foresees the End of Banking and the Triumph of Cryptocurrency," *FEE.org*, Foundation for Economic Education, 30 Sept. 2017. fee.org/articles/imf-head-predicts-the-end-of-banking-and-the-triumph-of-cryptocurrency, accessed 9 Jan. 2018.

303. Chris Skinner, "Will the Blockchain Replace Swift?" *American Banker*, SourceMedia, an Observer Capital Company, 8 March 2016. americanbanker.com/opinion/will-the-blockchain-replace-swift, accessed 9 Jan. 2018.

304. "Magnr Savings Earn 1.28% Annual Interest on Your Bitcoin," *Magnr.com*, Magnr, n.d. magnr.com/bitcoin-savings, accessed 9 Jan. 2018.

305. Krakenfx, "What Does It Really Cost to Buy and Sell Bitcoins?" *Kraken Blog*, Kraken Digital Asset Exchange, 9 Sept. 2014. blog.kraken.com/post/281/what-does-it-really-cost-to-buy-and-sell-bitcoins, accessed 9 Jan. 2018.

306. Camila Russo, "Bitcoin Options Will Be Available This Fall," *Bloomberg.com*, Bloomberg LP, 24 July 2017. bloomberg.com/news/articles/2017-07-24/bitcoin-options-to-become-available-in-fall-after-cftc-approval, accessed 9 Jan. 2018.

307. Camila Russo, "Bitcoin Futures Could Open the Floodgates for Institutional Investors," *Bloomberg.com*, Bloomberg LP, 31 Oct. 2017.

bloomberg.com/news/articles/2017-10-31/bitcoin-futures-could-open-to-floodgates-of-institutional-money, accessed 9 Jan. 2018.

308. Christine Lagarde, "Central Banking and Fintech—A Brave New World?" Speech, Bank of England, London, 29 Sept. 2017. International Monetary Fund, imf.org/en/News/Articles/2017/09/28/sp092917-central-banking-and-fintech-a-brave-new-world, accessed 9 Jan. 2018.

309. Christine Lagarde, "Central Banking and Fintech—A Brave New World?" Speech.

310. Josh Horwitz, "North Korea Is Bullish on Bitcoin, and State Hackers Are Getting in on the Action," *Quartz*, Quartz Media LLC, 12 Sept. 2017. qz.com/1074881/north-korea-is-bullish-on-bitcoin-and-state-hackers-are-getting-in-on-the-action, accessed 9 Jan. 2018.

311. Rishi Iyengar, "NiceHash: More than $70 Million Stolen in Bitcoin Hack," *CNN Money*, Cable News Network, 8 Dec. 2017. money.cnn.com/2017/12/07/technology/nicehash-bitcoin-theft-hacking/index.html, accessed 9 Jan. 2018. Oren Dorell, "North Korea Cyber Attacks like 'WannaCry' Are Increasingly Ploys for Money, Analysts Say," *USA Today*, Gannett Satellite Information Network, 20 Dec. 2017. usatoday.com/story/news/world/2017/12/20/north-korea-wannacry-cyber-attack-ploy-money-white-house/970138001, accessed 13 Jan. 2018.

312. Ben Chapman, "Bitcoin Latest: North Korea Suspected of South Korean Cryptocurrency Exchange Hack," *The Independent*, Independent Digital News and Media Ltd., 21 Dec. 2017. independent.co.uk/news/business/news/bitcoin-latest-updates-north-korea-south-youbit-exchange-hack-cryptocurrency-a8121781.html, accessed 9 Jan. 2018.

313. Bradley Wilkes, "National Digital Currency Platform Proposed for the Federal Reserve," *WingCash Faster Payments Network*, WingCash, 2017. fasterpaymentsnetwork.com, accessed 8 Jan. 2018.

314. "Energy Currency," *The Perfect Currency*, John Meyer, n.d. theperfectcurrency.org/main-energy-currency/energy-currency, accessed 9 Jan. 2018.

315. ADB, Oliver Wyman, and MicroSave, "Accelerating Financial Inclusion in South-East Asia with Digital Finance," *ADB.org*, Asian Development Bank, 16 Nov. 2017. adb.org/sites/default/files/publication/222061/financial-inclusion-se-asia.pdf, accessed 9 Jan. 2018.

316. Matthew Leising, "The Ether Thief," *Bloomberg.com*, Bloomberg LP, 13 June 2017. bloomberg.com/features/2017-the-ether-thief, accessed 9 Jan. 2018.

317. Faster Payments Task Force, "The US Path to Faster Payments: Faster Payments Final Report, Part Two: A Call to Action," Federal Reserve

Banks, July 2017. fasterpaymentstaskforce.org/wp-content/uploads/faster-payments-task-force-final-report-part-two.pdf, accessed 9 Jan. 2018.

318. OECD, "Government at a Glance 2017: Estonia," Organisation for Economic Co-operation and Development, 2017. oecd.org/gov/gov-at-a-glance-2017-estonia.pdf, accessed 20 March 2018.

319. @e_Residents, Twitter post, 23 Jan. 2018, 4:08 am. twitter.com/e_Residents/status/955728839791038465, accessed 20 March 2018.

320. Funderbeam, "Start-up Investment Report: Estonia," IFuturo.org, Institución Futuro, Dec. 2017, with data from 2 Oct. 2016. ifuturo.org/sites/default/files/docs/startup_investment_report_estonia.pdf, accessed 20 March 2018.

321. "e-Identity," *e-Estonia.com*, e-Estonia Briefing Centre, n.d. e-estonia.com/solutions/e-identity/id-card, accessed 17 Oct. 2019.

322. "KSI Blockchain," Solutions, *e-Estonia.com*, e-Estonia Briefing Centre, n.d. e-estonia.com/solutions/security-and-safety/ksi-blockchain, accessed 17 Oct. 2019.

323. Nathan Heller, "Estonia, the Digital Republic," *The New Yorker*, Condé Nast, 18 Dec. 2017. newyorker.com/magazine/2017/12/18/estonia-the-digital-republic, accessed 20 March 2018.

324. Nathan Heller, "Estonia, the Digital Republic."

325. Nathan Heller, "Estonia, the Digital Republic."

326. US General Services Administration, "FY 2019 Congressional Justification," 12 Feb. 2018. gsa.gov/cdnstatic/GSA%20FY%202019%20CJ.pdf, accessed 3 April 2018.

327. Jose Arrieta, Remarks delivered at the ACT IAC Blockchain Forum, 31 Jan. 2018. actiac.org/2018-blockchain-forum-0, accessed 3 April 2018.

328. Steven Kelman, "GSA's Blockchain Blockbuster," *LinkedIn*, LinkedIn Corp., 18 Oct. 2017. linkedin.com/pulse/gsas-blockchain-blockbuster-steven-kelman, accessed 17 Oct. 2019.

329. Steven Kelman, "GSA's Blockchain Blockbuster."

330. David Thornton, "GSA Experimenting with Blockchain to Cut Contracting Time," Federal News Radio, 16 Nov. 2017. federalnewsradio.com/it-modernization-2017/2017/11/gsa-experimenting-with-blockchain-to-cut-contracting-time, accessed 3 April 2018.

331. Jose Arrieta, remarks during Panel 1, "Blockchain and the Importance of Modernization," ACT IAC Blockchain Forum, Mayflower Hotel, Washington DC, 3 April 2018. actiac.org/2018-blockchain-forum-0, accessed 3 April 2018.

332. Steven Kelman, "GSA's Blockchain Blockbuster."

333. David Thornton, "GSA Experimenting with Blockchain to Cut Contracting Time."

334. "Corporate Headquarters," Division of Small Business, State of Delaware, n.d. dedo.delaware.gov/Industries/Corporate-Headquarters, accessed 6 April 2018.

335. Jeffrey W. Bullock, "Delaware Division of Corporations 2016 Annual Report," Delaware Division of Corporations, 2016. corp.delaware. gov/2016AnnualReport.pdf, accessed 6 April 2018.

336. John Williams, "Stock Ledgers Revolutionized with Delaware Corporate Blockchain Legislation," *Delaware Business Times*, 28 June 2017. delawarebusinesstimes.com/stock-ledgers-revolutionized-delaware-corporate-blockchain-legislation, accessed 6 April 2018.

337. Sara Merken, "Delaware Blockchain Move Drawing in Companies, Law Firms," *The Bureau of National Affairs*, Bloomberg Next, 11 Aug. 2017. biglawbusiness.com/delaware-blockchain-move-drawing-in-private-companies-law-firms, accessed 17 Oct. 2019.

338. Caroline Heider and April Connelly, "Why Land Registration Matters for Development," World Bank Group, 28 June 2016. ieg. worldbankgroup.org/blog/why-land-administration-matters-development, accessed 9 April 2018.

339. Joon Ian Wong, "Sweden's Blockchain-Powered Land Registry Is Inching toward Reality," *Quartz*, Quartz Media Inc., 3 April 2017. qz.com/947064/sweden-is-turning-a-blockchain-powered-land-registry-into-a-reality, accessed 17 Oct. 2019.

340. For the full report, see "The Land Registry in the Blockchain," Kairos Future, March 2017. chromaway.com/papers/Blockchain_Landregistry_Report_2017.pdf, accessed 9 April 2018.

341. Joon Ian Wong, "Sweden's Blockchain-Powered Land Registry Is Inching toward Reality."

342. Mark White, Jason Killmeyer, and Bruce Chew, "Will Blockchain Transform the Public Sector?" *Deloitte Insights*, Deloitte Touche Tohmatsu Ltd., 11 Sept. 2017. deloitte.com/us/en/insights/industry/public-sector/understanding-basics-of-blockchain-in-government.html, accessed 17 Oct. 2019.

343. For an excellent demonstration of how blockchain works, see Anders Brownworth, "1. How Blockchain Works," *Blockchain.MIT.edu*, Massachusetts Institute of Technology, n.d. blockchain.mit.edu/how-blockchain-works, accessed 17 Oct. 2019.

344. Miguel Castro and Barbara Liskov, "Practical Byzantine Fault Tolerance," *Third Symposium on Operating Systems Design and Implementation*, New

Orleans, Louisiana, Feb. 1999. MIT Computer Science and Artificial Intelligence Laboratory, pmg.csail.mit.edu/papers/osdi99.pdf, accessed 17 Oct. 2019.

345. For more on *internal state*, see Roger Hartley, "Internal State," *C++ Concept Map*, Robert Hartley's Home Page, Computer Science, New Mexico State University, 2003. cs.nmsu.edu/~rth/cs/cs177/map/intstate. html, accessed 17 Oct. 2019.

346. Andre Boaventura, "Demystifying Blockchain and Consensus Mechanisms: Everything You Wanted to Know but Were Never Told," *Medium*, Oracle Developers, 14 May 2018. medium.com/oracledevs/ demystifying-blockchain-and-consensus-mechanisms-everything-you-wanted-to-know-but-were-never-aabe62145128, accessed 17 Oct. 2019.

347. "Endorsement Policies," Operational Guides, *Hyperledger Fabric Release-1.4*, Hyperledger, n.d. hyperledger-fabric.readthedocs.io/en/ release-1.4/endorsement-policies.html, accessed 19 Oct. 2019.

348. Blockchain Working Group, "Enabling Blockchain Innovation in the US Federal Government: A Blockchain Primer," *ACTIAC.org*, American Council for Technology–Industry Advisory Council, 16 Oct. 2017. actiac. org/system/files/ACT-IAC%20ENABLING%20BLOCKCHAIN%20 INNOVATION_3.pdf, accessed 17 Oct. 2019.

349. Yuji Ijiri, "Triple-entry Bookkeeping and Income Momentum," American Accounting Association, Sarasota, FL, 1982.

350. Richard Mattessich, *Two Hundred Years of Accounting Research: An International Survey of Personalities, Ideas, and Publications (from the Beginning of the Nineteenth Century to the Beginning of the Twenty-First Century)* (London, UK: Routledge, 2008): 201, 239-240, 247, 336.

351. Ian Grigg, "Triple Entry Accounting," Working Paper, 25 Dec. 2005. iang.org/papers/triple_entry.html, accessed 12 June 2018.

352. Ben Taylor, "Triple-Entry Accounting and Blockchain: A Common Misconception," *Forbes*, Forbes Media LLC, 28 Nov. 2017. forbes.com/ sites/forbesfinancecouncil/2017/11/28/triple-entry-accounting-and-blockchain-a-common-misconception/#15f854f0190f, accessed 12 June 2018.

353. See, for example, Daniel Jeffries, "Why Everyone Missed the Most Important Invention of the last 500 Years," *Hackernoon*, Artmap Inc., 22 June 2017. hackernoon.com/why-everyone-missed-the-most-important-invention-in-the-last-500-years-c90b0151c169, accessed 12 June 2018.

354. Blockchain ABC, "Triple Entry Accounting," n.d. blockchainabc. blogspot.com/p/blog-page.html, accessed 12 June 2018. The post claims

that Ian Grigg invented the term; Grigg did not. See Mattessich, *Two Hundred Years of Accounting Research*.

355. For example, Enron had founded numerous "Special Purpose Entities" (SPE), companies that are (legally) founded for limited time horizons to allow the management of a particular risk. Usually, these SPEs are funded by separate equity investors. Enron had used its own equity, thereby fully exposing Enron shareholders to the risk that the SPE allegedly hedged. This activity would be visible if the SPE transactions were recorded on a blockchain.

356. Michael Minnis, "The Value of Financial Statement Verification in Debt Financing: Evidence from Private US Firms," *Journal of Accounting Research* 49, No. 2 (May 2011). onlinelibrary.wiley.com/doi/10.1111/j.1475-679X.2011.00411.x/epdf, accessed 30 Oct. 2017. According to Minnis, small-and medium-sized firms that have their books audited by a certified public accountant increase their chances significantly of obtaining a loan and receive on average a 69 basis points lower interest rate. An audit costs between $15,000 and $25,000. An audit of blockchain-based entries would be entirely automated at nominal costs.

357. There are some interesting wrinkles in the ownership and recording of ownership of stocks. Formally, all US stocks are owned by the DTCC, and shareholders merely hold a claim on the original certificates. In Canada, CDS records ownership and transfers, but these transfers are recorded only at the broker level. This procedure has important implications for issuers. For example, suppose CIBC customers buy 100,000 shares of Barrick Gold and sell 80,000. Then CDS records only the net transfer of 20,000. When Barrick needs to contact its owner for, say, the annual shareholder meeting, it needs to contact another third party, Broadridge, to collect the information on the current holders. Being a monopolist, Broadridge's service comes at considerable cost.

358. In contrast to these examples of centralized ledgers, a distributed ledger stores all information at all locations.

359. Richard Gendal Brown, "A Simple Explanation of Enterprise Blockchains for Cryptocurrency Experts," *Richard Gendal Brown Blog*, WordPress, 7 July 2017. gendal.me/2017/07/07/a-simple-explanation-of-enterprise-blockchains-for-cryptocurrency-experts, accessed 30 Oct. 2017.

360. Here is a simple mathematical description. The public key PUK is essentially a *hash* of the private key PRK, where a hash is a conversion of arbitrary-length text into a fixed-length combination of letters and numbers. For all practical purposes, this hash cannot be inverted, and so no one can derive PRK from PUK. Mathematically, we write

H(PRK)=PUK. Next, combining the text of the transaction (MSG) with the hash of the private key and then hashing both delivers the signature SIG, H(MSG+H(PRK))=SIG. So how does verification work? Well, the verifier has SIG, MSG, and PUK, so all she has to do is check if H(MSG+PUK)=SIG.

361. Creating an address on a public blockchain is straightforward: (1) go to the website MyEtherWallet.com and (2) enter an arbitrary string and a password. The website then creates a public ID and a private ID from this information.

362. Some of the regulations introduced after the 2008 financial crisis have severely limited the ability of financial institutions to absorb client orders. Specifically, the Volcker Rule limits banks' proprietary trading to market-making activities only. In illiquid markets, in particular, drawing the line between taking a position as part of a market-making activity and taking it to speculate on price changes can be difficult. Dealers may therefore appreciate technological advances that allow them to shorten the time they expect to hold an inventory.

363. Maureen O'Hara, Yihui Wang, and Xing (Alex) Zhou, "The Execution Quality of Corporate Bonds," Fordham University School of Business Research Paper No. 2680480, *SSRN.com*, 1 June 2016. Elsevier, ssrn.com/abstract=2680480, accessed 30 Oct. 2017. See also Gjergji Cici, Scott Gibson, Yalin Gündüz, and John J. Merrick, "Market Transparency and the Marking Precision of Bond Mutual Fund Managers," Bundesbank Discussion Paper No. 9 (2014). Elsevier, ssrn.com/abstract=2796963, accessed 30 Oct. 2017.

364. Susan Kerr Christoffersen, Erfan Danesh, and David K. Musto, "Why Do Institutions Delay Reporting Their Shareholdings? Evidence from Form 13F," Rotman School of Management Working Paper No. 2661535, University of Toronto, Ontario, 15 Aug. 2015. Elsevier, papers.ssrn.com/sol3/papers.cfm?abstract_id=2661535, accessed 30 Oct. 2017.

365. Vincent van Kerveland and Albert J. Menkveld, "High-Frequency Trading around Large Institutional Orders," WFA Paper, 29 Jan. 2016. Elsevier, ssrn.com/abstract=2619686, accessed 30 Oct. 2017.

366. Geoff Colvin, "Take this Market and Shove It," *Fortune*, Fortune Media IP Ltd., 17 May 2016. fortune.com/going-private, accessed 30 Oct. 2017.

367. Nancy L. Sanborn, Phillip R. Mills, and Saswat Bohidar, "Going Private Transactions: Overview," Practical Law Company, 2010. Davis Polk & Wardwell LLP, davispolk.com/files/uploads/davis.polk.going.private.pdf, accessed 30 Oct. 2017. They assert that "the Exchange Act and the Sarbanes-Oxley Act, [...] require[s], among other things, periodic disclosure of what may be competitive or strategic business

information and impose inflexible corporate governance requirements." Indeed, much literature studies whether the Sarbanes-Oxley Act caused the increased prevalence of going-private deals; see Ellen Engel, Rachel M. Hayes, and Xue Wang, "The Sarbanes–Oxley Act and Firms' Going-Private Decisions," *Journal of Accounting and Economics* 44, No. 1–2 (2007): 116–145. doi.org/10.1007/BF03342753 or leeds-faculty.colorado.edu/Bhagat/SOX-GoingPrivate.pdf, accessed 17 Oct. 2019.

368. Denise L. Parris et al., "Exploring Transparency: A New Framework for Responsible Business Management," *Management Decision* 54, No. 1(2016): 222–247. doi.org/10.1108/MD-07-2015-0279, accessed 30 Oct. 2017.

369. Don Tapscott, "Transparency as a Business Imperative," *Association Management* 57, No. 4 (April 2005): 17–18. EBSCO, connection.ebscohost.com/c/articles/16701312/transparency-as-business-imperative, accessed 30 Oct. 2017.

370. Denise L. Parris et al., "Exploring Transparency."

371. The first DAO was launched with a crowdfunding campaign in fall 2015. At the time, it was the largest crowdfunded project. See David Z. Morris, "Leaderless, Blockchain-Based Venture Capital Fund Raises $100 Million, and Counting," *Fortune*, Fortune Media IP Ltd., 15 May 2016. fortune.com/2016/05/15/leaderless-blockchain-vc-fund, accessed 16 May 2016.

372. From a game-theoretic perspective, it is not clear at all whether DAO voting structures lead to desirable outcomes. Following Kenneth Arrow's insights from his work on his Impossibility Theorem, a large body of literature on game theory explores the implication of voting on alternatives. The main insight is that there are numerous pitfalls in designing a voting system, and that care is needed to get it right.

373. Jack Bao, Maureen O'Hara, and Xing (Alex) Zhou, "The Volcker Rule and Market-Making in Times of Stress," Finance and Economics Discussion Series 2016-102 (8 Dec. 2016). Washington: Board of Governors of the Federal Reserve System. doi.org/10.17016/FEDS.2016.102, accessed 30 Oct. 2017.

374. Katya Malinova and Andreas Park, "Market Design with Blockchain Technology," *SSRN.com*, 26 July 2017. Elsevier, ssrn.com/abstract=2785626, accessed 30 Oct. 2017.

375. Jay Ritter and Donghang Zhang, for instance, provide some evidence for this type of nepotism during the height of the dot-com bubble; see Jay R. Ritter and Donghang Zhang, "Affiliated Mutual Funds and the Allocation of Initial Public Offerings," *Journal of Financial Economics* 86, No. 2 (Nov. 2007): 337–368.

doi.org/10.1016/j.jfineco.2006.08.005, accessed 30 Oct. 2017. Also see Tim Jenkinson and Alexander P. Ljungqvist, *Going Public: The Theory and Evidence on How Companies Raise Equity Finance*, 2nd ed. (New York: Oxford University Press, 2001).

376. Qing Hao, "Laddering in Initial Public Offerings," *Journal of Financial Economics* 85, No. 1 (2007): 102–122. doi.org/10.1016/j. jfineco.2006.05.008, accessed 30 Oct. 2017.

377. There is a gray zone as to what exactly a token is. The so-called US *Howey* test determines whether a transaction is a security: Is there an investment of money? An expectation of profit? Is the investment in a common enterprise? Does profit come from the efforts of the promoter? Many tokens are set up as "usage" coins, but my reading is that (a) there is a tacit promise of value and thus price appreciation of the coin and (b) these coins are meant as compensation for firm insiders. The first point generates capital gains profits, the second implies a financial reward and hints at option value. In practice, tokens are traded like stocks on crypto security exchanges. Indeed, the SEC stated that DAO tokens were securities (sec.gov/news/press-release/2017-131). Similarly, in its investor advisory section, the SEC highlights that tokens are often securities and should be treated as such (investor.gov/additional-resources/news-alerts/alerts-bulletins/investor-bulletin-initial-coin-offerings).

378. Discussing the mechanism of an ICO goes beyond the scope of this piece. The basic idea, however, is this: most ICOs to date involve the issuance of tokens using the Ethereum blockchain. For this blockchain, a token is a smart contract written in Ethereum smart contract language Solidity. This contract or code governs the issuance protocol. Commonly, the contract specifies a particular time (measured in block numbers) during which it accepts payment, and it specifies who receives the tokens once payment has been received (e.g., pro-rate, first come first serve, etc). The contract's code is publicly visible. For more information, see blockgeeks. com/guides/ico-basics.

379. David Yermack, "Corporate Governance and Blockchains," *Review of Finance* 21, No. 1 (1 March 2017): 7–31. doi.org/10.1093/rof/rfw074, accessed 30 Oct. 2017.

380. Susan E.K. Christoffersen et al., "A. Vote Trading and Information Aggregation," *Journal of Finance* 62 (2007): 2897–2927. Univ. of Penn. Scholarly Commons, repository.upenn.edu/cgi/viewcontent. cgi?article=1132&context=fnce_papers, accessed 30 Oct. 2017.

381. An example is the 2012 dispute between Telus and the US hedge fund Mason Capital. Mason had taken a long position in Telus' voting stock and it had offset this position with a short position in Telus non-voting stock. Consequently, Mason had a voting interest but no economic interest.

382. In Canada, insider filings are submitted to the System for Electronic Disclosure by Insiders (SEDI), and insiders must disclose transactions within five calendar days. In the United States, insiders must file Form 4 by the 10th of the month following the transaction. In addition to insider trading, there is also a long history of illegal insider trading, the type that usually makes it to the news. A recent study found that 25 percent of M&A deals show heightened levels of informed trading in options. When insiders would be required to reveal their blockchain IDs, such trades would be visible. See Patrick Augustin, Menachem Brenner, and Marti G. Subrahmanyam, "Informed Options Trading Prior to M&A Announcements: Insider Trading?" *SSRN.com*, 26 Oct. 2015. Elsevier, papers.ssrn.com/sol3/papers.cfm?abstract_id=2441606, accessed 30 Oct. 2017.

383. There is one caveat to this argument: currently, trades occur at specialized exchanges. To trade there, one transfers holdings to an exchange wallet. Formally, this wallet then owns the shares and trades on the exchange that can occur within this wallet. Moreover, an exchange wallet is not necessarily exclusive for a person but instead may mix ownership of several entities. A person only truly and irrevocably owns a digital item when it is transferred out of the exchange wallet to a "normal" wallet and settled on the blockchain; see also the appendix to Chapter 6.

384. Lin William Cong and Zhiguo He, "Blockchain Disruption and Smart Contracts," *SSRN.com*, 10 July 2017, last revised 17 March 2019. Elsevier, ssrn.com/abstract=2985764, accessed 7 Oct. 2019.

385. IBM Institute for Business Value, "Forward Together: Three Ways Blockchain Explorers Chart a New Direction," *Global C-suite Study* 19th ed., May 2017. public.dhe.ibm.com/common/ssi/ecm/gb/en/gbe03835usen/GBE03835USEN.PDF, accessed 30 Oct. 2017.

386. In a 2013 article, Forbes (tinyurl.com/ycavqqpd) describes in detail how their illicit endeavors with the infamous Silk Road were largely traceable. At the time, they relied on a method developed by Sarah Meiklejohn from University of California at San Diego; at around the same time, Ivan Pustogarov developed techniques to deanonymize transactions on the Bitcoin blockchain (see crypto.stanford.edu/seclab/sem-14-15/pustogarov.html).

387. The solution here is related to the so-called "CoinJoin" approach; see Vitalik Buterin, "Ethereum: Platform Review; Opportunities and Challenges for Private and Consortium Blockchains," Ethereum Foundation, 2 June 2016. static1.squarespace.com/static/55f73743e4b051cfcc0b02cf/t/57506f387da24ff6bdecb3c1/1464889147417/Ethereum_Paper.pdf, accessed 30 Oct. 2017.

388. "What iIs zkSNARKs: Spooky Moon Math," *Blockgeeks*, Blockgeeks Inc., n.d. blockgeeks.com/guides/what-is-zksnarks, accessed 30 Oct. 2017.

389. The underlying logic of zero-knowledge proofs is usually spelled out in mathematical terms, and the reader need not worry that, for instance, text-based information of statements are incompatible with the concept. Indeed, in the practical-mathematical application, strings are converted using so-called hash functions, which allow a concise mathematical representation of relations. Furthermore, as I depict the situation, there would be a constant back and forth between prover and validator—which is not practical. There are, of course, cryptographic protocols in place that are non-interactive.

390. Examples are corporate bond markets where information about past trades and quotes information are sparse, and dealers showed strong resistence to the collection and publication of such information. For instance, the implementation of the Trade Reporting and Compliance Engine (TRACE) was met with much resistance. In Canada, corporate bond trading data has only been published since 2016, and this information covers only a subset of trades. In the United States, data on trades in treasuries have only been included this July in TRACE—even though the system has been around since 2002.

391. My personal view is that, conceptually, Corda is, in fact, not a distributed ledger at all. For instance, a ledger records transactions, whereas Corda records current balances.

392. Wei-Tek Tsai, Xiaoying Bai, and Lian Yu, "Design Issues in Permissioned Blockchains for Trusted Computing," 2017 IEEE Symposium on Service-Oriented System Engineering, 6–9 April 2017. ieeexplore.ieee.org/document/7943306/?reload=true, accessed 30 Oct. 2017.

393. Alex Tapscott, "Blockchain Is Eating Wall Street," Presentation, TEDx San Francisco, 6 Oct. 2016, Video published by TED Talks, *YouTube.com*, 26 Oct. 2016. youtube.com/watch?v=WnEYakUxsHU, accessed 10 Dec. 2019.

394. "Distinguished Achievement Awards 2017," *Thinkers50*, Thinkers50 Ltd., n.d. thinkers50.com/t50-awards/awards-2017, accessed 8 Sept. 2019.

INDEX

F

G

T

U